LEARN
M I C R O S O F T®
WORD
NOW

Special Edition

Microsoft
P R E S S

JANET RAMPA

PUBLISHED BY
Microsoft Press
A Division of Microsoft Corporation
One Microsoft Way
Redmond, Washington 98052-6399

Library of Congress Cataloging-in-Publication Data

Rampa, Janet, 1948–
      Learn Microsoft Word now / Janet Rampa.
          p.   cm.
      ISBN 1-55615-296-5 : $29.95
      1. Microsoft Word (Computer program)   2. Word processing.
      I. Title.
      Z52.5.M52R37   1990
      652.5'5369--dc20   90-6677
                                                                                CIP

Printed and bound in the United States of America.

1 2 3 4 5 6 7 8 9   FGFG   4 3 2 1 0

Epson® is a registered trademark of Epson America, Inc. AT® IBM® and
PS/2® are registered trademarks of International Business Machines Corporation. Word Finder® is a registered trademark of Microlytics, Inc. Microsoft®
is a registered trademark of Microsoft Corporation.

Dedication

To my parents,
Marjorie and Peter Rampa,
with love

Acknowledgments

Special thanks go to Jack Litewka, a perceptive, sensitive, and good-humored editor, who fine-tuned this manuscript and generously offered me intelligent advice and enthusiastic support. Dail Magee, Jr., the technical editor, tracked changes to the Word program as they occurred and rigorously checked the accuracy of this book. He eliminated the usual lag time between software release and book publication. Debbie Kem and Cathy Thompson in word processing expertly and patiently waded through what was frequently a tangled jungle of markups.

Jim Brown, marketing director, and Claudette Moore, acquisitions editor, recognized the need for this book and got the wheels in motion to make it happen.

At home, Haluk Ozdemir, my husband, and Perrin and Nina, our daughters, endured me, delighted me, and inspired me.

CONTENTS

INTRODUCTION

Word processing is, today, the most widely used application for microcomputers. You might feel, however, that you don't have the time to stop and learn how to use the latest word-processing technology. Whether you've never touched a computer before or are an old hand at operating one, this book and the enclosed disk show you how to use Microsoft Word—a powerful yet friendly word processing program—without investing a lot of time or effort.

The enclosed disk contains a Working Model version of Microsoft Word that you can use to learn the product as you work through this book, which was written for use with the full retail version 5.0 of Microsoft Word. For instructions on how to install and use the Working Model with this book, refer to the section at the end of this Introduction titled "Using the Working Model Disk."

HOW THIS BOOK IS ORGANIZED

The first part of *Learn Microsoft Word Now,* "A Short Course in Word," conveys most of the information you need to use Microsoft Word and prepares you for the more sophisticated tools presented in the second and third parts of this book—"Advanced Word" and "Super Word."

Part I: A Short Course in Word

The first four chapters of this book ease you into Word. In Chapter 1, you learn what word processing is, why Microsoft Word stands out among other word-processing programs, and what kind of equipment you need to work with Word.

To demonstrate how easy it is to start working with Word, the next three chapters walk you through the steps of processing a document from start to finish. In Chapters 2, 3, and 4, you learn how to create, edit, store, retrieve, and print a document. After you finish reading the first part of this book, you'll be ready to put Word to work for you.

Part II: Advanced Word

After you're comfortable with the basics of the program, the second part of this book gently introduces you to the extra speed and power that Microsoft Word offers you. Chapter 5 provides an overview of Word's menus (lists of commands) and shows how to select commands from a menu. Chapters 6 through 12 explain how to revise documents, find and replace text, manage your files, and print documents with more control over what is printed and how it is printed.

Part III: Super Word

The third part of this book introduces you to the special features and enhancements that make Microsoft Word an exceptional word processor. You learn about merge printing, the spelling checker, automatic hyphenation, the built-in thesaurus, document retrieval, macros, and style sheets. With these features, you'll be able to reduce complicated or time-consuming tasks that require many keystrokes to simple tasks that require few keystrokes.

Part IV: Appendixes

In the fourth part of this book, you'll find six appendixes for quick reference when you need help with using DOS (the Disk Operating System), setting up Microsoft Word to fit your computer system, or remembering which commands, keys, or mouse maneuvers to use for a particular task.

At the end of the book is a comprehensive index that quickly directs you to the correct page when you want help with any of Word's features.

USING THE WORKING MODEL DISK

The disk bound into the back of this book contains the Working Model version of Microsoft Word. The Working Model has a few restrictions built into it. For a list of additional features you receive when you buy the full retail version of Microsoft Word, see "Additional Features in the Full Retail Version of Microsoft Word." **Because this book was written for the full retail version of Word, some parts of the book do not apply to the Working Model.** For a list of the topics that do not apply, see "Text Differences for the Working Model." For a list of the differences between the Working Model screens and the screen illustrations in this book, see "Visual Differences for the Working Model."

Hardware Requirements for the Working Model

The Working Model and the full retail version of Microsoft Word version 5.0 require 384 kilobytes of conventional memory. The Working Model is designed to be installed on a fixed (hard) disk. You need about 1.5 megabytes of free space on your fixed disk to install the Working Model.

Setting Up the Working Model

Before you can use the Working Model of Word for the first time, you need to set it up on your fixed disk. The Install program found on the Working Model disk helps you do this. The Install program creates a directory named WORD5DEM on your fixed disk and changes to that directory. It then copies the Word files from the Working Model disk to the WORD5DEM directory on your fixed disk.

To run the Install program, you first need to start DOS (as explained in Appendix A). When you see the DOS prompt C>, insert the Working Model disk in a high density (1.2 megabytes) 5¼-inch floppy-disk drive. Include the name of that drive when you type the command to start the Install program. For example, if the Working Model disk is in drive A, type:

A:INSTALL

and press the Enter key. Install displays messages to guide you through the installation procedure and returns you to the DOS prompt.

After the Install program copies the files from the Working Model disk to your fixed disk, it runs a program called Setup. The Setup program will ask you to identify what kind of video display is installed in your computer. Simply choose the appropriate type from a list of choices and Setup will set up Word to make the best use of your display.

Starting the Working Model

If you have just finished setting up the Working Model on your fixed disk, type:

WORD

and press the Enter key to start the Working Model of the Word program.

At other times, you must first start DOS and tell DOS to look for the Working Model on the WORD5DEM directory. Here is the step-by-step procedure you would follow.

1. Start DOS if it isn't already started.

2. When you see the *C>* prompt, change to the directory where the Working Model is stored. Type:

    CD \WORD5DEM

    and press the Enter key.

3. Finally, type:

    WORD

    and press the Enter key.

4. If you need to run the Setup program again to install a different type of video display, follow steps 1 and 2 above and then type:

    SETUP

    and press the Enter key. Choose the appropriate display type, and Setup will return you to the *C>* prompt.

The Working Model and the Microsoft Mouse

The Working Model disk contains revised mouse drivers for the Microsoft Mouse. **Be sure your computer uses the driver on the Working Model disk so that you avoid display problems caused by older versions of Microsoft Mouse drivers.** Copy the MOUSE.SYS or MOUS8514.SYS file to the directory that contains your current mouse-driver file. If your system uses the file MOUSE.COM to load the mouse driver, add the following line to your CONFIG.SYS file:

DEVICE=C:\WORD5DEM\MOUSE.SYS

Additional Features in the Full Retail Version of Microsoft Word

You get the following additional features when you purchase the full retail version of Microsoft Word:

- Ability to create documents as large as you have disk space to store. In the Working Model, you can store and print only about the first 6,000 characters of a document.

- Ability to print on all the printers that Microsoft Word supports— more than 100 printers. In the Working Model, you can print on only about a half dozen types of printers.

- Access to on-line Help, the on-line Tutorial, the spelling checker, the Thesaurus, and hyphenation. These features are not included with the Working Model.

- Access to an on-line glossary of useful macros and to additional sample documents and style sheets. These resources are not included with the Working Model.

- Product documentation.

- Product support from Microsoft. Microsoft's Product Support Department or Microsoft Press is not staffed to answer questions about the Working Model.

Text Differences for the Working Model

The following chapters and sections of *Learn Microsoft Word Now* do not apply to, or are different for, the Microsoft Word Working Model:

- Chapter 5, "On-Screen Commands"
  "Cancelling and Undoing Commands"—The Working Model does not support Library Hyphenate, Library Spell, or Library Thesaurus commands.
  "Getting Help with Commands"—The Working Model does not support the Help command, so you cannot perform the examples in this section.

- Chapter 9, "Formatting"
  "Line Breaks"—Nonbreaking spaces, nonbreaking hyphens, and non-required hyphens are not supported, so you cannot perform the examples in this section. In addition, the Library Hyphenate feature is not available in the Working Model.

- Chapter 11 "Filing Documents"
  "Automatic Saving"—The AutoSave feature is not supported in the Working Model.

- Chapter 12 "Printing Documents"
  "Printing Part of a Document"—You cannot print selected portions of a document with the Working Model. Because you can print only a full document, you cannot perform the examples in this section.

- Chapter 14, "Spelling, Hyphenation, and the Thesaurus"
  "Checking Spelling"—The Working Model does not supply the spelling checker, so you cannot perform the examples in this section.

"Automatic Hyphenation"—The Working Model does not supply the hyphenation dictionary, so you cannot perform the examples in this section.

"Using the Thesaurus"—The Working Model does not supply the thesaurus, so you cannot perform the examples in this section.

■ Chapter 16, "Macros"

"The Ready-Made Macros"—The Working Model does not supply the ready-made macros.

"How to Record Macros"—The example in this section records a macro that includes the Hyphenate command, which is not available in the Working Model. You can, however, use the instructions in this section to record macros that include any commands and features that are available.

"To Print What?"—Because the Working Model does not allow you to print only part of a document, you cannot successfully run this macro.

■ Appendix A "Getting Acquainted with DOS"

Because this appendix assumes you have the full retail version, certain parts do not apply. For example, there is no file named README.DOC included with the Working Model.

■ Appendix B "Setting Up and Starting Word"

This appendix applies ONLY to the full retail version of Microsoft Word. Use the instructions in this Introduction to set up and run the Working Model included with this book.

■ Appendix C "Summary of Commands" and Appendix D "Shortcut and Toggle Keys"

Because certain features are not included in the Working Model, not all commands listed in these appendixes are supported.

Visual Differences for the Working Model

The following are noticeable differences between the Working Model screens and the screen illustrations in this book:

■ The name of the program appears as "MS Word Demo" instead of as "Microsoft Word."

■ Lists of available fonts and point sizes, documents, directories, and printers on the Working Model screen might be different from the lists shown in this book.

Comments About the Working Model

If you have a question or comment about the text or programs in *Learn Microsoft Word Now,* or if the disk in your package is defective, write to Microsoft Press, Attn: Learn Word Now Editor, One Microsoft Way, Redmond, WA 98052-6399. No phone calls, please.

PART I

A SHORT COURSE IN WORD

Chapter 1

Getting Acquainted

Microsoft Word turns your computer into a
word processor. As a word processor, your computer can do everything a typewriter can do—
and much more. With Word, you can use your
computer to prepare any kind of document, from
memos to letters, reports, brochures, and even
entire books.

When you use a computer to prepare a document, you type on a keyboard much like that of a typewriter, but your words appear on a TV–like screen, instead of on paper. As you type, a small block of light, called a cursor (or highlight), marks your place in the document on the screen. You can tell the computer to print what you've typed at any time, but typing on the keyboard and printing on paper are separate events.

WHY USE A WORD PROCESSOR INSTEAD OF A TYPEWRITER?

A word processor is much more forgiving than a typewriter. You can review and easily change what you type *before* you print it on paper. Your paper copy of a document is always free from erasures, strips of correction tape, and blotches of white-out. A good word processor even helps you find the words you want to change. It removes anything you want to erase, closes up the gaps, and makes room for anything you want to add. You can easily move words or large sections of text from one place to another.

Even if you never make mistakes or change your mind, typing a document on a word processor is still easier than typing it on a typewriter. You can type without worrying about typing beyond the edge of the paper. As you approach the end of a line, you don't have to slow down to decide how many letters of the next word will fit in the remaining space. When you get to the bottom of a page, you don't have to stop to change the paper. When it's time to start a new line or a new page, a word processor automatically starts it for you, while you continue typing.

You can change the appearance of a document, reshaping it to fit your needs or tastes, as easily as you can change the words. For example, you can change the margins, change the spacing between lines, or justify the text (to make the right edge as straight as the left). You can also select special printing effects, such as boldfacing and underlining.

Compared to what a typewriter can do, all these word-processing features are marvels. But today, they are commonplace marvels. You can expect to get them with any reasonably good word-processing program. Microsoft Word goes beyond these basic offerings to give you more than a commonplace word processor.

WHAT MAKES WORD SPECIAL?

Microsoft Word is an extremely versatile and powerful word-processing program. Designed to be used with the IBM family of personal computers, Word takes full advantage of the considerable resources offered by these machines.

Flexible and Easy to Use

Whatever task is at hand, Word offers you a variety of ways to accomplish it. Word strives to accommodate you—your preferences and work habits—rather than forcing you to adapt to it. More than any other word processor, Word lets you control what you see and what you do.

You can give instructions to Word by choosing a plain English command from a list called a menu that's visible on the screen. If you don't like selecting commands from menus, you can use function keys or other special-purpose keys to perform word-processing tasks. You can even decide what each special-purpose key will do if you don't like Word's key assignments.

Word also offers an alternative to using the keyboard. If you purchase a mouse, a hand-held pointing device, you can point to words that you want to change and choose commands from a menu on the screen.

Powerful Editing

Each step of the way, whether you use the keyboard, menus, or the mouse to make changes to a document, Word safeguards your work by making text difficult to lose and easy to recover. For example, before you erase any amount of text, Word highlights it so there is no question about what you are removing. After you erase something, Word holds on to it, so you can plug it back into place if you change your mind. In fact, an Undo command lets you undo most changes you make—not only deletions.

You can view up to eight documents in separate windows at the same time, and you can easily move text from one document to another. When you want to see more of a document in one of the windows, simply zoom the window to enlarge it to full-screen size. Word puts no limit on the size of the document you can create. Commands that let you move quickly to any part of a document make long documents easy to work with. You can even look at different parts of the same document at the same time.

Instead of retyping frequently used names, phrases, or paragraphs, put them in a special storage area called a glossary. Once there, you can copy these pieces of text at any time, to insert in any document.

Not good at spelling? Want some help in finding typing errors? With Word's built-in Spell program, you can check a single word or an entire document for spelling errors and typos without leaving the Word program. Unsure where to hyphenate a word? Let Word do it for you. It will hyphenate a single word or all the words in a document that need it. Trying to think of a better word to use? Look it up in the built-in Thesaurus to find a good alternative.

Word can search through an entire document for anything you want to find and can replace each occurrence with something else. Every imaginable safeguard has been built into Word's search-and-replace feature to help you avoid finding or replacing the wrong text. In addition to searching for text, you can search for and replace formatting instructions or search for entire documents.

Exceptional Formatting

Word is unmatched in the number of formatting features it offers. The control you have over the appearance of a printed document is limited more by the capabilities of your printer than it is by the capabilities of Word. How much you get involved with formatting depends on your needs and interests: All formatting parameters have been conveniently preset for you, but you can view the settings and easily change them.

Word goes much further than other word-processing programs in show-ing you on the screen what your document will look like when it's printed. If you boldface a word, it's boldfaced on the screen. If you underline a word, it's underlined on the screen. As soon as you make a formatting change, you see the results on the screen, so you can experiment with different formats, polishing the appearance of a document before you print it.

If your printer can manage it, Word can give you proportionally spaced text, similar to the text in this book, in which the amount of space taken up by each letter varies according to its shape and size. And in addition to bold-facing and underlining, you can get italics, double underlining, small capi-tals, strikethroughs, subscripts, and superscripts.

Some formatting features make typing easier. If you type a word and then decide you want it in uppercase (capital) letters, you can reformat the word without retyping it. You can automatically indent the first line of each paragraph in a document without once pressing the Tab key, or you can put a blank line between all paragraphs with a single formatting command.

You can instruct Word to add headings in the top and bottom margins of each printed page, and you can specify different headings for alternate pages. Word lets you control the exact positions of both headings and page numbers.

Word also makes it easy to add footnotes to a document: It can automatically number the footnotes for you and can print them on the page where they are referenced. No matter how many changes you make to a document or to the number or the order of your footnotes, Word sees that they are numbered correctly and that each is printed on the correct page.

You can set tabs anywhere and control how text is aligned in the columns of a table. For example, you can ask Word to line up the decimal points in a column of numbers, or you can ask it to center the column headings in a table. Need to rearrange a table? You can delete, move, or copy entire columns.

To reduce time spent formatting documents, you can record and store often-used formats in style sheets and then apply the styles to any document.

Merge Printing

Word's Print Merge feature makes mass mailings easy and gives you control over what goes in each letter. If you want to send the same (or a similar) letter to a number of different people, you just type the letter once. Word will stop the printer at the appropriate places and ask you to type in the name and address (and any other variable information) for each letter. Or, you can give Word a mailing list of names and addresses, and Word will plug in the names and addresses for you.

Document Retrieval

Word does not limit you to an 8-character filename for identifying and finding files. You can append a summary sheet to each document, containing such information as the name of the author or person who prepared the document, the creation date, the revision date, and keywords and comments that help identify the document. Then you can conduct a search for documents based on this summary information or on text included within the document.

Macros

With macros, you can reduce complicated tasks to a few keystrokes. You can record any sequence of keystrokes and commands that you use repeatedly. Then, when you need to repeat the task they perform, you can play back the entire sequence included in the macro by pressing a few keys.

You can create macros that almost think for themselves: Macros can remind you of tasks to do, ask you for information needed to complete a task, calculate, repeat themselves as long as specified conditions are met, and perform alternative tasks if those conditions are not met.

Help Is Never Far Away

If you have the Special Edition with disks included, consult the Introduction

If you're working with Word and you forget how to do something, you can get help without searching through the manual. When help is requested, Word displays instructions, reminders, and explanations about almost every aspect of itself. You can get help with a specific command without having to read through screenful after screenful of unrelated information.

In addition to narrative instructions and information, you can ask for a tutorial that guides you through each step as you try out a feature. When you're done, Word takes you back to the document you were working on when you asked for help.

The List Goes On

The list of features seems endless. It goes on to include line and box drawing; math and sorting capabilities; indexing; outlining; and linking Word with spreadsheets and other programs.

The makers of Word aren't done yet. They are committed to keeping Word a state-of-the-art word processor: As computing power continues to grow, word-processing power with Word will grow too.

WHAT DO YOU NEED TO USE WORD?

To use Word, you need a computer with at least two floppy-disk drives, a keyboard, a display unit, a printer, Disk Operating System software, and several blank disks for storing documents.

The computer must be a member of the IBM family of personal computers, or it must work like an IBM personal computer. This group of machines includes the various models manufactured by IBM as well as equivalent computers manufactured by other companies.

Once you have Word up and running on one of these computers, Word will manage the computer for you. You don't need to know how a computer works in order to use Word, but you'll probably find it helpful to have a general understanding of what the various components do and the role each plays in word processing. For purposes of illustration, we'll look at the personal-computer system shown in Figure 1-1. Your computer may not look exactly like the one pictured here, but the basic components will be the same. Let's begin with the keyboard and the mouse.

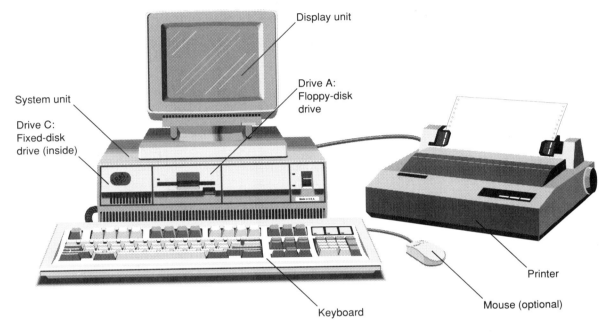

Figure 1-1. *A complete personal-computer system.*

The Keyboard and the Mouse

You talk to your computer through the *keyboard* or the *mouse*. By pressing keys or maneuvering the mouse, you can tell the computer when to start and stop the Word program, what words you want processed, and how you want them processed. The keyboard comes with the computer, but the mouse is an optional device that can be purchased from Microsoft or from your dealer.

The keyboard has all the keys that you find on a typewriter, plus a lot of special-purpose keys. The special-purpose keys let you tell the computer what to do by pressing one or two keys, instead of typing a long command.

The mouse is a small device that fits neatly under the hand. The mouse makes most of the special-purpose keys unnecessary, because it lets you give most commands without using the keyboard. As you slide the mouse around your desktop, a pointer (similar to the cursor) moves around the screen. The location, text, or command you point to on the screen determines the instruction you give to the computer when you press one or both of the buttons found on top of the mouse.

The mouse needs a clean, dry surface to glide over. There is a rotating ball on its underside: If it gets clogged with desktop debris and stops rotating freely, refer to the *Microsoft Mouse User's Guide* for instructions on removing and cleaning the ball.

The Display Unit

What you type on the keyboard shows up on the *display unit.* Also called a monitor, CRT (cathode-ray tube), VDU (visual display unit), or screen, the display unit lets you see your words before you commit them to paper. The computer speaks to you through the display unit: It prompts you to do things, tells you what commands you can give, tells you if it's having problems, and shows you the results of your joint efforts.

The display unit is connected to an adapter card that is inserted in a slot in the computer. The quality and the graphics capabilities of the display depend on both the type of monitor and the type of adapter attached to it. In the *Using Microsoft Word* manual, you'll find a list of possible combinations with specific brand names identified.

The various combinations of display units and adapter cards fall into two main categories: those that have graphics capabilities and those that don't. If you have a graphics monitor and adapter, you'll be able to use Word in two different modes: graphics mode or text mode. In *graphics mode,* you are treated to some special graphics that Word uses to illustrate what the mouse is doing. You also see special printing effects, such as italics and small caps, displayed on the screen. In *text mode,* you have increased speed but you forfeit the special graphics capabilities of the monitor. With Word, you can easily switch from one mode to another.

Some display units are automatically turned on when you turn on the computer; others you must turn on separately. You'll spend many hours looking at the display unit, so find the brightness and contrast controls and adjust them to suit yourself.

The Printer

The *printer* delivers the final product—a paper copy of your document. Printers come in two basic varieties: serial and parallel. The difference is based on how they are designed to receive signals from the computer. It's important for your computer—and therefore for you—to know which kind you have, but in terms of word-processing performance, there is no significant difference between parallel and serial printers.

Printers also differ in how they put images on paper. *Impact printers,* the most common and economical, employ mechanisms that strike the paper through an inked ribbon. Among impact printers, there are dot-matrix and formed-character printers. *Dot-matrix printers* form characters out of dots. As the printhead passes over the paper, individual pins in the printhead strike the paper to print dots in various patterns. Dot-matrix printers are usually faster and less expensive than formed-character printers, but the print quality is generally not as good. *Formed-character printers* are like typewriters in that preformed characters on a printing element strike the paper. The printing element is usually a daisy wheel or a thimble. A daisy wheel is a round, flat disk with spokes radiating from the center of the disk. At the end of each spoke is a character. A thimble is a cup-shaped printing element similar to a daisy wheel.

Among *nonimpact printers,* laser printers and ink-jet printers are becoming increasingly popular. Although considerably more expensive than dot-matrix or formed-character printers, they combine the best features of both—speed and quality of printing. *Laser printers* use light beams to produce images on paper somewhat like photocopiers do. *Ink-jet printers* print characters by spraying dots of ink on the paper through a printhead. Both laser printers and ink-jet printers give you quiet operation and a wide selection of fonts, styles, and sizes. With them, you can produce text that approaches typeset quality. Microsoft Word was the first major word-processing program to take advantage of all the features that laser and ink-jet printers offer.

Your printer plays a key role in the word-processing cycle. Get to know it well by reading the manual that comes with it.

The Computer Itself

At the center of a computer system is the computer itself. In most personal computers, the vital electronic parts that make the computer seem intelligent are housed in a flat case called the *system unit.* Within the system unit are the CPU (central processing unit) and the memory. The CPU enables the computer to interpret and follow instructions, carry out commands, perform calculations, and manipulate text. But the CPU can handle only one instruction or a small amount of information at a time. So the memory helps out by storing the instructions and information that are either waiting in line to be processed or have already been processed.

What you type on the keyboard goes to the computer's memory, where the CPU can access it. From the memory, it can be sent to the display unit, to the printer, or to permanent storage on disk.

The part of the memory that is available to you is called RAM (random access memory). Its size is measured in bytes: A byte is the amount of storage needed to hold one character. RAM is a temporary storage place. Each time you turn off the power, the contents of RAM disappear. If you want to keep what you've typed, you must store your work on a disk before you turn off the power.

If you have the Special Edition with disk included, consult the Introduction

The amount of memory you have in your computer depends on how much you purchased or added on to your computer. To use version 5.0 of Word you need at least 320 kilobytes (320 KB) of RAM. (1 KB = 1024 bytes.) Version 4.0 of Word requires only 256 KB, but to use the on-screen tutorials you need 320 KB. If you have more than the required memory, Word can speed up its own operation by making use of the extra memory.

The Disks and Their Drives

You create or edit a document in the computer's temporary memory and then copy it onto a disk, where it can be stored permanently. Transferring a copy of a document from memory to a disk is called *saving* a document. Transfering a copy of a document from a disk back to memory is called *loading* a document.

Programs are also stored on disks and are usually purchased on disks. Before you can use a program, a copy of it must be loaded into the computer's memory. A program is a set of instructions that tell the computer how to perform specific tasks. The Microsoft Word program tells the computer how to process the words you type.

Documents and programs are stored in *files* on a disk, much as papers are organized in file folders in a filing cabinet. Each file is given a name and usually holds one document, one program, or one section of a large program. The length of a file and the number of files you can store on a disk are limited primarily by the amount of space that is available on the disk. The total amount of space available on a disk depends on what type of disk it is.

Two types of disk can be used with personal computers: *floppy* (or flexible) *disks* and *fixed* (or hard) *disks*. Both types of disk have a magnetic recording surface on which information can be erased, as well as recorded. Floppy disks have either a 5¼-inch or 3½-inch diameter and are enclosed in covers. (See Figure 1-2.) Fixed disks, made of rigid metal and permanently fixed in place inside the system unit, have much higher storage capacities and are much faster than floppy disks.

The standard 5¼-inch floppy disk is double-sided (having a recording surface on both sides) and double-density (holding twice as much information as the older-style disks). It holds about 360,000 characters (360 kilobytes or 360 KB). The higher-capacity floppy disks can hold much more—such as 5¼-inch quad-density disks, which hold 1.2 million characters (1.2 megabytes or 1.2 MB).

The 3½-inch floppy disks can hold 720 KB or 1.44 MB. Fixed disks commonly hold from 10 to 40 MB.

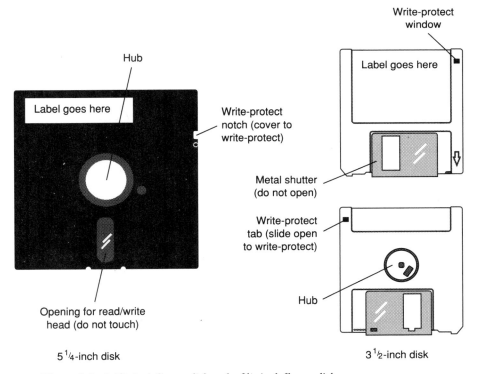

Figure 1-2. *A 5¼-inch floppy disk and a 3½-inch floppy disk.*

The type of disk your computer uses depends on the type of *disk drive* you have. A disk drive is the device that writes information on disks and reads information from them. Disk drives are identified by letters. The top or leftmost floppy-disk drive on a two-drive system is called drive A, and the second floppy-disk drive is called drive B. If you have only one floppy-disk drive, it is both drive A and drive B. Drive C refers to a fixed disk.

Because the Word program has grown to include so many features, operating Word with two standard 5¼-inch floppy-disk drives is becoming impractical. To take full advantage of Word's features and to avoid awkward disk switching, you need the higher-capacity floppy disks or a fixed disk.

Handling floppy disks

All disks must be protected from temperature extremes, moisture, smoke, and magnetic fields. Floppy disks that are not encased in a rigid sleeve need extra care. Do not bend, press, or touch their exposed surfaces. Keep their dust jackets on when the disks are not in use. Use a soft felt-tip pen when writing on their labels.

You can erase what's recorded on a disk, and you can write over a previous recording. Files stored on floppy disks can be protected from accidental erasing or changing by write-protecting them. When a disk is write-protected, the computer can read information from the disk but cannot write on it. To write-protect a 5¼-inch disk, put a write-protect tab or a piece of opaque tape over the write-protect notch found on the side of the disk. To write-protect a 3½-inch disk, slide the tab in the write-protect window until the window is open. (See Figure 1-2.)

A 5¼-inch floppy-disk drive has a *door* or latch that must be opened before you insert the disk and closed afterward. Never open the door or remove a disk when the light on the disk drive is on. The light indicates that the disk is in use—the computer is reading from it or writing on it—and you can lose information if you try to move it at this time.

To insert a 5¼-inch disk in a disk drive, gently hold the disk by its edge and insert it, label side up, with the long oval access slot pointing toward the rear of the drive and the write-protect notch on the left, as shown in Figure 1-3. (For a vertical drive, insert the disk with the label facing left and the write-protect notch on the bottom.) Slide the disk all the way into the drive and then close the door.

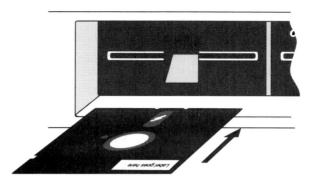

Figure 1-3. *Inserting a 5¹/₄-inch floppy disk.*

A 3¹/₂-inch disk will only go in one way. Hold the disk with the circular hub facing down and the arrow stamped on the disk pointing toward the drive, as shown in Figure 1-4. Push the disk into the drive until it clicks into place. To remove the disk, press the eject button on the drive.

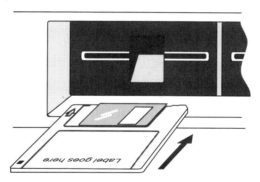

Figure 1-4. *Inserting a 3¹/₂-inch floppy disk.*

The Disk Operating System

When you first purchase a disk drive, you also purchase a Disk Operating System, which comes on a floppy disk. If your computer has a fixed disk, the Disk Operating System needs to be installed on it. The documentation that comes with the operating system tells you how to do this, but usually your computer dealer will install it for you.

Referred to as DOS (pronounced ''doss''), the Disk Operating System is a complex set of instructions that tells the computer how to do basic tasks, such as how to read other programs found on disks, how to organize disk space, and how to work cooperatively with all the other components of the system, including you. In short, DOS makes your computer operable. Before you can start Word, you must start DOS. Microsoft Word must be run with version 2.0 or later of MS-DOS, the Microsoft version of DOS.

In addition to making your computer operable, DOS comes with a toolkit of commands and small programs that are helpful to word processing. If you're not familiar with DOS, read Appendix A to find out how to use the most useful DOS commands: DIR (Directory), which shows you a list of files stored on a disk; FORMAT, which prepares a floppy disk so that you can store documents on it; DEL, which deletes files; REN, which renames files; COPY and DISKCOPY, which let you copy individual files or an entire floppy disk; and CHKDSK, which tells you how much memory your computer has and how much is available for use.

If you have a fixed disk or the higher-capacity floppy disks, be sure to learn the DOS commands that help you organize and access your storage space: MD (Make Directory), CD (Change Directory), RD (Remove Directory), PROMPT, and PATH. These commands are also covered in Appendix A.

THE WORD PACKAGE

If you have the Special Edition with disk included, consult the Introduction

In addition to an array of documentation, you find a handful of floppy disks when you open the Word package. Don't be alarmed. You won't be juggling all of these disks every day. Several of them are used only to set up Word to fit your system and to learn how to use the Word program. After you set up your copy of the Word program and learn how to use Word, you'll need only one program disk to run Word and do most of your work. If you have a fixed disk, everything you need can be put on your fixed disk.

In Appendix B, you'll find a description of each of the disks you receive with the Microsoft Word 5.0 package.

Before You Use Word

Before you use Word, the first thing you need to do is to make backup copies of the disks you received in the Word package. No matter how careful you are in handling floppy disks, accidents do happen, and with daily use over a long period of time, a disk can become worn and therefore less reliable. Protect your software by copying the contents of each disk onto a second disk and storing the originals where they won't be damaged. To make backup copies of Word disks, use the DOS command DISKCOPY described in Appendix A.

After you make backup copies of Word, the next thing you need to do is to run the Setup program. This enables Word to make the best use of your equipment. In most cases, you only have to use the Setup program once—before you use Word for the first time.

If your copy of Word has not been set up for your system, turn to Appendix B. There you'll learn the details of what the Setup program does and how to use it. Once these initial preparations are out of the way, you'll find that starting Word is a simple ceremony and that using Word requires minimal disk handling.

Chapter 2

Starting Word and Creating a Document

After you've made backup copies of the Word disks and used the Setup program to set up Word, you're ready to start using Word. In this chapter, you learn how to start the Word program and how to create a document.

HOW TO START WORD

The Setup program creates a working copy of your Word Program disk and, if necessary, modifies your working copy of DOS. Always use these working copies to start DOS and then Word.

If you have the Special Edition with disk included, consult the Introduction

If you have a fixed-disk system, note that I'm assuming both DOS and Word have been installed on your fixed disk in drive C. The copy of DOS and the copy of Word that reside on your fixed disk are your working copies.

Starting DOS

Before you can start Word, you must first start DOS. Ordinarily, if DOS is already up and running, you don't need to restart it. But you must restart DOS if it was not initially started with your working copy of DOS. In particular, the first time you use Word after running the Setup program, you must restart DOS so that the computer will be notified of any changes made to DOS files during setup.

To start DOS:

1. If you have a floppy-disk system and if you do not have DOS on your working copy of the Word Program disk, put your *working copy* of the DOS disk in drive A. If you do have DOS on your Word disk, insert your Word disk in drive A. (Recall that drive A is the leftmost or top drive of a two-drive system.)

   If you have a fixed-disk system, leave drive A empty with the door open.

2. If your computer is off, turn it on. If your computer is already on, restart it by holding down the Control (Ctrl) and Alternate (Alt) keys as you press the Delete (Del) key.

3. If the current date displayed by DOS is correct, press the Enter (↵) key to confirm it. If it needs to be changed, type in the correct date and then press the Enter key. Use hyphens or slashes to separate parts of the date.

4. If the current time displayed is correct, press the Enter key to confirm it. If it needs to be changed, type in the correct time and then press the Enter key. Use colons to separate units of time.

When you see the *A>* prompt (on a floppy-disk system) or the *C>* prompt (on a fixed-disk system), you know that DOS is running and ready for you to give the command to start Word.

Starting Word on a Floppy-Disk System

To start Word on a two-drive floppy-disk system after you've started DOS:

If you have the Special Edition with disk included, consult the Introduction

1. When you see the *A>* prompt, remove your DOS disk and insert your working copy of the Word Program disk in drive A (if it isn't already there). Put a formatted disk for storing documents in drive B.

2. If you have multiple directories, change to the directory where Word is stored. For example, if you told the Setup program to copy the Word program files to a directory called *word*, type:

   CD \WORD

   (As explained in Appendix B, this step isn't necessary if you include the Word program directory in the DOS PATH command within your AUTOEXEC.BAT file.)

3. At the *A>* prompt, type:

   WORD

   and press the Enter key to start Word.

If you see a message saying *Bad command or file name*, try it again. Take care to insert the correct disk and, if you have multiple directories, be sure to type the correct directory name.

❑ REMINDER: *You can type uppercase letters or lowercase letters when giving commands to DOS or Word.*

Starting Word on a Fixed-Disk System

To start Word on a fixed-disk system after you've started DOS:

1. When you see the *C>* prompt, change to the directory where Word is stored. For example, if you told the Setup program to copy the Word program files to a directory called *word*, type:

   CD \WORD

   (As explained in Appendix B, this step isn't necessary if you include the Word program directory in the DOS PATH command within your AUTOEXEC.BAT file.)

2. When the *C>* prompt reappears, type:

   WORD

   and press the Enter key to start Word.

If you see a message saying *Bad command or file name*, try it again. Be sure to type the correct directory name so that DOS can find the Word program.

❑ REMINDER: *You can type uppercase letters or lowercase letters when giving commands to DOS or Word.*

What You See After You Start Word

After you start up Word, the program introduces itself and draws a box, called a *window,* on the screen.

If you have the Special Edition with disk included, consult the Introduction

```
COMMAND: Copy Delete Format Gallery Help Insert Jump Library
         Options Print Quit Replace Search Transfer Undo Window
Edit document or press Esc to use menu
Pg1 Co1            {}              ?                    Microsoft Word
```

You look through this window to see what you've typed on the keyboard. The symbols in and around the window help you keep track of where you are. The small block of light in the upper left corner is called a *cursor,* or *highlight.* It moves along as you type to mark the place where the next character that you type will appear. The four lines of text below the window remind you what to do, explain your options, tell you where you are, and tell you if something has gone wrong. You'll take a closer look at these symbols and the text under the window later—when you need to know what they mean. For the time being, what you need to know is how to create a document.

CREATING A DOCUMENT

Because word processing makes it so easy to change a document without retyping it, it's now more feasible to create and compose while you're typing. You don't have to worry about getting it right the first time. You can change and rearrange your words to your heart's content by tapping some keys or maneuvering the mouse. You can polish and refine your words until they say exactly what you want them to say—without paying a tremendous price in typing time. You can spend more time creating and less time typing.

Whether you compose your words as you're typing them or you type from prewritten copy, the method for typing a document with Word is the same, and that's what the rest of this chapter is about. The next chapter is about changing what you've typed.

Before you start typing on a typewriter, you have to make some basic formatting decisions that affect the way your document looks on paper. Frequently, you need to adjust your typewriter to make typing easier. You set a left and a right margin so that the document doesn't look like it's falling off the paper and so that the typewriter reminds you, by ringing a bell, when it's time to start a new line. You set tabs so that you don't have to press the spacebar repeatedly when you want to indent paragraphs or lines or when you want to leave space between columns in a table.

No mention of formatting is made in this chapter because Word lets you start producing documents without knowing anything about formatting. You can start typing as soon as you start the program. Word formats the document for you as you type it. The margins and tabs have already been set to meet most word-processing needs. If they don't meet your needs, you can change them either before or after you type a document.

You'll learn what your formatting alternatives are in later chapters. For now, let Word do the formatting for you.

About the Keyboard

Personal-computer keyboards have a lot of special-purpose keys, but you can ignore them for now. If you're familiar with a typewriter, you already know all the keys that you need to type a document. The keys that you use to type a document are highlighted in Figures 2-1 and 2-2 on the following page. Some of these keys—the Shift, Caps Lock, Tab, Spacebar, Backspace, and Enter (or Return) keys—look or behave differently from the way they work on a typewriter.

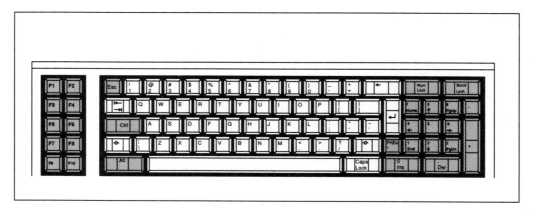

Figure 2-1. *The typing keys as they appear on the 83-key keyboard.*

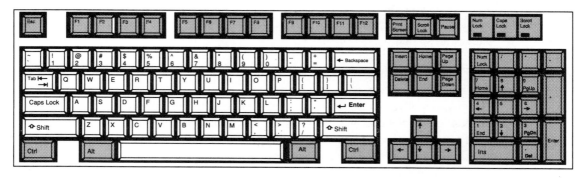

Figure 2-2. *The typing keys as they appear on the 101-key extended keyboard.*

The Shift keys

The two Shift keys behave as they do on a typewriter. Use them in combination with other keys to type uppercase letters, the symbols above the numbers, and anything else that is shown on the upper half of a key top. (Note that if the Caps Lock key is on, using the Shift key produces *lower*case letters.)

⇧ Shift

The Caps Lock key

When you want to type words in all uppercase (capital) letters, press the Caps Lock key so that you don't have to hold down the Shift key. Unlike the shift-lock key on a typewriter, Caps Lock affects the letter keys only. Caps Lock is a toggle key: Press it once, and it's turned on. Press it again, and it's turned off.

The Tab key

Use the Tab key as you would on a typewriter to type tables or to type facts and figures arranged in columns. You can also use the Tab key to indent the first line of a paragraph. (In Chapter 9, you'll learn how to get Word to automatically indent the first line of each paragraph in a document.)

On a typewriter, the Tab key simply moves the typing element (or carriage) to a fixed position, skipping over any previously typed letters on the way. With Word, you cannot use the Tab key to skip over previously typed characters because the Tab key inserts a tab character. A tab character is a special space-making character that you can delete like any other character.

The Spacebar

Use the Spacebar as you would on a typewriter to add space after words or punctuation. Similar to the Tab key, the Spacebar cannot be used to skip over previously typed characters as it can on a typewriter. Pressing the Spacebar inserts a space. A space in Word is a character that can be deleted like any other character.

Spacebar

The Backspace key

Unlike the backspace key on a typewriter, the Backspace key in Word erases characters as you back up over them. It's useful for correcting an error while you're typing, right after you make a mistake.

The Enter (or Return) key

On an electric typewriter, you press a carriage-return key at the end of each line you type in order to start a new line. On most computer keyboards, the return key is called the Enter key. With Word, you do not press the Enter key at the end of each line. Word knows where the right margin is and automatically starts a new line when you reach the right margin. (If you press the Enter key at the end of each line, you may end up with some very short lines when you revise or reformat what you've typed.)

When you're typing short documents or documents that won't need extensive formatting, it's easiest to use the Enter key as follows:

■ Press Enter to end a paragraph. Do not press Enter to end each line in a paragraph.

■ Press Enter twice to create a blank line between paragraphs. (In Chapter 9, you'll learn how to get Word to *automatically* insert extra space between paragraphs.)

■ Press Enter to end a line at a definite place. For example, when you're typing a table, a poem, or the address in a letter, you want to end each line after a particular word or number, regardless of how far it is from the right margin.

The Enter key inserts a nonprinting character, called a paragraph mark, that can be deleted like any other character.

The New Page keys

When using a typewriter, have you ever typed off the bottom edge of a sheet of paper before you remembered to start a new page? With Word, you don't have to worry about starting new pages. Just keep typing. When printing your document, Word automatically starts a new page for you when the current page is filled.

Occasionally, you might want to start a new page at a particular place—before the page you're currently typing is filled. For example, if you're typing a letter that includes a list of employee names and you want the list to be on a separate page, then you'd start a new page after the letter.

Three keys are used together to start a new page at a particular place: Hold down the Shift key and the Ctrl key while you press the Enter key.

A dotted line, called a new page mark, will appear across the window to show where the new page starts. The new page mark is a nonprinting character that can be deleted like any other character.

What You Do

Just start typing. Try out Word by typing the letter in Figure 2-3 on the following page, and remember:

- Don't press Enter at the end of each line in a paragraph. Just keep typing until you get to the end of the paragraph.

- To make a blank line between paragraphs, press Enter twice.

- When you get to the bottom of the screen, keep typing. Your text automatically moves up on the screen so that you always see the part that you are currently typing.

- No loitering allowed on any of the keys when you're typing: If you hold down any key, it repeats itself until you release it.

- If you make any errors, try out the Backspace key to correct a few of them. But save some errors to correct later.

Dear Western Allies,

This is just a quick note to let you know that all is fine
on the Eastern Front. Winter has been very picturesque here.
Lots of fluffy white snow on trees, houses, and hillsides.
Wreaths with bows on every colonial door. No horsedrawn
sleighs but lots of kids on sleds.

Adjusting to our new life on the other side of the continent
was difficult at first. We now understand why people resist
moving. Friendship is dear--all the more dear when not
there. We've finally met some people we feel comfortable
with and enjoy being with.

Our neighbors have stopped eyeing us, and our California
license plates, with distrust. After 6 months of proving
ourselves to be worthy neighbors without any unusual living
habits, we are now being rewarded with friendly greetings on
the street and even some prolonged chit-chat.

Time to go shovel some snow. Our very best wishes to you.

Love,

The Eastern Alliance

Figure 2-3. *A sample letter.*

In the next chapter, you'll learn how to correct mistakes and revise the letter
you've just typed. If you want to take a break now before you start editing
the letter, skip to Chapter 4 to learn how to save a document, quit Word, and
start again later.

Chapter 3

Editing a Document

So far, nothing that you've done is very different from typing on a typewriter. Not having to press a return key at the end of each line saves you time and effort, but the real value of word processing lies in being able to make changes to a document without retyping it. In this chapter, you'll learn how to correct errors, revise wording, rearrange a document, and add new text at any place by using the keyboard, the mouse, or some combination of both. Before you start editing, let's take a closer look at the Microsoft Word editing screen.

THE EDITING SCREEN

The editing screen has two parts: the text area at the top and the command area at the bottom.

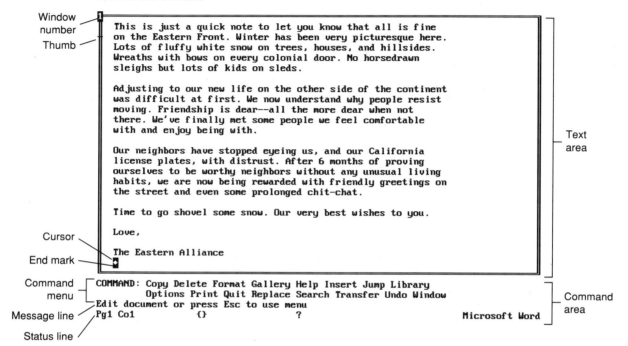

The Text Area

In addition to the window and the part of the document that's in the window, the text area displays these symbols: ▮, ♦, ▯, and −. If you have a mouse installed, you also see ▸ or ▮, depending on your system's graphics capability.

▮ The *cursor,* or *highlight,* is a small, rectangular block of light that marks the spot where the next character you type will appear or that highlights what you want to change. You can move the cursor anywhere in a document.

♦ The *end mark* is a diamond-shaped symbol that marks the end of your document. When you first see the window, and when the cursor is at the end of your document, the end mark and the cursor are superimposed like this: ▯.

■ The *window number* in the top left corner of the window frame tells you which window you're looking through. It's of no real importance until you open additional windows. (In Chapter 6, you'll learn how to open additional windows so that you can see more than one document or different parts of the same document at the same time. Then you can easily compare them or move text between them.)

− The position of the dash-like horizontal line, called the *thumb,* on the left window border tells you what part of a document you see in the window. If it's at the top of the left border, you're looking at the beginning of a document. If it's at the bottom, you're looking at the end. The distance of the dash from the top or bottom of the window border is proportional to the distance that you are from the beginning or the end of the document. This is particularly useful for working with long documents.

▶ *or* ■ If you have a mouse installed, you'll see an additional symbol in the text window: the *mouse pointer.* The shape of the mouse pointer depends on your system's graphics capability. When you first start Word, you see either an arrow pointing up and to the left or a bright rectangle.

The corners and borders of the window, as well as the column of space between the left border and your text, are special places for the mouse. Once you install a mouse, you can point to these places to perform a variety of tasks. When the mouse pointer is in any one of these special places, it changes its shape or its size. This is a graphic signal to you that the mouse is ready to perform a special task. Until you learn what all these special tasks are, avoid pressing the mouse buttons when the mouse pointer is not its usual shape or size.

The Command Area

The command area is below the window and includes the command menu, the message line, and the status line.

The *command menu,* the first two lines of text in the command area, lists all the main commands for editing, formatting, filing, and printing your document.

```
COMMAND: Copy Delete Format Gallery Help Insert Jump Library
         Options Print Quit Replace Search Transfer Undo Window
```

The *message line,* the third line, is the message center. Look here for instructions from the Word program whenever you're puzzled about what to do next or when something seems to have gone wrong.

```
Edit document or press Esc to use menu
```

The *status line,* the bottom line in the command area, offers you assorted information. It tells you the page number and the column that the cursor is in, the last piece of text you deleted or copied, and the abbreviation of whatever toggle key (such as CL for the Caps Lock key) that is turned on. (See Appendix D for a complete list of toggle keys and their abbreviations.) When the word *SAVE* appears in the middle of the status line, it's time to do just that— save your work. The *SAVE* indicator warns you when you're running out of working space in memory or on the Word Program disk.

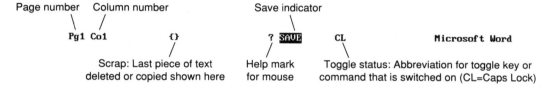

If you have a mouse installed, you see a question mark in the middle of the status line. Whenever you have a question about how things work, you can move the mouse pointer to the *?* and then press and release either mouse button to ask for help.

❑ NOTE: *After you become more familiar with Word, you might want more room on the screen for text display. You can increase the text area by using the Options command to turn off the menu or to remove the double-lined window borders. You can also use the Options command to make normally invisible characters—such as paragraph marks, tab characters, and spaces—visible. (See Chapter 6.)*

EDITING WITH THE KEYBOARD

To make changes to a document, whether you're using the keyboard or the mouse, you need to be able to:

■ Look at any part of your document.

■ Select and highlight what you want to change.

To edit a document with the keyboard, you'll begin to use some of the special-purpose editing keys.

The Editing Keys

You'll find most of the keys that you need to edit a document on the sides of the keyboard. They are highlighted in Figure 3-1 (which shows the 83-key keyboard) and in Figure 3-2 (which shows the 101-key keyboard). Most references in this book to individual keys are based on the 101-key extended

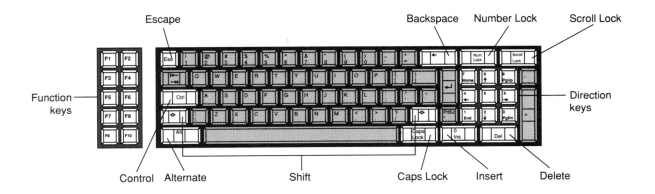

Figure 3-1. *The editing keys on the 83-key keyboard.*

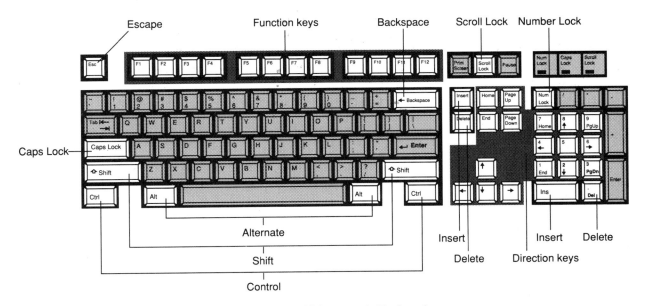

Figure 3-2. *The editing keys on the 101-key extended keyboard.*

keyboard, but the differences between the individual keys on the 101-key keyboard and the 83-key keyboard are minor.

The function keys

On the left side of the 83-key keyboard is a block of 10 *function keys,* labeled F1 to F10. The 101-key extended keyboard has a row of 12 function keys at the top of the keyboard. Most of these keys have four functions each. Just as you can get a different result from a letter key by holding down the Shift key as you press it, you can shift a function key to do something else. In addition to changing the purpose of a function key with a Shift key, you can alter a function key with the Control (Ctrl) key and with the Alternate (Alt) key.

The Shift, Control, and Alternate keys

Similar to the Shift key, the *Control key* and the *Alternate key* do nothing by themselves; but when coupled with other keys, they change the behavior of those keys. The Control key and the Alternate key are used exactly like the Shift key: Press the Ctrl or Alt key first, and hold it down while you press the second key.

The direction keys

On the right side of your keyboard are number keys arranged as they appear on a 10-key adding machine. These are great for typing in numbers when you're typing more numbers than words. However, their primary role is to help you edit. They are called *direction keys:* The arrows and words on the key tops indicate the direction in which they move the cursor or move the window (to see more of the document). The extended keyboard includes an extra set of direction keys that is separate from the block of number keys and easier to use.

You can shift direction keys to perform different tasks. They are shifted with the Shift key, the Control key, the Number Lock (Num Lock) key, and the Scroll Lock key.

When you press the Shift key in combination with one of the direction keys in the number keypad, the cursor not only moves, it highlights everything it passes over. (Note that this won't work with the extra set of direction keys on the extended keyboard.) The Control key *amplifies* the effect of the direction keys, allowing you to move through the text farther and faster.

The Number Lock and the Scroll Lock keys *change* the effect of the direction keys. The Number Lock key lets you type numbers with the direction keys in the number keypad. The Scroll Lock key enables you to use the cursor-moving keys to flip through a document so that you can view all parts of it. As explained in the next section, the Number Lock key and the Scroll Lock key are toggle keys and are used just like the Caps Lock key.

The toggle keys

Number Lock, Scroll Lock, and Caps Lock are called *toggle keys* because they alternate between turning something on and turning it off, the way a light switch does. Press them once to turn on a new function, and press them again to turn it off.

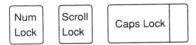

Toggle keys usually change the behavior of other keys. Caps Lock, for example, turns all letters that you type into uppercase letters. It's easy to forget to turn toggle keys off, and on some computers you can't tell whether they're on or off until you press a key that's affected by them. Word helps you by displaying in the status line an abbreviation for the toggle key that is on—for example, NL for Number Lock. Some keyboards have light indicators to remind you if the Caps Lock, Number Lock, and Scroll Lock keys are on.

Later in this book, you'll learn about several other toggle keys. In the meantime, you need to know how to turn off toggle keys in case you accidentally turn one on. If typing or editing keys aren't doing what you think they should, check the status line for a two-letter abbreviation. If you find an abbreviation in the status line and you don't know what it stands for, look it up in Appendix B to find out which key(s) you press to turn the toggle off.

The Insert and Delete keys

Below the number keypad are the Insert (Ins) key and the Delete (Del) key. For convenience, the 101-key extended keyboard has an additional set of Insert and Delete keys to the right of the Backspace key. Along with the Backspace (←) key, these are the keys you use to change text.

Now that you know where all the editing keys are and have a general idea of what they do, let's see how they're used.

Just Looking

To decide what editing changes you want to make, you need to be able to review your work. The letter you typed in Chapter 2, as well as most documents you create, can't be viewed all at once through the text window. Imagine that your document is on one long, continuous sheet of paper—a scroll—instead of on separate sheets of paper. Because you can only look at your document through the window, you have to move the window to see all parts of the document. This operation is called *scrolling*.

Word lets you scroll vertically (up and down) or horizontally (left and right). To scroll horizontally, your text must be wider than the screen. The sample letter you're working on and most documents you prepare aren't wider than the screen, so we'll wait until Chapter 6 to learn about scrolling horizontally.

Scrolling up and down

In Word, when you scroll up, you move the window up toward the beginning of a document. When you scroll down, you move the window down toward the end of a document. You can scroll up or down one windowful at a time, or you can scroll all the way to the beginning or end of a document in one step.

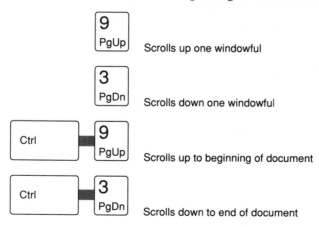

Scrolls up one windowful

Scrolls down one windowful

Scrolls up to beginning of document

Scrolls down to end of document

❑ REMINDER: *A gray horizontal bar connecting two or more keys indicates that those keys are pressed at the same time.*

Try out the scroll keys now to see how they work. Simply press them to see what they do.

Moving the Cursor and Highlighting Text

Before you can change anything in a document, you must first select what you want to change. You indicate to Word what you've selected by highlighting your selection with the cursor.

While you were typing the letter, you probably noticed the cursor jumping ahead with every keystroke, moving to where the next character you type would appear. You can move the cursor to any place in the document, and you can stretch the cursor so that it highlights more than one character.

Moving the cursor

To move the cursor one character or one line at a time, use the direction keys marked with arrows.

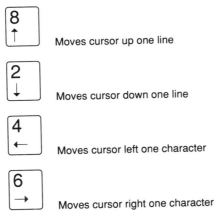

Moves cursor up one line

Moves cursor down one line

Moves cursor left one character

Moves cursor right one character

All keys repeat themselves when held down. Try holding down the direction keys one at a time to see what happens.

To move to the beginning of a line with one keystroke, use the Home key. To move to the end of a line, press the End key.

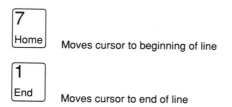

To move quickly to the top or bottom of the window, use the Ctrl key in combination with the Home key or the End key.

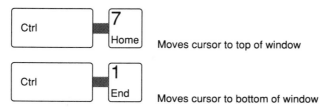

To move all the way to the beginning or the end of the document, use the Ctrl key in combination with the PageUp (PgUp) key or the PageDown (PgDn) key.

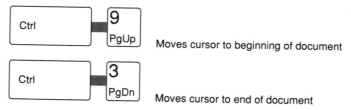

Test-drive the cursor-moving keys until you feel comfortable steering your way around a document.

Highlighting what you want to change

Each cursor-moving key that you've tried so far moves the cursor and leaves it highlighting one character. You can stretch the cursor so that it highlights whole words, parts of words, lines, sentences, paragraphs, and even the whole document. This speeds up editing and reduces the number of editing commands you have to learn. Once you learn how to stretch the cursor, you can use one delete command, for example, to delete a word, a sentence, a paragraph, or as much text as you want.

The function keys F7 to F10 extend the cursor to highlight a whole word or paragraph. F7 and F8 extend the cursor to highlight the word that the cursor is in. If the cursor is not in a word or if the cursor is already highlighting a whole word, F7 moves the cursor to highlight the word to its left and F8 moves the cursor to highlight the word to its right.

F9 and F10 expand the cursor to highlight the paragraph that the cursor is in. If the cursor is already highlighting a whole paragraph, F9 moves the cursor to highlight the previous paragraph and F10 moves the cursor to highlight the next paragraph.

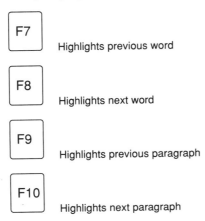

F7   Highlights previous word

F8   Highlights next word

F9   Highlights previous paragraph

F10   Highlights next paragraph

The Shift key gives these keys a different function. By shifting these keys, you can highlight an entire sentence, the line the cursor is in, or the whole document.

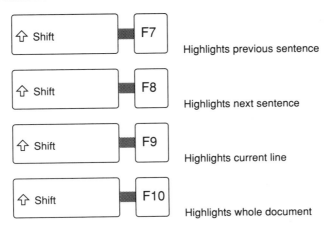

Shift + F7   Highlights previous sentence

Shift + F8   Highlights next sentence

Shift + F9   Highlights current line

Shift + F10   Highlights whole document

Try each of these keys now. Notice that Word highlights the space after a word when you highlight a word, and it highlights the space(s) after a sentence when you highlight a sentence.

When you've finished experimenting, shrink the cursor back to its single-character size by pressing any direction key.

Highlighting a block of text

To highlight a block of text that is not necessarily a word, sentence, or paragraph, you can extend the cursor from one end of the block to the other. The block can be any size. To highlight a block of text:

1. Move the cursor to one end of the block.

2. Press F6, the Extend toggle key, to turn it on.

3. Move the cursor, using *any* cursor-moving key that takes you to the other end of the block. If you go too far, you can back up to reduce the amount of text highlighted.

The F6 key is a toggle key that turns the Extend function on and off. Word automatically turns it off for you after you make an editing change that affects the highlighted text. If you decide not to make a change, press F6 again to stop the cursor from extending every time you try to move it. (To shrink the cursor back to its one-character size, press any direction key.) An *EX* in the bottom line of the screen tells you that the Extend function is turned on.

You can experiment with extending the cursor now, but it will be easier if you wait to see how it's done in the next section.

Making Changes

Now that you know how to scroll to any part of a document and highlight what you want to change, you're ready to learn the most essential editing features of any word processor: inserting and deleting text. Other, more powerful editing features are simply faster and easier ways to insert and delete. Eventually, you'll want to use these features; for now, let's stick to the basics.

Inserting new text

When you want to add new text, all you have to do is move the cursor to where you want to insert the text and start typing. The new text is inserted *to the left of* the cursor, pushing the cursor to the right.

Let's add a postscript to the letter.

1. *Move the cursor to where you want to insert text:* Press Ctrl-PgDn (hold down the Ctrl key while you press the Page Down key) to move the cursor to the end of the document.

2. *Type in the new text:* Press the Enter key (twice, if necessary) to leave a blank line between the closing of the letter and the postscript. Then, type:

   P.S. We're no longer sure we want to be nomads.

```
┌─────────────────────────────────────────────────────────────┐
│1                                                             │
│  The Eastern Alliance                                        │
│                                                              │
│  P.S. We're no longer sure we want to be nomads.▮            │
│                                                              │
│                                                              │
│                                                              │
│                                                              │
│                                                              │
│                                                              │
│                                                              │
│                                                              │
│                                                              │
└─────────────────────────────────────────────────────────────┘
COMMAND: Copy Delete Format Gallery Help Insert Jump Library
         Options Print Quit Replace Search Transfer Undo Window
Edit document or press Esc to use menu
Pg1 Co48          {}              ?              Microsoft Word
```

Deleting text

The Backspace key deletes one character to the left of the cursor. You might have already used the Backspace key to erase errors when you were typing the letter. Let's see how it works when you're editing.

```
┌──────────────────┐
│ ← Backspace      │
└──────────────────┘
```

Let's change "hillsides" to "hills" in the first paragraph of the letter.

1. *Scroll to bring the text into view:* Press Ctrl-PgUp. The cursor now highlights *D*, the first character in the first line.

```
┌──────────────────────────────────────────────────────────────┐
│▒ear Western Allies,                                            │
│                                                                │
│This is just a quick note to let you know that all is fine      │
│on the Eastern Front. Winter has been very picturesque here.    │
│Lots of fluffy white snow on trees, houses, and hillsides.      │
│Wreaths with bows on every colonial door. No horsedrawn         │
│sleighs but lots of kids on sleds.                              │
│                                                                │
│Adjusting to our new life on the other side of the continent    │
│was difficult at first. We now understand why people resist     │
│moving. Friendship is dear--all the more dear when not          │
│there. We've finally met some people we feel comfortable        │
│with and enjoy being with.                                      │
│                                                                │
│Our neighbors have stopped eyeing us, and our California        │
│license plates, with distrust. After 6 months of proving        │
│ourselves to be worthy neighbors without any unusual living     │
│habits, we are now being rewarded with friendly greetings on    │
│the street and even some prolonged chit-chat.                   │
│                                                                │
│Time to go shovel some snow. Our very best wishes to you.       │
│                                                                │
│Love,                                                           │
│                                                                │
└──────────────────────────────────────────────────────────────┘
COMMAND: Copy Delete Format Gallery Help Insert Jump Library
         Options Print Quit Replace Search Transfer Undo Window
Edit document or press Esc to use menu
Pg1 Co1              {}                    ?                    Microsoft Word
```

2. *Move the cursor to the right of the characters you want to delete:* Use the Down direction key to move down to the line that starts with "Lots of fluffy." Press the End key to move to the end of the line, and then press the Left direction key twice to back up until the cursor highlights the period after "hillsides."

   Lots of fluffy white snow on trees, houses, and hillsides█

3. *Delete characters to the left:* Press the Backspace key until "hillsides" is changed to "hills."

   Lots of fluffy white snow on trees, houses, and hills█

The Delete key deletes whatever is highlighted by the cursor. Word calls the piece of text you cut out of your document with the Delete key a *scrap* of text, and it temporarily saves the scrap in case you want to paste it back into your document.

Let's use the Delete (Del) key to change ''friendly greetings on the street'' to just plain ''friendly greetings.''

1. *Highlight what you want to delete:* Use the Down direction key to move down to the line that ends with ''greetings on'' in the third paragraph. Press F8 to move right until the word ''on'' is highlighted.

2. *Extend the cursor:* Press F6 to turn on the Extend function, and then press F8 twice to move right so that the three words ''on the street'' are highlighted. The space after ''street'' will also be highlighted.

```
Dear Western Allies,

This is just a quick note to let you know that all is fine
on the Eastern Front. Winter has been very picturesque here.
Lots of fluffy white snow on trees, houses, and hills.
Wreaths with bows on every colonial door. No horsedrawn
sleighs but lots of kids on sleds.

Adjusting to our new life on the other side of the continent
was difficult at first. We now understand why people resist
moving. Friendship is dear--all the more dear when not
there. We've finally met some people we feel comfortable
with and enjoy being with.

Our neighbors have stopped eyeing us, and our California
license plates, with distrust. After 6 months of proving
ourselves to be worthy neighbors without any unusual living
habits, we are now being rewarded with friendly greetings on
the street and even some prolonged chit-chat.

Time to go shovel some snow. Our very best wishes to you.

Love,
```

```
COMMAND: Copy Delete Format Gallery Help Insert Jump Library
         Options Print Quit Replace Search Transfer Undo Window
Edit document or press Esc to use menu
Pg1 Co11           {}              ?              EX      Microsoft Word
```

3. *Delete the highlighted text:* Press the Del key once to delete all three words. Notice how the surrounding text immediately adjusts itself so that there is no sign that text was erased.

```
┌─────────────────────────────────────────────────────────┐
│▌                                                         │
│  Dear Western Allies,                                    │
│                                                          │
│  This is just a quick note to let you know that all is fine
│  on the Eastern Front. Winter has been very picturesque here.
│  Lots of fluffy white snow on trees, houses, and hills. │
│  Wreaths with bows on every colonial door. No horsedrawn│
│  sleighs but lots of kids on sleds.                     │
│                                                          │
│  Adjusting to our new life on the other side of the continent
│  was difficult at first. We now understand why people resist
│  moving. Friendship is dear--all the more dear when not │
│  there. We've finally met some people we feel comfortable
│  with and enjoy being with.                             │
│                                                          │
│  Our neighbors have stopped eyeing us, and our California
│  license plates, with distrust. After 6 months of proving
│  ourselves to be worthy neighbors without any unusual living
│  habits, we are now being rewarded with friendly greetings
│  ▌nd even some prolonged chit-chat.                     │
│                                                          │
│  Time to go shovel some snow. Our very best wishes to you.
│                                                          │
│  Love,                                                   │
│                                                          │
└─────────────────────────────────────────────────────────┘
COMMAND: Copy Delete Format Gallery Help Insert Jump Library
         Options Print Quit Replace Search Transfer Undo Window
Edit document or press Esc to use menu
Pg1 Co1            {on·the·street·}   ?                    Microsoft Word
```

Look at the bottom line in the command area of your screen to see the scrap of text that you've just deleted enclosed in braces ⟨⟩ :

{on·the·street·}

Scrap   Space (raised dot)

Word saves this scrap until you delete another piece of text with the Delete key or the Delete command. Notice how spaces between words are represented by raised dots. Word displays nonprinting characters with special symbols. For example, a space is shown as a ·, a tab is shown as a → , and a paragraph mark as a ¶ . (For a list of symbols that appear in the scrap, see Appendix F.)

Changing your mind

Suppose you change your mind about the last deletion. If you haven't moved the cursor since you deleted the text, you can press the Ins key to paste it back in place. The Insert key inserts *to the left of* the cursor a copy of whatever is enclosed in ⟨⟩ on the status line.

```
┌─────────────┐
│ 0           │
│ Ins         │
└─────────────┘
```

If you've moved the cursor since you deleted the text, you can use the Undo command to retrieve the deleted text. With the Undo command, the deleted text reappears in the place it was deleted from (and disappears from the scrap)—regardless of where the cursor is. You can use the Undo command to reverse any kind of editing change, including the insertion of new text. If the last change you made was with the Undo command, you can even undo that. Undo reverses the *last* editing change only.

If you haven't already reinserted "on the street," try doing it now with the Undo command:

1. Press the Esc key to go to the command area.

2. Press U for Undo.

Moving text

To *move* text, you need to delete it from one place and insert it in another. Let's move "on the street" to the next paragraph instead of deleting it.

1. *Highlight the text you want to move:* Include the space before "on" when you highlight the phrase " on the street" (but not the space after "street"). Use any of the cursor-moving keys to move the cursor to either end of the phrase. Press F6 to turn on the Extend function (*EX* appears on the status line), and then move the cursor to the other end of the phrase. If you go too far, back up using keys that move the cursor in the opposite direction.

    ```
    habits, we are now being rewarded with friendly greetings on
    the street and even some prolonged chit-chat.
    ```

2. *Delete what you want to move:* Press the Del key.

    ```
    habits, we are now being rewarded with friendly greetings
    and even some prolonged chit-chat.
    ```

3. *Move the cursor to the new location:* Press the Down direction key until the cursor moves down to the next paragraph. Then press F7 to move left one word at a time until the period (and the space) after "some snow" is highlighted.

    ```
    Time to go shovel some snow. Our very best wishes to you.
    ```

4. *Insert the text at the new location:* Press the Ins key. Notice how the text to the right of the cursor moves over and down to make room for the inserted text.

```
Dear Western Allies,

This is just a quick note to let you know that all is fine
on the Eastern Front. Winter has been very picturesque here.
Lots of fluffy white snow on trees, houses, and hills.
Wreaths with bows on every colonial door. No horsedrawn
sleighs but lots of kids on sleds.

Adjusting to our new life on the other side of the continent
was difficult at first. We now understand why people resist
moving. Friendship is dear--all the more dear when not
there. We've finally met some people we feel comfortable
with and enjoy being with.

Our neighbors have stopped eyeing us, and our California
license plates, with distrust. After 6 months of proving
ourselves to be worthy neighbors without any unusual living
habits, we are now being rewarded with friendly greetings
and even some prolonged chit-chat.

Time to go shovel some snow on the street█ Our very best
wishes to you.

Love,
```

```
COMMAND: Copy Delete Format Gallery Help Insert Jump Library
         Options Print Quit Replace Search Transfer Undo Window
Edit document or press Esc to use menu
Pg1 Co42           {·on·the·street}  ?                Microsoft Word
```

Joining paragraphs

Recall that you pressed the Enter key twice after each paragraph to start a new paragraph and to leave a blank line. Each time you press the Enter key, it inserts a nonprinting character, called a paragraph mark, that can be deleted like any other character. Let's join the second and third paragraphs of the letter by removing the normally invisible paragraph marks that separate them.

1. *Move the cursor to the beginning of the second paragraph you want joined:* Press the Up direction key to move the cursor up to the line starting with "Our neighbors." Press the Home key to go to the beginning of the line. The cursor now highlights the "O" in "Our."

```
with and enjoy being with.

█ur neighbors have stopped eyeing us, and our California
```

2. *Delete the paragraph mark(s) between the paragraphs you want joined:* Press the Backspace key. Press it twice if you pressed the Enter key twice to leave a blank line between paragraphs. The paragraph starting with ''Our neighbors'' scoots up on the screen to merge with the previous paragraph.

```
Dear Western Allies,

This is just a quick note to let you know that all is fine
on the Eastern Front. Winter has been very picturesque here.
Lots of fluffy white snow on trees, houses, and hills.
Wreaths with bows on every colonial door. No horsedrawn
sleighs but lots of kids on sleds.

Adjusting to our new life on the other side of the continent
was difficult at first. We now understand why people resist
moving. Friendship is dear--all the more dear when not
there. We've finally met some people we feel comfortable
with and enjoy being with.Our neighbors have stopped eyeing
us, and our California license plates, with distrust. After
6 months of proving ourselves to be worthy neighbors without
any unusual living habits, we are now being rewarded with
friendly greetings and even some prolonged chit-chat.

Time to go shovel some snow on the street. Our very best
wishes to you.

Love,

The Eastern Alliance
```

```
COMMAND: Copy Delete Format Gallery Help Insert Jump Library
         Options Print Quit Replace Search Transfer Undo Window
Edit document or press Esc to use menu
Pg1 Co27            {·on·the·street}  ?                    Microsoft Word
```

3. *Add a space, if necessary:* If there is no space between the sentences where the paragraphs were joined, press the Spacebar to insert one.

Splitting paragraphs

Suppose you're not satisfied with the long paragraph you created and you want to break it into two shorter paragraphs. Let's start a new paragraph before the sentence that begins with ''We've finally....''

1. *Move the cursor to where you want the new paragraph to start:* Use the direction keys to move the cursor to the first letter of the previous sentence: ''W.''

```
there. We've finally met some people we feel comfortable
with and enjoy being with. Our neighbors have stopped eyeing
```

2. *Press the Enter key:* Press it twice if you want to separate the paragraphs with a blank line.

```
Dear Western Allies,

This is just a quick note to let you know that all is fine
on the Eastern Front. Winter has been very picturesque here.
Lots of fluffy white snow on trees, houses, and hills.
Wreaths with bows on every colonial door. No horsedrawn
sleighs but lots of kids on sleds.

Adjusting to our new life on the other side of the continent
was difficult at first. We now understand why people resist
moving. Friendship is dear--all the more dear when not
there.

We've finally met some people we feel comfortable with and
enjoy being with. Our neighbors have stopped eyeing us, and
our California license plates, with distrust. After 6 months
of proving ourselves to be worthy neighbors without any
unusual living habits, we are now being rewarded with
friendly greetings and even some prolonged chit-chat.

Time to go shovel some snow on the street. Our very best
wishes to you.

Love,
```

```
COMMAND: Copy Delete Format Gallery Help Insert Jump Library
         Options Print Quit Replace Search Transfer Undo Window
Edit document or press Esc to use menu
Pg1 Co1               {·on·the·street}  ?                      Microsoft Word
```

Moving to and from the command area

The Escape (Esc) key takes you to and from the command area. When you start Word, you're in the text area. You can move to the command area to use the commands listed on the menu by pressing the Escape key. Once you're in the command area, you won't be able to type: When you press a letter key, you'll be choosing a command instead of typing that letter. After you choose and carry out a command, you're automatically returned to the text area where you can resume typing. If you do not want to choose and carry out a command, you must press the Esc key to return to the text area.

Except for the Undo command, you won't need to use the commands to do basic editing, but it's important that you know how to cancel a command chosen by mistake or out of curiosity and how to return to the text area.

To cancel a command, press the Esc key. If you want to choose another command at this point, you must press the Esc key again to go back to the command area.

❑ NOTE: *If you choose the Gallery command, the Library Document-retrieval command, the Library Spell command, or the Print preView command, the Escape key won't take you back to the text area. You must choose the Exit command (press E for Exit) to continue typing.*

EDITING WITH THE MOUSE

Except for adding new text, you can do all your editing with the mouse. It offers you greater speed and flexibility, and it's often easier to use than the keyboard.

The Mouse

The mouse, as shown in Figure 3-3, has two buttons on top and a rotating ball underneath. What the mouse does depends on where you position the mouse pointer on the screen and which of the mouse buttons you press.

Figure 3-3. *The mouse.*

To move the pointer around on your screen, slide the mouse around on your desktop. You can move the mouse in any direction, even diagonally. If the mouse runs off the edge of your desk before you get where you want to go, pick it up and put it down again—farther from the edge this time. Then continue moving it until you get to your destination.

To tell you which button to press and whether you press and release the button or hold it down and release it later, the following symbols are used:

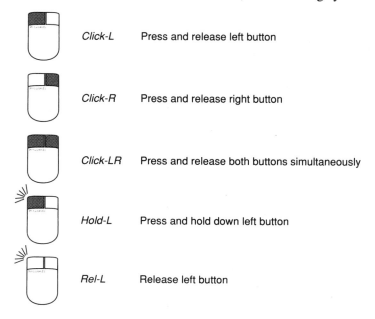

Click-L   Press and release left button

Click-R   Press and release right button

Click-LR   Press and release both buttons simultaneously

Hold-L   Press and hold down left button

Rel-L   Release left button

Just Looking

You can see any part of your document by scrolling with the mouse. The mouse gives you much more control over the distance that you scroll than the keyboard does.

Scrolling up and down

To scroll up or down with the mouse, move the mouse pointer to the *vertical scroll bar* (the left window border). The pointer changes its shape to ✦ or ▯ to indicate that it's ready to scroll.

The distance that you scroll depends on where you place the mouse pointer on the scroll bar. Position the pointer on the scroll bar at a distance from the top that matches the distance you want to scroll. For example, if you want to scroll up or down a few lines, place the pointer a few lines from the top of the scroll bar. If you want to scroll up or down one windowful, place the pointer at the bottom of the scroll bar.

Point here to scroll up or down a few lines

Position of pointer determines how far you scroll

Point here to scroll up or down one windowful

The direction that you scroll depends on which mouse button you press: Click-L to *scroll up* toward the beginning of the document, and Click-R to *scroll down* toward the end of the document.

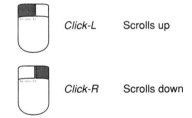

Click-L   Scrolls up

Click-R   Scrolls down

You can also scroll sideways with the mouse, and you'll learn how to do that in Chapter 6.

Thumbing through a document

Just as you can use your thumb to open a book at a particular place, rather than flipping through the book page by page, you can *thumb* directly to any part of your document with the mouse's help. Thumbing is a form of scrolling that allows you to quickly find a particular place in a document without knowing whether you have to scroll up or scroll down to get there. It is especially useful in long documents.

When you are thumbing, the top of the vertical scroll bar represents the beginning of your document and the bottom represents the end. The pointer's position on the scroll bar determines where you thumb to in the document. For example, if you want to see the middle of the document, place the pointer halfway between the top and the bottom of the vertical scroll bar.

Point here
to thumb
to beginning
of document

Position
of pointer
determines
where you
thumb to

Point here
to thumb
to end of
document

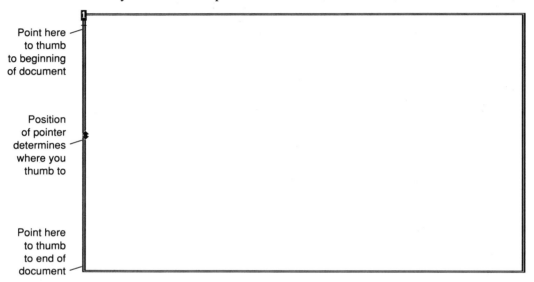

After you position the pointer, Click-LR to indicate that you want to thumb.

Click-LR   Scrolls up *or* down to particular place

Try scrolling to different places in the letter by moving the pointer to various positions on the vertical scroll bar and clicking the left or right button. You can also try thumbing. Although it will be difficult to see the difference between thumbing and scrolling on such a short document, you will be able to see that thumbing is a fast and easy way to move directly to the beginning or end of a document.

Highlighting What You Want to Change

The mouse lets you highlight any character, word, sentence, or larger piece of text you want to change with greater ease and flexibility than the keyboard-cursor combination. What you highlight depends on where you move the mouse pointer and which mouse button(s) you press.

Highlighting a character, a word, or a sentence

To highlight a single character, first move the mouse pointer to that character. To highlight a whole word or whole sentence, first move the pointer to any character in the word or sentence. Then Click-L to highlight a single character, Click-R to highlight the whole word, or Click-LR to highlight the whole sentence.

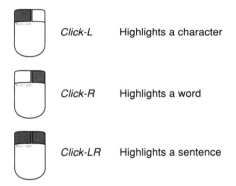

Click-L	Highlights a character
Click-R	Highlights a word
Click-LR	Highlights a sentence

Highlighting a line, a paragraph, or the whole document

When the mouse pointer is in the *selection bar* (the blank column to the left of your text), you can highlight a line, a paragraph, or the whole document. You know that the pointer is in the selection bar when it changes its shape to ◢ or dims to half its usual brightness (▮).

With the mouse pointer in the selection bar, Click-L to highlight the line next to the pointer, Click-R to highlight the paragraph next to the pointer, or Click-LR to highlight the whole document.

```
┌─┬──────────────────────────────────────────────────────────┐
│1│Dear Western Allies,                                       │
│ │                                                           │
│ │This is just a quick note to let you know that all is fine │
│ │on the Eastern Front. Winter has been very picturesque here.│
│ │Lots of fluffy white snow on trees, houses, and hills.     │
│ │Wreaths with bows on every colonial door. No horsedrawn    │
│ │sleighs but lots of kids on sleds.                         │
│ │                                                           │
│ │Adjusting to our new life on the other side of the continent│
│ │was difficult at first. We now understand why people resist│
│ │moving. Friendship is dear--all the more dear when not     │
│ │there.                                                     │
│ │                                                           │
│ │We've finally met some people we feel comfortable with and │
│ │enjoy being with. Our neighbors have stopped eyeing us, and│
│ │our California license plates, with distrust. After 6 months│
│ │of proving ourselves to be worthy neighbors without any    │
│ │unusual living habits, we are now being rewarded with      │
│ │friendly greetings and even some prolonged chit-chat.      │
│ │                                                           │
│ │Time to go shovel some snow on the street. Our very best   │
│ │wishes to you.                                             │
│ │                                                           │
│ │Love,                                                      │
│ │                                                           │
└─┴──────────────────────────────────────────────────────────┘
```

Selection bar — (left label)

Mouse pointer changes its shape in selection bar — (left label)

```
COMMAND: Copy Delete Format Gallery Help Insert Jump Library
         Options Print Quit Replace Search Transfer Undo Window
Edit document or press Esc to use menu
Pg1 Co1              {·on·the·street}  ?              Microsoft Word
```

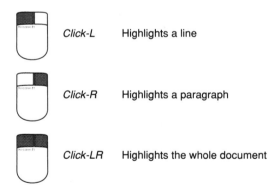

Click-L	Highlights a line
Click-R	Highlights a paragraph
Click-LR	Highlights the whole document

Highlighting any block of characters

To highlight a block or sequence of characters of any length:

1. Move the pointer to one end of the block and Hold-L.

2. Move the pointer to the other end of the block and Rel-L.

Making Changes

To make editing changes with the mouse, you choose commands from the command menu below the window. Because Word lets you highlight whatever you want to change, you can do all your editing with two commands: the Delete command and the Insert command.

To see how both of these commands work, let's delete a piece of text from one place and insert it in another. We'll move the first sentence of the letter from the first paragraph to the last paragraph. Before you start, bring the beginning of the letter into view if it is not visible. Thumb to the beginning by moving the mouse pointer to the top of the vertical scroll bar and clicking both buttons.

Deleting and moving text

The Delete command removes whatever is highlighted by the cursor. The text you delete is saved as a scrap until you delete something else with either the Delete key or the Delete command. To delete the first sentence in the letter:

1. *Highlight what you want to delete:* Move the mouse pointer to any character in the first sentence and Click-LR to highlight the sentence.

Mouse pointer

```
Dear Western Allies,

This is just a quick note to let you know that all is fine
on the Eastern Front. Winter has been very picturesque here.
Lots of fluffy white snow on trees, houses, and hills.
Wreaths with bows on every colonial door. No horsedrawn
sleighs but lots of kids on sleds.

Adjusting to our new life on the other side of the continent
was difficult at first. We now understand why people resist
moving. Friendship is dear--all the more dear when not
there.

We've finally met some people we feel comfortable with and
enjoy being with. Our neighbors have stopped eyeing us, and
our California license plates, with distrust. After 6 months
of proving ourselves to be worthy neighbors without any
unusual living habits, we are now being rewarded with
friendly greetings and even some prolonged chit-chat.

Time to go shovel some snow on the street. Our very best
wishes to you.

Love,
```

```
COMMAND: Copy Delete Format Gallery Help Insert Jump Library
         Options Print Quit Replace Search Transfer Undo Window
Edit document or press Esc to use menu
Pg1 Co22          {·on·the·street}  ?                    Microsoft Word
```

2. *Choose and carry out the Delete command:* Move the mouse pointer to the Delete command in the command menu and Click-R.

```
COMMAND: Copy Delete Format Gallery Help Insert Jump Library
         Options Print Quit Replace Search Transfer Undo Window
```

                              Click-R

You now see parts of the deleted sentence at the bottom of the screen, enclosed in ⟨⟩.

```
┌──────────────────────────────────────────────────────────────┐
│ Dear Western Allies,                                         │
│                                                              │
│ Winter has been very picturesque here.  Lots of fluffy white │
│ snow on trees, houses, and hills.  Wreaths with bows on      │
│ every colonial door. No horsedrawn sleighs but lots of kids  │
│ on sleds.                                                    │
│                                                              │
│ Adjusting to our new life on the other side of the continent │
│ was difficult at first. We now understand why people resist  │
│ moving. Friendship is dear--all the more dear when not       │
│ there.                                                       │
│                                                              │
│ We've finally met some people we feel comfortable with and   │
│ enjoy being with. Our neighbors have stopped eyeing us, and  │
│ our California license plates, with distrust. After 6 months │
│ of proving ourselves to be worthy neighbors without any      │
│ unusual living habits, we are now being rewarded with        │
│ friendly greetings and even some prolonged chit-chat.        │
│                                                              │
│ Time to go shovel some snow on the street. Our very best     │
│ wishes to you.                                               │
│                                                              │
│ Love,                                                        │
│                                                              │
└──────────────────────────────────────────────────────────────┘
COMMAND: Copy Delete Format Gallery Help Insert Jump Library
         Options Print Quit Replace Search Transfer Undo Window
Edit document or press Esc to use menu
Pg1 Co1            {This·i...ront.·} ?                Microsoft Word
```

                    Deleted sentence

You can retrieve the sentence you just deleted and move it to a new location with the Insert command. The Insert command pastes the last scrap of deleted text back into the document. Before you insert text with the Insert command, you must move the cursor to the place where you want to insert it. The Insert command inserts text to the left of the cursor. To insert text that is in the scrap:

3. *If necessary, scroll to find a new location:* Move the mouse pointer to the left window border and position it about three lines from the top. Click-R to scroll down a few lines.

4. *Move the cursor to where you want to insert, or move, the text:* Move the mouse pointer to the ''T'' in ''Time'' and Click-L. The cursor moves to highlight the ''T.''

```
Winter has been very picturesque here.  Lots of fluffy white
snow on trees, houses, and hills.  Wreaths with bows on
every colonial door. No horsedrawn sleighs but lots of kids
on sleds.

Adjusting to our new life on the other side of the continent
was difficult at first. We now understand why people resist
moving. Friendship is dear--all the more dear when not
there.

We've finally met some people we feel comfortable with and
enjoy being with. Our neighbors have stopped eyeing us, and
our California license plates, with distrust. After 6 months
of proving ourselves to be worthy neighbors without any
unusual living habits, we are now being rewarded with
friendly greetings and even some prolonged chit-chat.

Time to go shovel some snow on the street. Our very best
wishes to you.

Love,

The Eastern Alliance
```

```
COMMAND: Copy Delete Format Gallery Help Insert Jump Library
         Options Print Quit Replace Search Transfer Undo Window
Edit document or press Esc to use menu
Pg1 Co1          {This·i...ront.·} ?              Microsoft Word
```

5. *Choose and carry out the Insert command:* Move the mouse pointer to the Insert command in the command menu and Click-R to insert the scrap of text.

```
COMMAND: Copy Delete Format Gallery Help Insert Jump Library
         Options Print Quit Replace Search Transfer Undo Window
```

Click-R

The sentence you deleted now appears to the left of the cursor.

```
┌─────────────────────────────────────────────────────────────┐
│█                                                             │
│ Winter has been very picturesque here.  Lots of fluffy white │
│ snow on trees, houses, and hills.  Wreaths with bows on      │
│ every colonial door. No horsedrawn sleighs but lots of kids  │
│ on sleds.                                                    │
│                                                              │
│ Adjusting to our new life on the other side of the continent │
│ was difficult at first. We now understand why people resist  │
│ moving. Friendship is dear--all the more dear when not       │
│ there.                                                       │
│                                                              │
│ We've finally met some people we feel comfortable with and   │
│ enjoy being with. Our neighbors have stopped eyeing us, and  │
│ our California license plates, with distrust. After 6 months │
│ of proving ourselves to be worthy neighbors without any      │
│ unusual living habits, we are now being rewarded with        │
│ friendly greetings and even some prolonged chit-chat.        │
│                                                              │
│ This is just a quick note to let you know that all is fine   │
│ on the Eastern Front. █ime to go shovel some snow on the     │
│ street. Our very best wishes to you.                         │
│                                                              │
│ Love,                                                        │
│                                                              │
│ The Eastern Alliance                                         │
└─────────────────────────────────────────────────────────────┘
COMMAND: Copy Delete Format Gallery Help Insert Jump Library
         Options Print Quit Replace Search Transfer Undo Window
Edit document or press Esc to use menu
Pg1 Co23         {This·i...ront.} ?                Microsoft Word
```

Changing your mind

Now that you've moved the sentence, suppose you're not sure it was a good move. You can instantly move it back with the Undo command.

- ■ *Choose and carry out the Undo command:* Point to the Undo command and Click-L.

```
COMMAND: Copy Delete Format Gallery Help Insert Jump Library
         Options Print Quit Replace Search Transfer Undo Window
                                                       ▲
                                                    Click-L
```

Still not sure? Undo the Undo command: Choose and carry out the Undo command again. Undo reverses the last editing change made. Use it freely whenever you change your mind (or can't make up your mind) about deleting text, inserting text (including inserting new text), or moving text.

Let's add a word to the sentence we just moved.

1. *Move the cursor to where you want to insert text:* Move the mouse pointer to the ''o'' in ''on the Eastern'' and then Click-L. The cursor moves to the ''o.''

```
This is just a quick note to let you know that all is fine
█n the Eastern Front. Time to go shovel some snow on the
```

2. *Type in the new text:* Type "here" plus a space. The text you type appears to the left of the cursor.

```
This is just a quick note to let you know that all is fine
here in the Eastern Front. Time to go shovel some snow on
```

Moving to and from the command area

With the mouse, you have free passage to the command area—you don't have to press the Escape key to leave the text area. But as soon as you point to a command and click a button, you're locked into the command area until you either carry out or cancel the command. Some commands, like the ones you've been using so far, can be chosen and carried out with one mouse maneuver. Other commands cannot, however, be carried out so quickly.

Until you learn what the commands do and how to carry them out, you need to know how to cancel any commands you've chosen by mistake or out of curiosity so that you can leave the command area and resume typing.

To cancel a command with the mouse:

1. Click-LR with the mouse pointer anywhere in the command area.

2. Continue typing or choose another command.

❑ NOTE: *If you choose the Gallery command, the Library Document-retrieval command, the Library Spell command, or the Print preView command, the usual method for canceling a command won't take you back to the text area. You must choose the Exit command (point to Exit and Click-L) to continue typing.*

Chapter 4

Saving and Printing Your Words

If you've just finished creating or editing a document, your words are sitting somewhat precariously in the computer's electronic memory. If the electricity goes off, or if you go off and someone else comes along and turns off your computer, your words will be lost. To protect yourself from losing your work, make a habit of saving your work every half hour. Then, if a mishap occurs, you lose only what you have done since you last saved. (Word has an *autosave* feature, which you can find by choosing the Options command. See Chapter 11 for more information.)

The first thing you'll learn in this chapter is how to save a document. Then you'll learn how to gracefully quit the Word program (without ruffling any electronic feathers) and how to restart it. You'll also learn how to print a document. Printing a document increases your chances of having at least one readable copy of your work. If you have a printed copy and your electronic copy gets damaged, you won't be starting from scratch. So, it's a good idea to print out anything in which you've invested a lot of time, thought, or effort.

SAVING A DOCUMENT

When you *save* a document, you're asking Word to transfer a copy of it from temporary memory to a more permanent storage place—a disk. You tell Word to save a file by using the Transfer command shown in the command menu below the text window.

Before filing it away, Word asks you to give the document a filename so that you can retrieve it by asking for that name. You can make up any name from one to eight characters long, using letters, numbers, and some symbols (! @ # $ % & ( ) - _ { } ' ` ~), but no spaces. The same rules that apply to DOS filenames apply to Word filenames.

You'll find that working with the commands that handle document files is easier if you use the filename extension .DOC. No need to type it in, though: Word automatically appends *.DOC* to a document filename, unless you type in a filename extension of your own.

If you're saving the document for the first time, Word presents you with a questionnaire titled *Summary Information* before completing the save. This information supplements the eight-character filename, which can be too cryptic for you to tell easily what's in a document. Instead of reviewing the entire document to see what's in it, you can review the summary information or you can search for a file or group of files based on any of the data provided in the summary. If you produce a lot of documents or if you are using a fixed-disk system, retrieving documents with the aid of summary information will be a big help in keeping track of files. (More details on summary information and document retrieval are given in Chapter 15.)

Saving with the Keyboard

To save a document with the keyboard:

1. Press the Esc key to go to the command area.

2. Press T to choose the Transfer command.

3. Press S to choose the Save subcommand.

4. When you see:

```
TRANSFER SAVE filename: █
                   format:(Word)Text-only Text-only-with-line-breaks RTF
```

type in a filename (in uppercase or lowercase letters) and press the Enter key. For example, type *SAMPLE* and press the Enter key to save the sample letter you created.

5. When you see the Summary Information questions, press the Enter key to skip the questions for now.

Saving with the Mouse

To save a document with the mouse:

1. Point to the Transfer command and Click-L:

```
COMMAND: Copy Delete Format Gallery Help Insert Jump Library
         Options Print Quit Replace Search Transfer Undo Window
                                                  ▲
                                              Click-L
```

2. When you see the following menu, point to the Save subcommand and Click-L:

```
TRANSFER: Load Save Clear Delete Merge Options Rename Glossary Allsave
               ▲
           Click-L
```

3. When you see:

```
TRANSFER SAVE filename: █
                   format:(Word)Text-only Text-only-with-line-breaks RTF
```

type in a filename (in uppercase or lowercase letters) and press the Enter key. For example, type *SAMPLE* and press the Enter key to save the sample letter you created.

4. When you see the Summary Information questions, press the Enter key to skip the questions for now.

After Saving

After Word is done saving the file, it displays the filename in the lower right corner of the text window and tells you in the message line how many characters were saved (including tabs and paragraph marks—each paragraph mark counts as two characters). If you saved the file on a floppy disk, Word tells you how many bytes of storage space are now available on that disk. You still see a copy of the document in the text window, so you can continue to edit it or you can print it. (If you want to work on another document, you must first load it. See ''Loading a Document'' later in this chapter.)

Where Is the Document Saved?

Just as DOS has a current drive and current directory, Word has a *current document drive* and *current document directory*. The current document drive and directory is the place where Word assumes you want to save a file, unless you tell it to save it elsewhere. If you're not maintaining multiple directories, you don't have to be concerned with the current document directory.

On a floppy-disk system, the current document drive is initially drive B and the current document directory is initially the root directory of drive B. On a fixed-disk system, the current document drive is initially drive C, and the current document directory is the one you were in when you started Word.

If you want to save a document in a different drive or directory, you must specify where you want it saved. There are two ways to do this. One way is to *override* the current document drive or directory by specifying where you want to save an individual file when you type its filename. The other way is to *change* the current document drive or directory for all files that will be saved.

Specifying where to save an individual file

To specify where you want to save an individual file, precede the filename with the desired location. For example, if you want to save a document called SAMPLE.DOC in drive A, type:

A:SAMPLE

Word observes the same conventions for specifying paths that DOS does. So if you're using multiple directories and you want to save a document in a directory called LETTERS rather than in the current directory, type:

\LETTERS\SAMPLE

Note that, in this example, the file will be saved in the current drive because none is specified.

You can specify both the drive and the directory where you want the file saved in this way:

B:\LETTERS\SAMPLE

Any directory that you specify must be an existing directory. Before you can store files in a directory, you have to create it with the DOS command MD (Make Directory), as explained in Appendix A.

Checking and changing the current document drive and directory

To change the current document drive or document directory for all files, you change the setup options offered by the Transfer command. To do this:

1. Press the Esc key to go to the command area.

2. Press T to choose the Transfer command.

3. Press O to choose the Options subcommand.

4. In the first line under the window, Word displays the current document drive and document directory and labels them the *setup*. For example, if your current drive is *C* and your current directory is *WORDIR*, you would see:

   `TRANSFER OPTIONS setup: C:\WORDIR`

5. Type the new drive or directory path. For example, if you have a fixed disk and you want most of your documents saved in an existing directory called LETTERS, type:

   C:\LETTERS

   and press the Enter key.

As soon as you start typing, the drive and directory displayed disappear. If the directory you specify doesn't exist, Word displays the message: *Not a valid drive or directory.*

Once you change the current document drive and directory, all files will be saved there unless you specify otherwise. You can override your new setup by specifying where to save an individual file (as described in the preceding section). Word remembers your setup throughout the work session.

If you're using multiple directories, you need to pay close attention to where you save files because it's easy to forget which directory you're in. The Transfer Options command provides an easy way to check where Word will save your documents before you save.

Try the Transfer Options command now to find out what your current document directory is. Follow the first four steps listed above. You can press the Escape key to cancel the command without changing the setup. If you use multiple directories, check (and change, if necessary) the current document drive and directory each time you start Word before you start saving files.

The Next Time You Save

If you revise a document that you previously saved, you need to save it again to preserve the changes. The next time you save it, you won't have to type in the filename or location and you won't be asked for summary information. After you choose the Transfer Save command, Word displays the name given to the document and the drive and directory it was saved in. For the sample letter you just saved, you see something like:

```
TRANSFER SAVE filename: B:\SAMPLE.DOC
```

if you're using a floppy-disk system. If you're using multiple directories, note that the single backslash (\) tells you the file was saved in the root directory.

If you're using a fixed disk, the display shows C as the drive. If the sample letter was saved in a directory called WORDIR, the Transfer Save display looks like this:

```
TRANSFER SAVE filename: C:\WORDIR\SAMPLE.DOC
```

You simply press the Enter key when you see the filename displayed. The document and any changes are saved with the same name in the same place where the document was previously saved. The previous version of the document is renamed with the filename extension .BAK. (In Chapter 11, you'll learn how to change a document's name or location.)

QUITTING GRACEFULLY

When you're ready to stop working with Word, choose the Quit command. Quitting Word takes you back to the DOS prompt (A> or C>). Once there, you can turn off the computer or start up other programs. If you have any un-saved work when you choose the Quit command, Word lets you know and gives you an opportunity to save it before you quit.

Try quitting now so that you can walk through the steps of quitting, restarting, and loading a document.

Quitting with the Keyboard

To quit with the keyboard:

1. Press the Esc key to go to the command area.

2. Press Q to choose the Quit command.

3. If you have any unsaved work, Word highlights the entire document and displays the message:

   `Enter Y to save changes to document, N to lose changes, or Esc to cancel` █

   Press Y to save your work before quitting. Press N only if you don't want to save a document, or if you don't want to save the changes made to a previously saved document. Press the Esc key if you want to cancel the command.

Quitting with the Mouse

To quit with the mouse:

1. Point to the Quit command and Click-L:

   `COMMAND: Copy Delete Format Gallery Help Insert Jump Library`
   `         Options Print Quit Replace Search Transfer Undo Window`
   `                        Click-L`

2. If you have any unsaved work, Word highlights the entire document and displays the message:

   `Enter Y to save changes to document, N to lose changes, or Esc to cancel` █

   With the mouse pointer anywhere in the command area, Click-L or Click-R to save your work before quitting. Press N if you don't want to save a document, or if you don't want to save the changes you've made to a previously saved document. Click-LR to cancel the command.

After Quitting

After Word carries out the Quit command, DOS takes over. (If you have a floppy-disk system and your computer can't find DOS in the A drive, it might ask you to insert the DOS disk before it displays the A>.) Once you see the *A>* prompt, you can turn off the computer or load another program.

RESTARTING WORD

To resume working with Word, you need to restart Word. You can restart Word the same way you started it. At the DOS prompt *A>* or *C>*, type:

WORD

and press the Enter key. If you have multiple directories, you may need to change the directory before you type the WORD startup command.

If you start Word with the WORD command, you see a blank text window. You can then create a new document or you can load a previously saved document that you want to work with. When you *load* a file, you transfer a copy of it from its permanent storage place—your document disk—to temporary memory.

You can load a document at the same time you start Word. To start the Word program and load the file that you last worked on, type:

WORD/L

If the file you want to load is not the one you last worked on, you can type the filename after you type *WORD*. For example, type:

WORD YOURFILE

and then press the Enter key to start Word and to load the file named YOURFILE.DOC. (When you don't type a filename extension, Word assumes the filename has the extension .DOC.) As usual, you must include the drive or directory path to the document file if it's not stored in the current document drive or directory.

Restart Word now with the simple WORD command so that you can walk through the steps of loading and printing a document in the next sections.

LOADING A DOCUMENT

After starting Word, you can load a previously saved document into the blank window or you can create a new document. Let's load the sample letter you created and saved under the name SAMPLE.DOC. You'll be using the Transfer command again with either the keyboard or the mouse.

Loading a Document with the Keyboard

To load a document with the keyboard:

1. Press the Esc key.

2. Press T to choose the Transfer command.

3. Press L to choose the Load subcommand.

4. When you see:

    `TRANSFER LOAD filename: █                    read only: Yes(No)`

    type the name of the file you want to load and press the Enter key. In this example, type:

    SAMPLE

    and press the Enter key.

What If Word Can't Find the File You Want to Load?

If Word can't find the file you request, it assumes you want to create a new file and displays the message: *File does not exist. Enter Y to create or Esc to cancel.* If this happens while you're attempting to load a previously saved file, press the Escape key to cancel the command.

Perhaps you typed the wrong filename. If you don't remember the exact name of a file that you want to load:

1. Choose the Transfer Load command.

2. Press the F1 key when you're asked to give a filename. Pressing the F1 key displays a list of the .DOC files on the disk in the current document drive and directory.

3. Select a file from the list using the direction keys to move the highlight to the file you want.

4. Press the Enter key to carry out the command.

Perhaps you gave Word the right filename but Word looked in the wrong place for the file. When you ask Word to load a document, Word looks for your document file in the current document drive and directory. When you start Word, the current document drive is drive B for a floppy-disk system or drive C for a fixed-disk system. If you have multiple directories, Word looks in the current document drive for the file in the directory you were in when you started Word.

If the file you want to load is not in the current document drive and directory, you must tell Word where to look for it. You can specify the drive or directory path for an individual file when you type the filename. Or you can change the current drive and directory with the Transfer Options command described earlier in this chapter in "Checking and Changing the Current Document Drive and Directory."

Loading a Document with the Mouse

To load a document with the mouse:

1. Point to the Transfer command and Click-L:

```
COMMAND: Copy Delete Format Gallery Help Insert Jump Library
         Options Print Quit Replace Search Transfer Undo Window
                                              Click-L
```

2. When you see the following menu, point to the Load subcommand and Click-L:

```
TRANSFER: Load Save Clear Delete Merge Options Rename Glossary Allsave
          Click-L
```

3. When you see:

```
TRANSFER LOAD filename: █                    read only: Yes(No)
```

point to the highlighted space to the right of *filename* and Click-R to see a list of the .DOC files in the current document drive and directory.

4. Point to the name of the file you want to see and Click-R. Try loading the letter you created: Point to the filename *SAMPLE.DOC* and Click-R.

If you don't see the name of the file you want to load in the list, perhaps it's on another floppy disk or in another directory. In that case, point anywhere in the command area and Click-LR to cancel the command. Check that you have inserted the correct floppy and change it, if necessary. If you have multiple directories, check and change the current document directory using the Transfer Options command, as described earlier in this chapter. Then try loading the file again.

After Loading

After a document is loaded, you see it in the text window, and you see its file-name in the window border. The message line tells you how many characters are in the document, including tabs and paragraph marks. If you load a file from a floppy disk, Word also tells you how many bytes of storage space are still available on that disk.

PRINTING A DOCUMENT

When you tell Word to *print* a document, you're asking it to transfer a copy of the document from the computer's temporary memory to the printer. This means the document must be visible in the text window when you give the print command. If you recently finished creating or editing a document, that's where it will be. But if you just started Word or if you're working with another document, you first have to load the document that you want to print. (See the previous section, called "Loading a Document.")

In most cases, following the steps below will give you a printed copy of your document. If you experience problems printing documents, Word might not have the correct information about your printer. In that case, turn to Chapter 12 to find out how to be sure that Word knows how to talk to your printer.

Printing a Document with the Keyboard

To print a document with the keyboard:

1. Load the document if it isn't already in the text window.

2. Be sure your printer is ready: Is the paper in position? Is the printer plugged in? Are the power switch and the on-line switch turned on?

3. Press the Esc key.

4. Press P to choose the Print command.

5. Press P to choose the Printer subcommand and to start printing.

To interrupt the printing, press the Esc key. To restart printing after you interrupt it, press Y. Or, to stop the printing altogether, press the Esc key again.

Printing a Document with the Mouse

To print a document with the mouse, move the mouse pointer to the Print command and Click-R:

```
COMMAND: Copy Delete Format Gallery Help Insert Jump Library
         Options Print Quit Replace Search Transfer Undo Window
                  ▲
                Click-R
```

This selects and carries out both the Print command and the Printer subcommand.

To interrupt the printing, press the Esc key. To restart printing after you interrupt it, press Y. Or, to stop the printing altogether, press the Esc key again.

WHERE TO GO FROM HERE

You can go back to the sample letter you prepared and use it to practice the editing techniques you learned in this part of the book. Try correcting any typing errors you might have made. Practice inserting new text and highlighting and deleting or moving different parts of the letter. Practice moving the cursor or moving the mouse pointer around until it seems like second nature to you. Don't be afraid to experiment. If you get stuck, you can always reset the computer by holding down the Ctrl, Alt, and Del keys simultaneously and start over. All you will have lost is some practice text, and you won't even lose all of that if it's been saved once.

Perhaps you don't have time to practice and experiment. If you've got some urgent work waiting for you, you're ready to start doing it. You can clear the sample letter out of your way and start creating your own document. Just press the Esc key and then press T for Transfer, C for Clear, and W for Window to give yourself a blank window to start typing in.

When you have more time, or when you find that you need more information or more tools, take a look at later chapters of this book. There you'll find out how to make editing changes faster and with more finesse. You'll also learn how to let Word check your spelling, hyphenate your words, and even suggest alternative words from its built-in thesaurus. You'll learn tricks that make creating a document easier and that reduce the amount of typing you have to do. You'll learn about formatting and printing alternatives, and you'll learn more about managing your files.

PART II

ADVANCED WORD

Chapter 5

On-Screen Commands

The commands you see on the screen increase the scope of what you can do and the speed with which you can do it. The rest of this book is about using the on-screen commands to process words more efficiently and to arrange them into attractive formats. Individual commands are explained in detail in later chapters. This chapter describes the dialogue you engage in when working with commands, gives an overview of what commands do for you, and shows how to choose them.

COMMAND DIALOGUE

Commands are presented to you on a menu. When you choose from a menu of commands, you tell the Word program to do a particular task. If you've ever ordered food in a restaurant, you're already familiar with the process of choosing from menus and giving commands.

There are 16 choices, called *commands,* on Word's main menu. In most cases, when you choose a command, Word prompts you to be more specific about what you want to do. It responds to your choice by displaying a new menu of choices, called *subcommands,* or by displaying questions related to the command, called *command fields,* which may or may not be accompanied by a list of possible answers. Sometimes you have to ask to see a list of possible answers. Usually, Word proposes a choice from a menu or a response to a question—like a waiter who speeds up the ordering process by recommending a particular dish. If you don't want to accept the *proposed response,* you can choose something else.

To *carry out the command,* you give Word a signal that says you've finished specifying what you want done. If you ask Word to do something it can't do, it will tell you in the message line.

WHAT'S ON THE MENU?

It's not a very enticing menu you see on your screen. The 16 commands are arranged in alphabetical order and are squeezed together to save space.

```
COMMAND: Copy Delete Format Gallery Help Insert Jump Library
         Options Print Quit Replace Search Transfer Undo Window
```

To make the menu more palatable, let's rearrange it so that related commands are grouped together.

Editing	Formatting	Filing	Printing	General Purpose
Copy	Format	Transfer	Print	Help
Delete	Gallery	Quit		Library
Insert				Options
Jump				Undo
Replace				
Search				
Window				

Our revised menu groups the commands according to what they help you do: edit, format, file, and print. The Help, Library, Options, and Undo commands are grouped together in a general-purpose category because they *supplement* the other commands.

Looking at this menu, you might think that there are more commands for editing than for formatting, filing, or printing. But there are, in fact, fewer editing commands than any others. Hiding behind the main formatting, filing, and printing commands are bunches of subcommands. (The Format command alone branches out into 14 subcommands, which branch out into a total of 22 more subcommands.) Because you need to use the editing commands more frequently than the others, most editing commands were made into *main* commands that are always visible and immediately available to you on the main menu.

The Editing Commands

The editing commands help you make changes to the text of a document.

Copy, *Delete*, and *Insert* are used for cutting text out and pasting text in. They are used to store text in and retrieve text from the scrap (a temporary storage place) or from a glossary (a permanent storage place for frequently used text).

Jump lets you leap to a particular page or footnote.

Search finds text and moves the cursor to it.

Replace finds text and substitutes other text for what it finds.

Window lets you open, close, and change the size of windows. With more than one window open, you can look at more than one document (or at different parts of the same document) at the same time and easily move text between them.

The Formatting Commands

The formatting commands help you to change the appearance of a document.

Format branches out into a menu of subcommands that determine the overall layout of a printed page and the appearance of particular paragraphs and individual characters. With these subcommands, you can change the margins, renumber pages, make footnotes and running heads, set tabs, justify lines, center lines, indent lines, adjust the line spacing, print line numbers, mark revisions, change the type size and style, and achieve special printing effects like boldface, italics, underline, subscripts, superscripts, and more. Format also leads to subcommands that search for and automatically replace formats.

Gallery takes you to an entirely different menu, similar to the main menu. The commands on the Gallery menu let you create, edit, print, and save style sheets instead of documents. Style sheets format text as do the Format commands; however, one style sheet can replace dozens of individual formatting subcommands. (To get out of the Gallery menu and go back to the main menu where you can resume working with a document, choose the *Exit* command.)

The Filing Commands

The filing commands control what goes in and out of temporary storage (memory) and permanent storage (disks). They arrange for the back-and-forth transfer of documents and glossaries between memory (where they can be changed and are initially created) and disks (where they can be stored indefinitely).

Transfer loads, saves, and merges documents and glossaries; deletes documents, glossaries, style sheets or any other kind of file; renames documents; and erases the contents of all or part of your work area in memory.

Quit erases your work area and stops the Word program. Before it erases anything that hasn't been saved, Quit gives you another chance to save it.

The Printing Command

The sole printing command, Print, single-handedly controls almost everything related to printing. That's a lot to take care of because Word offers you a lot of printing alternatives.

Print lets you print all or part of a document; merge documents while printing; edit a document while printing; choose a printer; print a glossary or a summary sheet; and more.

General-Purpose Commands

Help gives you helpful information about each of the commands as well as about the keyboard, the mouse, and editing techniques.

Library branches out into a menu of subcommands that let you perform special tasks: check and correct spelling; automatically hyphenate words; find synonyms from a built-in thesaurus; create a table of contents or an index; automatically number items in an outline or in text; sort text; sort, update, and print summary information about documents; run other programs and DOS commands without leaving Word; and link Word with spreadsheets, graphics, or other documents so that your document will be automatically updated when the other files are updated.

Options lets you change the way the program behaves when you're editing and formatting. With the wide assortment of options offered to you, you can, for example, turn off the menu display and remove the window borders; make invisible characters visible so that you can easily edit them or edit around them; turn off the audible alarm that usually beeps when you try to do something illegal; adjust the speed at which the cursor moves; and show line breaks as they will occur during printing.

Undo lets you change your mind and recover from mistakes. It reverses the last editing or formatting change made, including changes made by the Undo command itself.

WORKING WITH MENUS

The procedure for using menu commands, with either the keyboard or the mouse, can be summarized in four steps:

1. Choose the command.

2. Choose the subcommand(s), if any.

3. Answer questions, if any, posed by command fields.

4. Carry out the command.

To see how it's done, we'll choose and carry out the Transfer Load command. This command has an example of each kind of menu and question you see when you're working with commands. In an earlier chapter, I hurried you through the steps for using this command so that you could use it right away. This time, I'll explain what you're seeing and what you're doing, and then go over the general rules for choosing and carrying out any menu command.

Choosing a Command

The command menu that's usually visible when you're typing or editing a document is called the Edit menu and is labeled *COMMAND*:

```
                        Commands
                           |
         ┌─────────────────┴──────────────────────────┐
COMMAND: Copy Delete Format Gallery Help Insert Jump Library
         Options Print Quit Replace Search Transfer Undo Window
```

When you're using the keyboard, the Escape key takes you to and from the Edit menu. After you press the Esc key, the first command on the main menu is highlighted:

```
COMMAND: Copy Delete Format Gallery Help Insert Jump Library
         Options Print Quit Replace Search Transfer Undo Window
```

This lets you know that you are in command mode and that you can now choose a command.

With the mouse, you have immediate access to the main command menu whenever it's visible. Just roll the mouse to move the mouse pointer to the command you want. After you select a command, you are in command mode.

For either the keyboard or the mouse, being in command mode means you cannot enter text in your document by pressing the letter keys. While in command mode, the letter keys can only be used to choose commands or command options.

If you would like to see a brief message telling you what a command does, use the keyboard to highlight the command: Press the Esc key to activate the menu and then move the highlight to the command by pressing the direction keys or the Spacebar. After highlighting the Transfer command, for example, you see the message:

```
Manages document files (loads, saves, etc). Sets default drive/directory
```

To access the menu and choose a command

With the keyboard:	With the mouse:
1. *Press the Esc key to access the menu.* The menu becomes visible if it was turned off (with the Options command) and the first command in the menu is highlighted.	1. *If the menu is turned off, point to any place on the status line except the help mark (?) and Click-L or Click-R, as shown in Figure 5-1.*
2. *Press the first letter of the command you want.* In this instance, press T (uppercase or lowercase) to choose the Transfer command.	2. *Point to the command and Click-L.* In this case, point to Transfer and Click-L, as shown in Figure 5-2.
(You can, instead, press the direction keys or the Spacebar to move the highlight to the command, and then press the Enter key to choose it.)	

Figure 5-1. *Using the mouse to temporarily make the menu visible.*

COMMAND: Copy Delete Format Gallery Help Insert Jump Library
            Options Print Quit Replace Search Transfer Undo Window

                                                   Click-L

Figure 5-2. *Choosing the Transfer command with the mouse.*

❑ KEYBOARD NOTE: *When choosing commands, use the keys that are easiest for you to remember or to reach. It's usually fastest to choose a command by typing the initial letter.*

Choosing a Subcommand

After you choose a command from the menu, a new menu of subcommands often appears. After you choose the Transfer command, you see this subcommand menu:

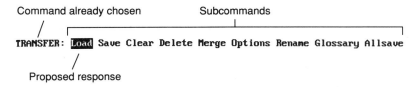

The word in capital letters on the left tells you which command you've already chosen. The first command or subcommand in a menu is always the proposed response and is highlighted. For the most part, subcommands are chosen the same way that commands are chosen.

As with main commands, you can highlight a subcommand (by pressing the direction keys or the Spacebar) to see a brief explanation of what the subcommand does. For example, when the Load subcommand is highlighted, Word displays the message:

Loads named document

To choose a subcommand

With the keyboard:

1. *Press the capitalized letter of the subcommand you want.* In this case, press L to choose the Load subcommand.

   Alternatively, you can press the direction keys or the Spacebar to move the highlight to the command, and then press the Enter key to choose it. (If you're choosing the proposed response, you can simply press the Enter key because it is already highlighted.)

With the mouse:

1. *Point to the subcommand and Click-L.* In this case, point to Load and Click-L, as shown in Figure 5-3.

```
TRANSFER: Load Save Clear Delete Merge Options Rename Glossary Allsave
          Click-L
```

Figure 5-3. *Choosing the Load subcommand with the mouse.*

❏ KEYBOARD NOTE: *With few exceptions, the first letter of a subcommand is also the capitalized letter. When two or more subcommands start with the same letter, a different letter is capitalized—as in, for example, Format sEarch. In these instances, press the capitalized letter, rather than the first letter.*

Answering Questions

If Word needs more information after you choose a command or a subcommand, you see a display of one or more command fields. For example, after you choose Load, you see two command fields, *filename* and *read only*:

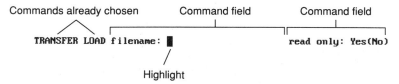

There are two kinds of questions posed by command fields: fill-in-the-blank and multiple choice. The *filename* field is a fill-in-the-blank question and asks, "What's the name of the file you want to load?" The *read only* field is a multiple-choice question and asks, ''Do you only want to read the file (and not make any changes)?''

You must move the highlight or the mouse pointer to a command field before you can answer the question it poses. With the keyboard, pressing the direction keys or the Tab key moves the highlight from field to field. With the mouse, sliding the mouse on your desktop moves the mouse pointer.

To save you time, there's usually a *proposed response* (or *default* answer) to both types of questions. It's marked either with the highlight or with parentheses. If there is a proposed response and it's acceptable, simply skip the question. After all questions have been answered to your satisfaction, you can carry out the command.

Fill-in-the-blank questions

You don't see a list of choices after a fill-in-the-blank question, but frequently a separate list is available. When answering a fill-in-the-blank question, you can either type in your response or select one from a list (if one is available). First we'll walk through the steps of requesting a list and choosing a response from it. Then I'll explain how you can type in a response.

Choosing from a list. You can ask Word to display a list of possible responses to a fill-in-the-blank question. If available, the list will appear at the top of the screen and the first item in the list will be highlighted as the proposed response. If you request a list when one is not available, Word immediately beeps to let you know you've asked for the impossible.

A list is available for the *filename* field of the Transfer Load command, so let's take a look at it. The list of possible responses for the *filename* field will include all the document files, if any, on the current document disk or in the current document directory.

To request and choose from a list

With the keyboard:	**With the mouse:**
1. *If necessary, press the direction keys or the Tab key to move the highlight to the command field*. In this example, it's not necessary because the *filename* command field is already highlighted.	1. *Point to the command field and Click-R to move to the command field and display the list*. In this example, point to the *filename* field and Click-R, as shown in Figure 5-4 on the following page.

With the keyboard:

2. *Press the F1 key to display the list.*

3. *Use the direction keys to move the highlight to your choice on the list.* For trial purposes, move the highlight to any filename.

4. *Press the Tab key to go back to the command fields and move to the next command field.* You can press the Enter key, instead, if you're ready to carry out the command. In this example, press the Tab key so that you can modify the next command field.

With the mouse:

2. *Point to your choice and Click-L.* You can Click-R, instead of Click-L, if you're ready to carry out the command. In this example, point to any filename in the list and Click-L so that you can take a look at the next command field.

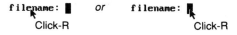

```
filename: █      or      filename: █
          Click-R                    Click-R
```

Figure 5-4. *Using the mouse to request a list of possible responses to the* filename *field.*

If you press the Tab key or Click-L to choose a response, the highlight moves to the next command field. As an example, if you chose a file named SAMPLE.DOC, your screen would now look like this:

Highlight has moved
to next field

```
TRANSFER LOAD filename: C:\WORDIR\SAMPLE.DOC  read only: Yes No
```

Typing in a response. Instead of choosing from a list, you can type in a response to a fill-in-the-blank question. You can correct errors with the Backspace key as you're typing.

To type in a response

With the keyboard:

1. *If necessary, press the direction keys or the Tab key to move the highlight to the command field.*

2. *Type your response.*

With the mouse:

1. *If necessary, point to the command field and Click-L to move the highlight to the command field.*

2. *Type your response.*

Multiple-choice questions

Multiple-choice questions are followed by a list of choices—another menu of sorts. Choosing a response to a multiple-choice question is exactly like choosing a command from a menu.

To choose a response to a command field

With the keyboard:

1. *If necessary, press the direction keys or the Tab key to move the highlight to the command field.* In this example, the *read only* command field is already highlighted.

2. *Press the first letter of your choice.* In this case, press Y. (Although you would rarely want to change the response in the *read only* field from the proposed *No* to *Yes*, try it now to see how it's done, and then change it back to *No*.)

   (Alternatively, you can press the Spacebar or the Backspace key to move the highlight to your choice.)

With the mouse:

1. *Point to your choice and Click-L.* Click-R, instead, if you're ready to carry out the command. In this example, the *read only* field is the last command field, so point to *No* and Click-R, as shown in Figure 5-5.

```
TRANSFER LOAD filename: C:\WORDIR\SAMPLE.DOC   read only: Yes No
                                                              Click-R
```

Figure 5-5. *Using the mouse to choose a response and carry out the command at the same time.*

When you're loading a file, you usually want to be able to write in it or make changes to it, so you can usually skip the *read only* command field by carrying out the command right after you choose or supply the filename.

Frequently, a multiple-choice question is not really asking you for more information. It tells you (with the proposed response) how Word ordinarily does something and gives you the option to do it differently.

Carrying Out Commands

If there are no command fields, Word carries out the command after you make all your menu selections. If there are command fields, you must tell Word when to carry out the command; otherwise, Word has no way of knowing when you're finished answering or changing answers to all the questions in the command fields.

To carry out a command

With the keyboard:

1. *Press the Enter key.*

With the mouse:

1. *Point to the capitalized command words and Click-L. As an example, you could point to TRANSFER LOAD and Click-L, as shown in Figure 5-6.*

   You can, instead, point to your choice in a list or multiple-choice command field and Click-R.

TRANSFER LOAD filename: `C:\WORDIR\SAMPLE.DOC` read only: Yes(No)
Click-L

Figure 5-6. *Using the mouse to carry out the Transfer Load command.*

After a command is carried out, you're automatically returned to type-in mode, where you can resume typing. If Word can't carry out the command, it beeps and lets you know why in the message line.

The Click-R Shortcut

Once you become familiar with the commands, you can speed up command selection immensely by taking the *Click-R shortcut* with the mouse.

Click-R chooses the command you're pointing to *plus* the proposed response to the next level. The next level might be a menu of subcommands, or it might be the command-field display. For example, if you want to load a file, you can choose Transfer with Click-R to choose both Transfer from the main menu and Load from the next menu. Or to print a file (without changing any of the options), choose the Print command with Click-R so that you can skip the menu of subcommands and immediately start printing.

The Delete, Insert, and Copy commands have only one command field and the proposed response is always the scrap. So when you want to Delete to, Copy to, or Insert from the scrap (which is what you usually want to do when you use these commands), Click-R to choose these commands. Click-R chooses the command, okays the proposed response to the single command field, and carries out the command for you—replacing three steps with one.

COMMAND SPECIALS

Word provides some special tools to help you work with commands. With these tools, you can repeat a command you've just carried out, cancel a command before you carry it out, undo a command after you carry it out, and get help with a specific command before you carry it out.

Repeating Commands

You can repeat many commands without having to work your way through menus, submenus, and command fields again.

To repeat the last command that was carried out, with all the same options:

Press   F4

To repeat the last command using the mouse:

1. Point to the word *COMMAND* in the command menu.

2. Click either button. For example:

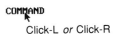

COMMAND
Click-L *or* Click-R

Before you repeat a command, you can move the cursor or highlight text. Pressing the F4 key or clicking the word *COMMAND* repeats the following commands:

Copy	Library Hyphenate
Delete	Library Index
Format subcommands	Library Table
Insert	Transfer Merge
Library Autosort	Undo

To repeat the last Search command, with all the same options:

Press

Canceling and Undoing Commands

You can cancel a command before it's carried out by pressing the Escape key. This takes you back to type-in mode. If you want to choose another command, you have to press the Esc key again to return to command mode. As an alternative, you can press Ctrl-Esc to cancel a command without leaving command mode.

Press

To cancel a command with the mouse, Click-LR when the mouse pointer is anywhere in the command area. If you cancel a command with the mouse, you return to type-in mode.

❑ NOTE: *To cancel the Gallery, Library Document-retrieval, Library Spell, Print preView, or Help command and return to type-in mode, you must choose the Exit command from the menu displayed.*

If you carry out a command by mistake, or if you change your mind about what you've just done, reach for the Undo command. It reverses the last editing or formatting change. For example, if you deleted text, Undo inserts it back in place. If you inserted text, Undo deletes it. If you replaced text, Undo restores it. If you changed a word from boldface to italics, Undo changes it back to boldface.

Undo works with the following commands:

Copy	Library Link
Delete	Library Number
Format	Library Spell
Format repLace	Library Table
Insert	Library thEsaurus
Library Autosort	Replace
Library Hyphenate	Transfer Merge
Library Index	Undo

Getting Help with Commands

If you try to carry out a command and get an error message that you don't understand, look up the message in the *Reference to Microsoft Word* manual. Here you will find out what went wrong and what you should do next.

If you have the Special Edition with disk included, consult the Introduction

If you don't remember what a specific command, subcommand, or command field does, you can get instant help on-screen. To get this kind of help, first highlight the command, subcommand, or command field (use the direction keys) and then press Alt-H.

If you're using the mouse, highlight the command, subcommand, or command field using the direction keys, and then point to the question mark at the bottom of the screen and Click-L.

After calling for help, the screen fills up with information and explanations (called Quick Help) specific to the highlighted command.

You can also get help by choosing the Help command from the main menu. Whichever way you access help, you see the Quick Help menu (labeled "Help") at the bottom of the help screen:

```
HELP: Exit Next Previous Basics
      Index Tutorial Keyboard Mouse
```

You can choose commands from the Quick Help menu just like you choose commands from the main editing menu. The *Exit* command takes you back to your document or to the menu you were at when you requested help. *Next* brings up the next help screen, and *Previous* lets you see the previous help screen. Choose the *Basics* command if you need help getting around the help screens themselves, and choose *Index* to see and choose from a list of Quick Help topics. *Keyboard* and *Mouse* allow you to directly access the help screens for the keyboard and the mouse.

If you also want tutorial help that provides guided practice lessons on using a command, subcommand, or command field, choose *Tutorial* from the Quick Help menu. This leads you to a menu of two subcommands: Lesson and Index. *Lesson* brings you hands-on exercise for the feature last described by Quick Help. *Index* shows you a long list of topics for which you can choose a tutorial lesson.

Instructions on the bottom of the tutorial screen tell you how to choose a lesson, lead you through the tutorial, and get you back to the Quick Help menu. Once there, you can choose the Exit command to get back to your document.

If you don't have a fixed disk, or if you haven't copied Learning Word to your fixed disk with the SETUP program, you will be asked to insert the Learning Word disk when you request tutorial help.

You must have at least 320 KB of available memory to use tutorial help. (You can use the DOS command CHKDSK, as described in Appendix A, to find out your system's available memory.) If you don't have enough memory, you see the message: *Insufficient memory.*

LEARNING COMMANDS

As you read through the remaining chapters of this book, take some time to try each command that you read about. You can't be sure that you understand what a command does until you see for yourself the effect it has. Try the commands on any document—the sample document you created in Chapter 2 of this book or a copy of any document that you created on your own. It doesn't matter what you practice on. In most cases, you only need some text, any text, to load into Word and experiment with. When you're done experimenting, you can quit without saving the changes so that the document you might have mangled by testing commands appears untouched. (To quit without saving, choose the Quit command and press N to confirm that you do not want to save the changes.)

When you're first starting out, don't load your memory down with all the steps you take, the keys you press, the mouse buttons you click, or the commands you choose to help you process words. Try to remember (in a general way) what can be done, rather than how to do it. When you need to make a particular change to a document, you can refer back to the sections in this book that tell you how to do it. After you've done something a few times, you'll be ready to rely more on the cues you get from the screen than on the guidance of this book.

If you're choosing commands with the keyboard, you can get by if you remember how to use these keys:

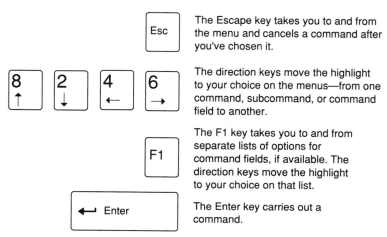

Esc	The Escape key takes you to and from the menu and cancels a command after you've chosen it.
8 ↑ 2 ↓ 4 ← 6 →	The direction keys move the highlight to your choice on the menus—from one command, subcommand, or command field to another.
F1	The F1 key takes you to and from separate lists of options for command fields, if available. The direction keys move the highlight to your choice on that list.
↵ Enter	The Enter key carries out a command.

If you're choosing commands with the mouse, you can do almost everything by moving the mouse pointer and clicking the left mouse button. If you also remember how to request a list of possible answers and how to cancel a command, you'll be well prepared for any situation.

Click-L Chooses anything that you're pointing to in a menu or a list.

Click-L Moves the highlight to the command field that you're pointing to.

Click-L Carries out a command if you're pointing to a capitalized command word in the command area.

Click-R Requests a list of possible responses for the command field that you're pointing to.

Click-LR Cancels a command if you're pointing anywhere in the command area.

Graphic Reminders

As you're learning what individual commands do, I'll frequently use graphics to remind you how to choose and carry out the commands. You're already familiar with some of these graphics. In earlier chapters, they were used to illustrate what was explained in words. In the remaining chapters, they'll be used instead of words to remind you what keys to press, or what to point at with the mouse pointer and which mouse button(s) to press.

When you see something like:

Press [Esc] [T] [L]

press and release the Esc key, then press and release the letter T key, and then press and release the letter L key. Press them in the order given as rapidly or as slowly as you like. Press them slowly if you want to see each menu or sub-menu that pops up.

When you see a shaded bar connecting two keys or a dash linking two key names, as in:

 *or* Ctrl-Esc

press and hold down the first key, and then press the second key. In this example, hold down the Ctrl key while you press the Esc key.

When you see something like:

point to the Transfer command and press and release the left mouse button. Then, when the submenu comes up, point to the Load subcommand and press and release the left mouse button.

In addition to using graphic symbols, I use some verbal short-forms to reduce the number of words you have to read. When you see something like:

Choose the Transfer Load command

choose Transfer from the main command menu, and then choose Load from the subcommand menu.

Whenever you see a reference to a two- or three-word command, as in the example above, remember that, strictly speaking, it refers to a command plus one or more subcommands.

WHAT IF YOU DON'T LIKE MENUS?

For those of you who don't like menus, Word offers some alternatives. You can invoke many of the most commonly used menu commands by pressing a function key in combination with the Shift, Alternate, or Control key. For example, when you want to load a file, you can press Ctrl-F7 instead of the Esc, T, L sequence to choose the Transfer Load command. You can invoke most formatting commands by pressing the Alt key in combination with a letter key. For example, to underline characters, you can press Alt-U instead of pressing the Esc, T, C sequence to choose the Format Character command and then pressing additional keys to move to the command field that controls underlining. If you're good at remembering key assignments, they will save you a few keystrokes.

If you don't like Word's key assignments, you can make up your own. You can make macros that reassign any of the function keys (F1 to F10), function-key combinations (such as Shift-F2, Alt-F2, and Ctrl-F2), and Ctrl-key combinations (such as Ctrl-A, Ctrl-AB, and Ctrl-1). If you're used to using another word processor that employed function keys or Ctrl-key combinations to give commands, this means you don't have to start over: You can redesign Word to issue commands like the word-processing program that you already know.

If alternatives to using the command menus interest you, see Appendix D for a list of preassigned shortcut keys. See Chapter 16 to find out how to make your own key assignments by recording macros.

Do give the menus a chance. I think you'll find that it's easier to actually use them than it is to read about using them.

Chapter 6

Cutting and Pasting

Not too long ago, the only way to revise and rearrange a typed document without retyping it was to cut out—using scissors—the parts you wanted to delete or move. You saved the scraps of paper that you could use elsewhere. When you found the place where you wanted to insert a scrap of text, you pasted, or glued, or taped it in place and hoped that your cut lines wouldn't show on the photocopy.

Electronic cut-and-paste is a lot easier, and the seams never show. In Word, it's done with the Delete, Copy, and Insert commands. These commands let you easily change and rearrange documents by erasing, moving, or copying any amount of text. The text that surrounds the deleted, copied, or moved text instantly adjusts itself to conceal any signs that a change was made. If you open an additional window, you can even move or copy text from one document to another.

Before you can delete, copy, or move text, you have to find it and highlight (select) it. Let's review what you've already learned about scrolling and highlighting text. As we review what you learned in Chapter 3, we'll add a few more tricks. Once you become adept at selecting text, cutting and pasting will be a breeze.

SCROLLING WITH THE KEYBOARD

Scrolling takes you to any part of a document that you want to see. You can scroll up and down (vertically), as you learned in Chapter 3, and you can also scroll sideways (horizontally).

Scrolling Up and Down

You can scroll up or down one line at a time or one windowful at a time. Or you can scroll all the way to the beginning or end of a document in one step.

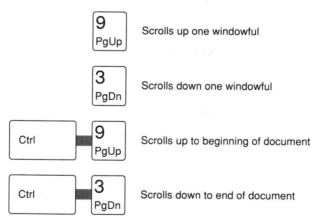

9 PgUp	Scrolls up one windowful
3 PgDn	Scrolls down one windowful
Ctrl — 9 PgUp	Scrolls up to beginning of document
Ctrl — 3 PgDn	Scrolls down to end of document

To scroll up or down one line at a time, press the Scroll Lock key to turn it on (*SL* appears on the status line), and then press the up or down direction key. When you're done scrolling, don't forget to turn off Scroll Lock by pressing it again.

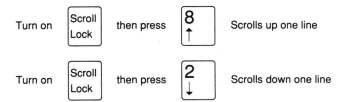

Scrolling Sideways

Word lets you create documents that are wider than the window. When you're working with wide documents, you see only the part of the line that you're currently working on. To see the part that doesn't fit in the window, you scroll horizontally to the left or to the right. You can scroll sideways one-third windowful at a time if at least one line is wider than the window.

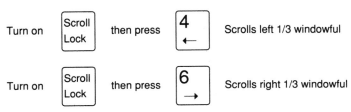

Regardless of how wide your document is, you can quickly scroll all the way to the left end of a line with the Home key or all the way to the right end with the End key.

SCROLLING AND THUMBING WITH THE MOUSE

To scroll with the mouse, you point to the left or bottom window border and click one or both mouse buttons, depending on which direction and how far you want to scroll.

Scrolling Up and Down

To scroll up or down with the mouse, move the mouse pointer to the *vertical scroll bar* (the left window border). The pointer changes its shape to ✦ or ▮ to indicate that it's ready to scroll. The distance that you scroll depends on where you place the mouse pointer on the scroll bar. Position the pointer on the scroll bar at the distance from the top that matches the distance you want to scroll. The direction that you scroll depends on which mouse button you press:

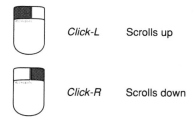

Click-L   Scrolls up

Click-R   Scrolls down

Thumbing Through a Document

As you learned in Chapter 3, you can thumb directly to any part of your document. When you are thumbing, the top of the vertical scroll bar (left window border) represents the beginning of your document and the bottom represents the end. The pointer's position on the scroll bar determines where you thumb to in the document. Point to the top of the vertical scroll bar to thumb to the beginning of the document, point to the bottom of the bar to thumb to the end of the document, or point to the middle of the bar to thumb to the middle of the document.

After you position the pointer, Click-LR to indicate you want to thumb, which means scroll to a particular place regardless of whether you have to scroll up or scroll down to get there.

Click-LR   Scrolls up *or* down to a particular place

Scrolling Sideways

When you have a document that is wider than the window, you can scroll sideways. Scrolling or thumbing horizontally with the mouse works like vertical scrolling and thumbing, except that you position the mouse pointer on the *horizontal scroll bar* (the bottom window border). To scroll left or right with the mouse, position the pointer at a distance from the left end of the horizontal scroll bar that matches the distance you want to scroll. The pointer changes its shape to ↔ or ▯ to indicate that it's ready to scroll.

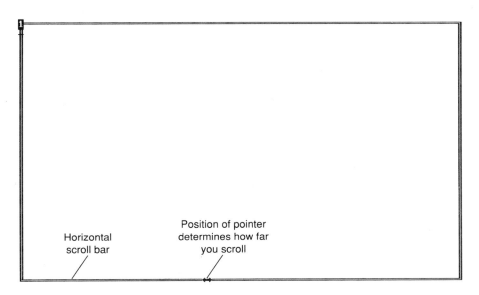

Click-L to scroll left toward the beginning of the line. Click-R to scroll right toward the end of the line.

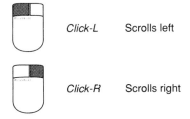

Click-L   Scrolls left

Click-R   Scrolls right

Thumbing Sideways

You can thumb directly to any part of a long line that exceeds the width of the window. When you're thumbing, the left end of the horizontal scroll bar represents the beginning of the line and the right end of the horizontal scroll bar represents the end of the line. Move the mouse pointer along the horizontal scroll bar to a position that represents the part of the line you want to see and Click-LR.

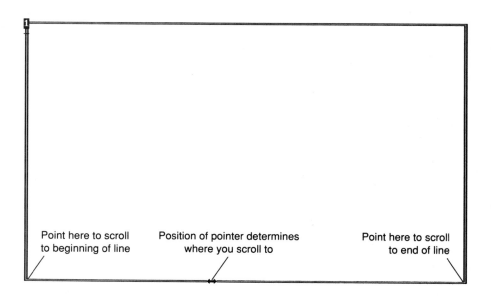

Point here to scroll to beginning of line   Position of pointer determines where you scroll to   Point here to scroll to end of line

Click-LR   Scrolls left *or* right to a particular place

You cannot scroll or thumb horizontally if none of the lines are wider than the window.

USING MENU COMMANDS TO FIND TEXT

Two menu commands help you find and select any text you want to change. When you know what you're looking for or where you want to go, the Search command and the Jump Page command can take you there in one leap, skipping over everything on the way.

The Search command lets you specify a word, phrase, or any single character or sequence of characters that you want to locate. Word moves the cursor to highlight the specified text when it finds it. The Search command and its close associate, the Replace command, deserve a chapter all to themselves. So they are described in detail in Chapter 7.

The Jump Page Command

The Jump Page command lets you quickly move to a particular page in a document. After you choose the Jump Page command, Word asks you what page number you want to go to:

```
JUMP PAGE number: 1
```

Type in a number and carry out the command. Use Arabic numerals—1, 2, 3, and so forth—regardless of what format you choose for printing your page numbers. (The Format Division Page-numbers command lets you choose Arabic numerals, Roman numerals, or letters instead of numbers.)

If a document has been formatted into more than one division and if it therefore has more than one page with the same number, you can include the division number along with the page. For example, type:

3d2

to jump to page three in the second division. (See Chapter 9 for more information on divisions and formatting.)

If you see the message *Pagination is required*, it means the document hasn't been divided into pages yet. Word normally determines where the pages will break as you type, but you can turn off this feature by choosing the Options command and changing the response to the *paginate* command field to *Manual*. You can then paginate the document manually by choosing the Print Repaginate command.

If you tell Word not to repaginate automatically, the page numbers of your document will correspond to the page numbers of the last printed copy. If you ask to jump to page 5, the cursor will move to the first character of what was page 5 in the last printout. This makes it easy to make changes that you've marked on a printed copy.

SELECTING TEXT WITH THE KEYBOARD

As you learned earlier, selecting text or highlighting what you want to change involves moving the cursor and, sometimes, stretching it to highlight all text that you want a command to act on.

Moving the Cursor

The basic cursor-moving keys that you learned earlier (plus a few more) are illustrated in Figure 6-1.

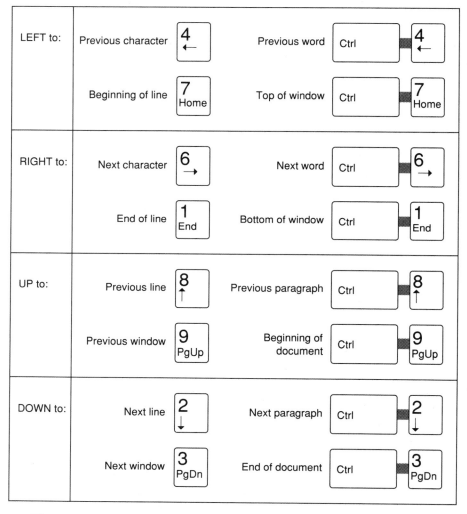

Figure 6-1. *The cursor-moving keys.*

Stretching the Cursor

As you learned in Chapter 3, the four function keys F7 to F10 extend the cursor to highlight a whole word or paragraph:

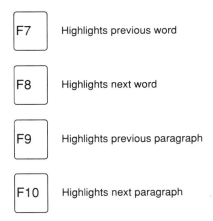

The Shift key gives each of these keys a different function:

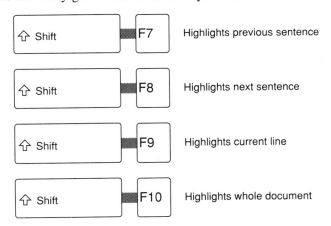

Notice how some of these function keys can also serve as cursor-moving keys. F7 and F8 move the cursor a word at a time in either direction. Shift-F7 and Shift-F8 move the cursor a sentence at a time in either direction. F9 and F10 scoot the cursor through the document a paragraph at a time.

Highlighting a block of text

You can highlight a block of text of any length by extending the cursor from one end of the block to the other:

1. Move the cursor to either end of the block.

2. Press F6, the Extend key, or hold down the Shift key.

3. Move the cursor to the other end of the block.

If you use the Shift key, use any of the direction keys to move the cursor to the other end of the block. The cursor stops extending as soon as you release the Shift key. If you use the Extend key, you can use both the direction keys and the function keys, F7 to F10, to move the cursor. Unlike the Shift key, the F6 key is a toggle key that turns the Extend function on and off. Word turns the toggle off for you after you choose and carry out a command. If you decide not to carry out a command, press the F6 key again to turn it off. When the Extend function is switched on, *EX* appears at the bottom of the screen.

In addition to using the cursor-moving keys, you can use the scroll keys to move the cursor to the other end of a large block of text. When you scroll with the keyboard, the cursor moves through the text in the direction that you scroll and, with the Extend function turned on or the Shift key held down, all text the cursor passes over is highlighted.

You can also use the Search command to extend the cursor. First press the F6 key, and then use the Search command to search for the text at the other end of the block that you wish to highlight.

When you're editing a document, frequently you want to select and delete the last or the first part of a word or sentence rather than the whole word or sentence. To highlight part of a word or sentence, press F6 to turn on the Extend function and then:

Press	*to extend the cursor to*
F7	the beginning of the word
F8	the end of the word
Shift-F7	the beginning of the sentence
Shift-F8	the end of the sentence

SELECTING TEXT WITH THE MOUSE

Selecting text is much faster and easier with the mouse than with the keyboard. You can move and stretch the cursor with one mouse action.

Moving and Stretching the Cursor

Just slide the mouse around your tabletop until the mouse pointer is where you want the cursor to be. With the mouse pointer in the text, you can highlight a character, word, or sentence:

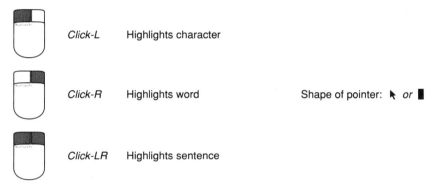

Click-L   Highlights character

Click-R   Highlights word   Shape of pointer: ▸ *or* ▮

Click-LR   Highlights sentence

If you move the mouse pointer to the selection bar to the left of your text, you can highlight a line, a paragraph, or the whole document:

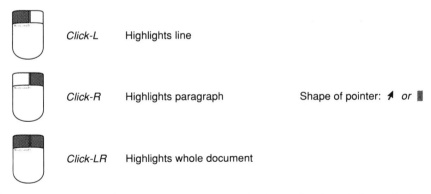

Click-L   Highlights line

Click-R   Highlights paragraph   Shape of pointer: ◢ *or* ▮

Click-LR   Highlights whole document

If you want to move the cursor to some text that's not in the window, first scroll to bring the text into view. Then move the pointer to where you want the cursor to be.

Highlighting a block of text

You can highlight a block of text of any length by extending the cursor from one end of the block to the other:

1. Move the pointer to one end of the block and Hold-L.

2. Move the pointer to the other end of the block and Rel-L.

If the other end is somewhere outside the window, you can drag the mouse pointer (while still holding down the left mouse button) across the window border to find it. The text will scroll as you cross over the border.

Another way to highlight a block of text is to:

1. Move the pointer to one end of the block and Click-L.

2. Press F6, the Extend key. *EX* appears at the bottom of the screen.

3. Move the pointer to the other end of the block and Click-L. If the other end is not in sight, scroll to it in the usual way: Move the pointer to the left window border or the bottom window border and Click-L or Click-R to scroll to the desired text.

Word turns off the Extend function after you carry out a command. If necessary, you can press the F6 key again to turn it off.

To quickly highlight the last part of a word or sentence:

1. Move the pointer to the beginning of the part you want to highlight and Click-L.

2. Press the F6 key. *EX* appears at the bottom of your screen.

3. Click-R to extend the cursor to the end of the word, or Click-LR to extend it to the end of the sentence.

USING THE SCRAP TO CUT AND PASTE

The *scrap* is a temporary holding cell for a scrap of text. When you cut out a piece of text, you can put it in the scrap so that you can retrieve it and paste it back in the document somewhere else. The scrap also allows you to delete text without losing it altogether. If you change your mind after you have deleted something, or if you delete something by mistake, you can retrieve it from the scrap.

The scrap can hold a piece of text of any length, but it can hold only one piece at a time. If you have text in the scrap and you then put in another piece, the new text displaces the existing text. You can always check what's currently in the scrap by looking at what's enclosed in braces (⟨⟩) on the status line. If it's longer than 15 characters, you'll see the beginning and the end, separated by an ellipsis (...). For example, if I deleted the first sentence of this paragraph to scrap, I would see this on the status line:

```
{The·sc...·time.}
```

You will see special symbols in the scrap that you may not recognize. As mentioned before, nonprintable characters—such as spaces, tabs, and paragraph marks—are always shown in the scrap with special symbols. A space character is shown as a raised dot (·); a tab character is displayed as a right arrow (→); and a paragraph mark looks like this: ¶ . (A complete list of special symbols that you might encounter in the scrap is found in Appendix F.)

Deleting Text to the Scrap

If you don't have a mouse, use the Delete key to delete, or remove, text. It's faster and easier than choosing and carrying out the Delete command.

If you have a mouse, take the Click-R shortcut when you use the Delete command. There is only one command field (*DELETE to*), and the proposed response is ⟨⟩, which is the scrap. So choose the Delete command, okay the proposed response, and carry out the command, all with one mouse maneuver: Point to the command and Click-R.

To delete any amount of text to the scrap:

1. Highlight the text you want to delete.

2. Delete the text:

The highlighted text disappears from the document and appears in the scrap. If you delete something by mistake or if you change your mind about deleting something, you can use the Undo command to put it back:

Press ☐ Esc ☐ ☐ U ☐   *or*   Undo
                                   Click-L

The text you deleted reappears in the same place. Undo reverses the *last* editing or formatting change only. If you made another change since you deleted the text you want to restore, Undo can't restore your deleted text.

Always check the contents of the scrap before you give up: If your deleted text is still there, you can insert it back into place with the Insert key or the Insert command:

1. Move the cursor to where you want the text to appear.

2. Insert the text:

Press    *or*   Insert Click-R

Deleting and Replacing Text

When you delete something in a document, you frequently want to insert something else in its place. For example, you might want to replace the word *labyrinth* with *maze* in the following sentence:

It's easy to get lost in a labyrinth.

The best way to make a one-time replacement of this sort is to delete the word and then type in the substitution. After you delete the text, the cursor is in the right place to start typing in the new text.

Word normally *inserts* anything you type, so you can move the cursor anywhere and start typing without typing over anything. If there is any text after the cursor, it will automatically move to the right to make room for the newly typed text. This works well for most editing needs.

Occasionally, you may prefer to delete and replace text by typing over it. The Overtype key, F5, lets you do that. F5 is a toggle key that must be turned on and off. When it is on, you see *OT* in the status line.

A third way to delete and replace text is with the Replace command. This command not only deletes and replaces specified text, but it also finds every occurrence of the text for you. Use it when you want to find and replace every occurrence (or several occurrences) of a piece of text throughout a document.

For example, if you repeatedly used the word *labyrinth* throughout a document, and you want to substitute each occurrence with the word *maze*, it's best to use the Replace command. Chapter 9 contains a detailed explanation of the Replace command.

Moving Text

To move text, you delete it from one place in the document and insert it in another. When you delete text, you erase it from the document and put it in the scrap. When you insert text (using the Insert key), you take a copy of it from the scrap and put it in the document.

Dear Western Allies,

This is just a quick note to let you know that all is fine
on the Eastern Front. Winter has been very picturesque here.
Lots of fluffy white snow on trees, houses, and hillsides.
Wreaths with bows on every colonial door. No horsedrawn
sleighs but lots of kids on sleds.

Adjusting to our new life on the other side of the continent
was difficult at first. We now understand why people resist
moving. Friendship is dear--all the more dear when not
there. We've finally met some people we feel comfortable
with and enjoy being with.

Our neighbors have stopped eyeing us, and our California
license plates, with distrust. After 6 months of proving
ourselves to be worthy neighbors without any unusual living
habits, we are now being rewarded with friendly greetings on
the street and even some prolonged chit-chat.

Time to go shovel some snow. Our very best wishes to you.

Love,

Delete to the scrap

COMMAND: Copy Delete Format Gallery Help Insert Jump Library
        Options Print Quit Replace Search Transfer Undo Window
Edit document or press Esc to use menu
Pg1 Co46   {}   ?   Microsoft Word

Dear Western Allies,

This is just a quick note to let you know that all is fine
on the Eastern Front. Winter has been very picturesque here.
Lots of fluffy white snow on trees, houses, and hillsides.
Wreaths with bows on every colonial door. No horsedrawn
sleighs but lots of kids on sleds.

Our neighbors have stopped eyeing us, and our California
license plates, with distrust. After 6 months of proving
ourselves to be worthy neighbors without any unusual living
habits, we are now being rewarded with friendly greetings on
the street and even some prolonged chit-chat.

Adjusting to our new life on the other side of the continent
was difficult at first. We now understand why people resist
moving. Friendship is dear--all the more dear when not
there. We've finally met some people we feel comfortable
with and enjoy being with.

Time to go shovel some snow. Our very best wishes to you.

Love,

Insert from the scrap

COMMAND: Copy Delete Format Gallery Help Insert Jump Library
        Options Print Quit Replace Search Transfer Undo Window
Edit document or press Esc to use menu
Pg1 Co1   {¶Our·...hat.¶}   ?   Microsoft Word

To move any amount of text:

1. Highlight the text you want to move.

2. Delete the text:

3. Move the cursor to the new location. (Use any of the cursor-moving keys, or point to the new location with the mouse and Click-L.)

4. Insert the text:

The text you deleted is inserted to the left of the cursor.

What if you lose the scrap?

As you're moving through the document to find the new location for deleted text, you'll probably spot something else that needs changing. As long as you don't delete or copy anything else to the scrap, you can make other editing or formatting changes on the way.

You can delete text without changing the contents of the scrap if you use the Backspace key or combine the Shift key with the Delete key. To delete highlighted text without putting it in the scrap:

If you accidentally delete or copy other text to the scrap before you complete a move, the text you want to move disappears from the scrap. You can recover it if you can undo the command that put new text in the scrap. (Remember, you can only undo the last command carried out.) Undoing a command that changes the contents of the scrap also undoes the change to the scrap. After you carry out the Undo command, the text that was previously in the scrap (which, hopefully, is the text you were planning to move) reappears in the scrap. Whenever you see valuable text in the scrap, you can salvage it with the Insert key or the Insert command.

Copying Text

Copying text is similar to moving text, except that you copy the text to the scrap without deleting it from the document. Once it's in the scrap, you can get a copy of it any number of times, to insert in any number of places. To copy any amount of text:

1. Highlight the text you want to copy.

2. Copy the text:

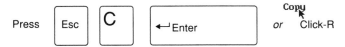

3. Move the cursor to the new location.

4. Insert the copy of the text:

A copy of the highlighted text appears in front of the cursor. You still have a copy of the text in scrap, so you can insert another copy elsewhere in the document. Think of the Insert key or the Insert command as a duplicating machine that can churn out as many copies of the text in scrap as you need. If you undo a copy operation with the Undo command, the copy disappears from the new location.

The Mouse Express for Moving and Copying Text

Using the mouse with the Control and Shift keys lets you directly move and copy text without going through the scrap. To move text with lightning speed:

1. Highlight the text.

2. Move the pointer to the new location.

3. Move the text to the new location:

To quickly copy text:

1. Highlight the text.

2. Move the pointer to the new location.

3. Copy the text to the new location:

Hold down | ⇧ Shift | and Click-L

USING A GLOSSARY TO CUT AND PASTE

You can avoid having to patrol the contents of the scrap by using a glossary, instead of the scrap, when you move or copy text. A glossary is a less volatile storage place for text than the scrap, but it's not quite as handy for cut-and-paste work. Using a glossary requires a few more keystrokes or mouse clicks.

What Is a Glossary?

A glossary, like the scrap, is a holding cell for pieces of text. But unlike the scrap, it can hold more than one piece of text at a time. Text put in a glossary stays there until you quit Word (with the Quit command) or clear the memory (with the Transfer Clear All command). This gives you more time to find the new location for text you want to move or copy. As you're traveling through a long document to find the new location, you can do other editing without worrying about losing your scrap of text.

You can permanently save the contents of a glossary by transferring the glossary to a file on disk, but it's usually not necessary to save a glossary that you use for cut-and-paste work. In fact, it's better not to clutter up your disks with scraps of text if you don't have a frequent and long-term use for them. (Saving and working with permanent glossaries is discussed in Chapter 8.) If you don't save a glossary, you'll be asked if you want to save it when you quit Word:

```
Enter Y to save changes to glossary, N to lose changes, or Esc to cancel █
```

If you're intentionally *not* saving the glossary, press N.

You can use the same commands to store and retrieve text in a glossary that you use to store and retrieve text in the scrap: Delete, Copy, and Insert. However, you cannot use the Insert and Delete *keys* or the Mouse Express described above to work with a glossary.

Moving Text and Copying Text Through a Glossary

To move any amount of text using a glossary, you first have to delete the text from the document and insert it in the glossary. To do this:

1. Highlight the text you want to move.

2. Choose the Delete command:

3. When you see the *DELETE to* prompt, type in a short name (up to 31 characters long) to represent the piece of text you're moving, and press the Enter key to carry out the command. (For example, if you're moving the section on educational background to another part of your résumé, you might type in a name like *education* or simply, *ed.*)

Your text is now safely tucked away in glossary memory, waiting for you to retrieve it. When you're ready to complete the move:

1. Move the cursor to the new location.

2. Choose the Insert command:

3. When you see the *INSERT from* prompt, type in the name you made up for the text when you deleted it, and press the Enter key. (The ✪ symbol for the scrap disappears as soon as you start typing.)

Instead of typing the name of your text in the *INSERT from* command field, you can press the F1 key to see a list of all names you used for pieces of text stored in the glossary and select one from the list. This is particularly helpful when you don't remember the name.

Copying text using the glossary is like moving text, except you choose the Copy command instead of the Delete command. You can undo a copy or move operation done through the glossary by using the Undo command.

OPENING WINDOWS TO CUT AND PASTE

The window you see when you start Word is one of eight windows that you can have open at one time. Opening another window lets you move or copy text from one document to another while both documents are in view. Or you can view different parts of the same document at the same time so that you see and compare where text is coming from and where it's going to. You can use any of the cut-and-paste techniques to move and copy text between windows.

To work with more than one window, you need to know how to:

- Open a window.

- Move from one window to another.

- Zoom (or enlarge) a window.

- Clear a window.

- Close a window.

A new window is opened by splitting an existing window either horizontally or vertically. A horizontal split seems to work best for most documents because you are able to see entire lines of the document in each window. You only have to scroll up and down in each window to see all of the text. With a vertical split, you may have to scroll sideways (as well as up and down) if your windows are not wide enough to show an entire line. A vertical split works well with a wide table because it allows you to easily compare columns of the table that aren't adjacent to each other.

If there is a document in the window that you split, the newly opened window displays part of that document—unless you specify that you want the new window cleared when you open it. You can load a different document into one of the windows. Or, you can clear the document out of one window so that you can create a brand new document.

You can work in only one window at a time, but you can easily move from one window to the next and back. When you're through working with an additional window, you'll want to close it so that you can reclaim the space it takes up on the screen. To give yourself more working space in a split window, you can zoom it to full size.

You can use either the mouse or the keyboard to open, move between, zoom, clear, and close windows. You'll find that the mouse is particularly handy for window work. First, I'll go over the steps for opening, moving between, zooming, clearing, and closing windows. Then, I'll explain how you go about using a second window to cut and paste.

Windows and the Keyboard

The Window command is your key to opening and closing windows with the keyboard. The F1 function key moves the cursor from one window to another, and the Transfer command leads to a subcommand for clearing windows.

Opening a window

To open a new window, you can split an existing window horizontally or vertically:

1. Choose the Window Split Horizontal or Window Split Vertical command:

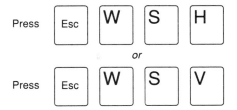

2. After you see either:

   `WINDOW SPLIT HORIZONTAL at line: 3`   `clear new window: Yes(No)`

   or:

   `WINDOW SPLIT VERTICAL at column: 1`   `clear new window: Yes(No)`

   press the F1 key. A cursor look-alike, called a *window-split pointer,* appears on the left side or top of the window you're splitting.

3. Use the direction keys (↑, ↓, ←, or →) to move the pointer to the place where you want to split the window. If you're doing a horizontal split, move the pointer to the *line* where you want the new window to start. If you're doing a vertical split, move the pointer to the *column* where you want the new window to start. As you move the pointer, the number shown in the *at line* or *at column* command field changes to correspond to the pointer's position.

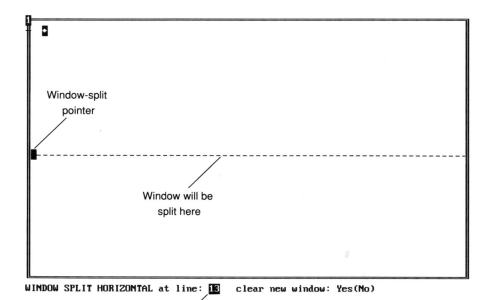

Window-split
pointer

Window will be
split here

WINDOW SPLIT HORIZONTAL at line: **13**   clear new window: Yes(No)

Number corresponds
to pointer location

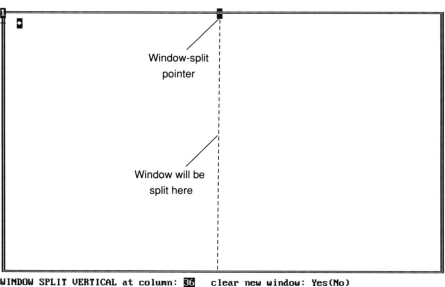

Window-split
pointer

Window will be
split here

WINDOW SPLIT VERTICAL at column: **36**   clear new window: Yes(No)

Number corresponds
to pointer location

116

4. If you want the new window to be empty so that you can use it to create a new document or to jot down notes, press the Tab key to move to the *clear new window* field. Then type *Y* to choose the *Yes* response. (If you want to use the window to view another part of the same document or if you plan to load another document into the newly opened window, you don't need to clear the window.)

5. Press the Enter key to carry out the command.

A new window instantly appears, and the cursor is in the new window. Notice that the window number in the upper left corner of the new window is highlighted. You'll find some intricate rules in the *Using Microsoft Word* manual about where you can open a window. It isn't worth trying to remember these rules. If Word refuses to split a window at the place you've indicated, simply choose the command again and try a different location.

Moving from window to window

You can work in only one window at a time—the active window. The window with the cursor and the highlighted window number is always the active window. To move the cursor to the other window (or to the next one, if you have more than two windows), press the F1 key.

Zooming a window

If you feel cramped working on or viewing a document in a split window, you can *zoom* (enlarge) it so that it fills the screen. When you no longer need the window to be full size, you can restore it to its previous size or zoom another window. To zoom a window to full size:

1. Press the F1 key to move the cursor to the window you want to zoom.

2. Press Ctrl-F1.

Ctrl-F1 is a toggle switch. After you press it, you see *ZM* in the status line. If you then want to zoom another window, you can press the F1 key to zoom the next window. When you're ready to restore all windows to their previous sizes, press Ctrl-F1 again to turn off the zoom switch.

If you choose Quit while a window is zoomed, Word restores all windows to their previous sizes and lets you know if you have any unsaved changes in any of the windows so that you can save them before quitting.

Clearing a window

You may want to empty a window that you've been working in so that you have a clean slate to write on. When you clear a window, the document displayed in it disappears from the window. It also disappears from memory unless it is also displayed in another window. To clear a window:

1. Press the F1 key to move the cursor to the window you want to clear.

2. Choose the Transfer Clear Window command:

If the document in the window has any unsaved changes, Word lets you know and gives you a chance to save them.

Closing a window

When you close a window, the document displayed in it disappears from the window. It also disappears from memory unless it is also displayed in another window. To close a window:

1. Choose the Window Close command:

2. When you see:

```
WINDOW CLOSE window number: 1
```

type in the number of the window you want to close.

3. Press the Enter key to carry out the command.

If the document in the window has any unsaved changes, you are notified and given a chance to save them.

Windows and the Mouse

With the mouse, you can instantly open and close windows by pointing to the top or the right window border. These two borders are called *window split bars*. To open or close windows, you first move the mouse pointer to one of these bars. The mouse pointer changes its shape to ▭ or ▮ to indicate that it's ready to open or close a window.

Opening a window

To open a new window, you can split an existing window horizontally or vertically. To split a window horizontally:

1. Move the pointer to the right window border at the line where you want the new window to start.

2. If you want the new window to display the same document that's in the window you're splitting, Click-L. If you want the new window to be empty, Click-R.

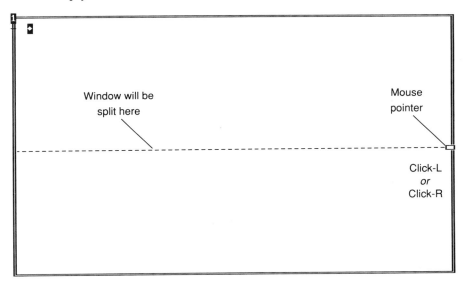

To split a window vertically:

1. Move the pointer to the top window border at the column where you want the new window to start.

2. Click-L to display the same document in both windows, or Click-R if you want the new window to be empty.

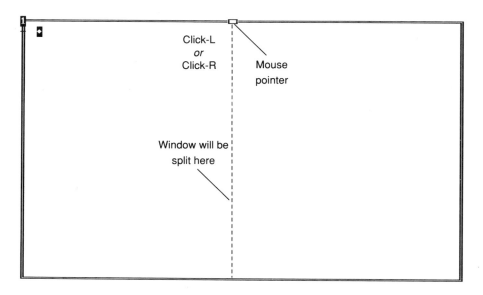

A new window instantly appears and the cursor is in the new window. If Word can't split the window at the place you indicated, it lets you know. Try it again at a different location.

Moving from window to window

You can work in only one window at a time—the active window. The window with the cursor and the highlighted window number is always the active window. To move the cursor to another window, simply move the pointer to the window and Click-L. The cursor moves to the location of the pointer.

Zooming a window

You can zoom (enlarge) a window so that it fills the screen. When you no longer need it to be full size, you can un-zoom it or zoom another window. To zoom a window to full size, move the pointer to the window number of the window you want to zoom and Click-R.

If you then want to zoom another window, point to the current window number and Click-L to zoom the next window, or hold down the Shift key and Click-L to zoom the previous window. When you're ready to shrink a window to its original size, point to its window number and Click-R.

Clearing a window

To clear a window:

1. Move the pointer to the window you want to clear and Click-L.

2. Choose the Transfer Clear Window command:

Transfer
Click-L   **Clear**
Click-L   **Window**
Click-L

If there are any unsaved changes to the document, you are notified and given a chance to save them.

Closing a window

To close a window:

1. Move the pointer to either the top or right window border of the window you want to close.

2. Click-LR.

If there are any unsaved changes to the document, you are notified and given a chance to save them.

Using a Second Window to Cut and Paste

In this section, we'll go over the procedure for using a second window to cut and paste between two parts of the same document or between two different documents. Although you might occasionally want more than two windows open, I think you'll find two windows enough for most cut-and-paste work. If you ever need to work with more than two windows, you'll be able to do it by applying the tools you learned about in the previous sections and the techniques you'll learn in this section.

Between two parts of a document

To cut and paste between two different parts of the same document:

1. Load the document you want to work with.

2. Open the second window. Leave the response to the *clear new window* field set to *No* so that the document that's in the first window will also be in the second window.

3. Scroll each window separately until you see both the text you want to move or copy and the place you want to move or copy it to.

4. Highlight the text to be moved or copied, and then delete or copy it to the scrap.

5. Move the cursor to the destination for the text in the other window, and insert the text from the scrap.

6. Close the window when you have no more use for it.

You don't have to save before closing the window because you have the same document in both windows. Any changes made to the document can be viewed and saved through the other window.

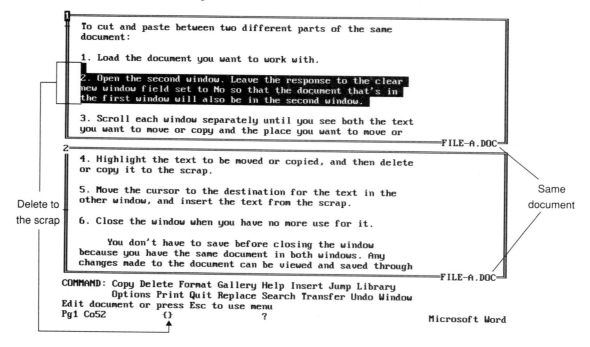

Delete to the scrap

Same document

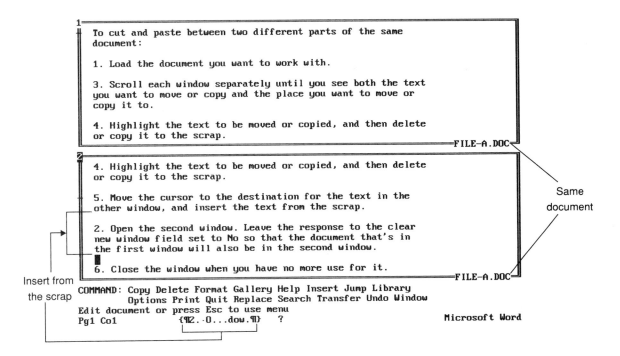

Between two documents

To cut and paste between two different documents:

1. Load one of the documents you're going to work with.

2. Open the second window. (You don't have to clear the new window when you open it because the next step will replace the contents of the second window.)

3. Load the second document into the new window with the Transfer Load command.

4. Scroll each window separately until you see both the source for the text you want to move or copy in one window/document and the destination for it in the other window/document.

5. Highlight the text to be moved or copied, and then delete or copy it to the scrap.

6. Move the cursor to the destination for the text in the other window, and insert the text from the scrap.

7. Before closing either one of the windows, save the document that's in it to save any changes you made to it.

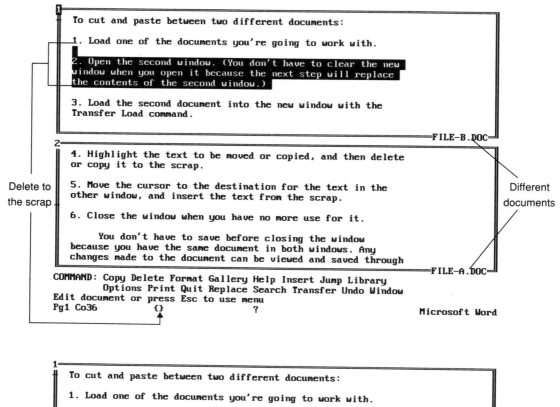

To cut and paste between two different documents:

1. Load one of the documents you're going to work with.

2. Open the second window. (You don't have to clear the new window when you open it because the next step will replace the contents of the second window.)

3. Load the second document into the new window with the Transfer Load command.

━━FILE-B.DOC━━

4. Highlight the text to be moved or copied, and then delete or copy it to the scrap.

5. Move the cursor to the destination for the text in the other window, and insert the text from the scrap.

6. Close the window when you have no more use for it.

You don't have to save before closing the window because you have the same document in both windows. Any changes made to the document can be viewed and saved through

━━FILE-A.DOC━━

COMMAND: Copy Delete Format Gallery Help Insert Jump Library
        Options Print Quit Replace Search Transfer Undo Window
Edit document or press Esc to use menu
Pg1 Co36   {}   ?   Microsoft Word

Delete to
the scrap

Different
documents

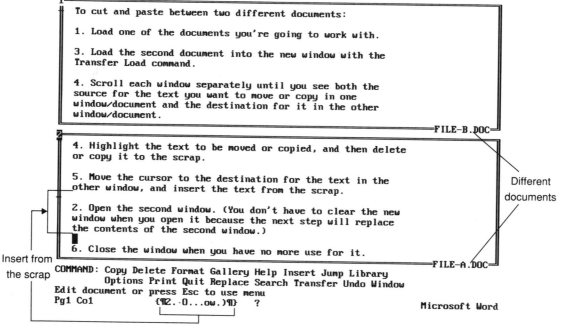

To cut and paste between two different documents:

1. Load one of the documents you're going to work with.

3. Load the second document into the new window with the Transfer Load command.

4. Scroll each window separately until you see both the source for the text you want to move or copy in one window/document and the destination for it in the other window/document.

━━FILE-B.DOC━━

4. Highlight the text to be moved or copied, and then delete or copy it to the scrap.

5. Move the cursor to the destination for the text in the other window, and insert the text from the scrap.

2. Open the second window. (You don't have to clear the new window when you open it because the next step will replace the contents of the second window.)

6. Close the window when you have no more use for it.

━━FILE-A.DOC━━

COMMAND: Copy Delete Format Gallery Help Insert Jump Library
        Options Print Quit Replace Search Transfer Undo Window
Edit document or press Esc to use menu
Pg1 Co1   {¶2..O...ow.)¶}   ?   Microsoft Word

Insert from
the scrap

Different
documents

After opening a window, you can clear out the text that's in it so that you have a blank screen to start creating a new document or to use for taking notes. You can then cut and paste between your new document or note pad in the second window and the document you loaded or created in the first window.

Undoing Window Work

You can undo any cutting and pasting that you do between windows, exactly as you can within a single window. But the Undo command has no effect on opening, closing, or clearing windows or on moving from window to window.

Customizing the Editing Screen

The Options command lets you control what you see on the editing screen and how the program operates. Here, I'll introduce you to the options most helpful to editing. In later chapters, you'll learn about other options as the need for them becomes apparent. (Appendix C contains a complete list of options titled "Operating Options.")

Turning off the menu and removing the window borders allow more room for text display. To turn off the menu, select the *No* response to the *show menu* command field of the Options command. You'll still be able to see the menu when you need it: Simply press the Esc key or point to the status line and Click-L. To remove the window borders, choose *No* in the *show borders* field. If you have more than one window open, each window is surrounded by borders, which you cannot remove.

Nonprinting characters like spaces, tabs, newline marks, and paragraph marks are usually indistinguishable from one another on the screen because they all look like blank space. To make some of them visible, choose *Partial* in the *show non-printing symbols* command field. With partial visibility, you see newline marks (↓), paragraph marks (¶), and optional hyphens (–). To make all nonprinting characters visible, choose *All* in the *show non-printing symbols* field. With complete visibility, you see spaces (·) and tabs (→) in addition to the others.

You can adjust the speed of the cursor with the *cursor speed* field. Enter a number from 0 to 9 (9 is the fastest, 3 is the default) to indicate how fast you want the cursor to move. Speeding up or slowing down the cursor is noticeable when you hold down a cursor-moving key for continuous movement.

Chapter 7

Searching and Replacing

Instead of scrolling through a document and scanning the lines to find text, let the computer do the searching for you. Searching is a shortcut that can eliminate the separate steps of scrolling, eye-scanning, moving the cursor, and highlighting text. The search ends with the cursor highlighting whatever you were looking for so that you can edit, format, or simply review it.

The Search command is an obvious tool to reach for when you want to find text. Think of it also as a tool for scrolling and moving the cursor quickly and precisely. It is often the fastest way to move the cursor to an exact spot, even if you know where that spot is or have it in view. You'll find that using the Search command to move the cursor can be a real time-saver.

The Replace command goes a step further than the Search command. In addition to quickly finding the text you're looking for, the Replace command deletes it and inserts other text in its place. With one command, you can replace every occurrence of a word in a document with another word. Or you can limit the replacements to a part of the document.

With other word processors, search and replace commands are powerful but often inflexible tools that can produce unexpected and unwanted results. Word's Search and Replace commands come with safeguards and easy-to-set options that let you prevent and recover from mishaps.

In addition to the Search command and the Replace command, which find and replace text, there are two commands that find and replace formats, instead of text: the Format sEarch command and the Format repLace command. You can, for example, find all italicized characters and replace them with boldface characters. The formatting search and replace commands are explained in Chapter 9, along with other formatting commands.

SEARCHING

A search starts from the cursor and continues in one direction until Word finds the first occurrence of the text you're looking for. You can specify which direction to search: up (toward the beginning of the document) or down (toward the end of the document).

Anything highlighted by the cursor is not included in the search. This usually isn't significant unless you have a big block of text highlighted. The search starts before the cursor if you're searching up, and it starts after the cursor if you're searching down. Because the cursor's location determines the starting point of a search, it might be necessary to move the cursor before you choose the Search command.

If you want to search through an entire document, move the cursor to the beginning or the end of the document—whichever is closest. If you only want to search through a certain section of a document, be sure the cursor is either at the beginning of the section (if you're searching forward) or at the end of the section (if you're searching backward) before you start the search. The search stops when Word finds the first occurrence of the text, but you can easily search again to find the next occurrence.

To start searching, choose the Search command from the main command menu:

Press [Esc] [S] *or* Click-L

Word responds with this display:

```
SEARCH text: █
       direction: Up(Down) case: Yes(No) whole word: Yes(No)
```

Fill in the *text* field by typing in the text you want to find. You can search for a single character, a word, a phrase, a sentence, or any string of text up to 252 characters long. The term *string* refers to any characters strung together in sequence. Like the term *block,* it's a convenient way of talking about any piece of text.

The symbols *?* and ^ have special meanings when put in the *text* field. They're used in codes to search for special characters, like tabs and paragraph marks, or unspecified characters. (More about search codes later.) To search for a question mark or caret, precede each of these symbols with a caret (^). By putting a caret in front of these symbols, you're signaling Word that you are searching for them—not using them as codes for something else. For example, type:

Do you understand^?

to find:

Do you understand?

and type:

^^*C*

to find:

^*C*

The other Search command fields—*direction, case,* and *whole word*—give the command flexibility and help you find exactly what you want. Word guesses what your most likely responses will be to these fields. The proposed responses, shown in parentheses, assume that you want to search forward, that you want to ignore whether letters are uppercase or lowercase when looking for a match, and that the text you're looking for is not necessarily a whole word. If these choices are right for you, carry out the command after you type in the search text. Otherwise, change the responses before you carry out the command. To carry out the Search command, you can:

Press | ⏎ Enter | *or*   SEARCH text:
Click-L

The following sections explain the various options provided by the command fields. Familiarize yourself with each option, but don't be afraid to use either the Search or the Replace command without inspecting each command field. The Search and Replace commands are serviceable whether you fine-tune them (by altering the command fields) or not. If you get unintended results, you can always undo them.

Searching Up or Down

The *direction* field tells Word which way to look.

```
SEARCH text:
        direction: Up Down  case: Yes(No) whole word: Yes(No)
```

Choose *Up* to search backward if the cursor is at the end of the document or after the part of the document you want to search through.

Choose *Down* to search forward if the cursor is at the beginning of the document or before the part of the document you want to search through.

Matching or Ignoring Case

The *case* field asks if you want Word to find only text that has the same uppercase and lowercase letters as the search text.

```
SEARCH text:
        direction: Up(Down) case: Yes No  whole word: Yes(No)
```

Choose *Yes* when you're looking for words that are definitely in all caps or initial caps, like acronyms, proper names, or the first word of a sentence. For example, choose *Yes* to match case if you want to find *WAVES* in uniform, not *waves* in the sea; or *China* in the Far East, not *china* on the shelf; or *Word* the word-processing program, and not any old *word*.

The proposed response is *No* because a word's letter case is usually determined by its position in a sentence; when you're searching for a word, you usually want to find it regardless of where it occurs in a sentence. For example, if you want to find *something scrumptious*, you probably want to find it regardless of whether it occurs at the beginning of a sentence with an uppercase *S*, in the middle of a sentence with a lowercase *s*, or in a special block of text that is in all uppercase letters. By choosing *No* to the case field, you would find *something scrumptious*, *Something scrumptious*, *Something Scrumptious*, and *SOMETHING SCRUMPTIOUS*. You would even find *SOMEthing scRUMPtious*, or other playful typing errors.

Looking for Whole Words

The *whole word* command field asks if the text you're looking for is a whole word.

```
SEARCH text:
        direction: Up(Down) case: Yes(No) whole word: Yes No
```

Choosing *Yes* lets you search for a word like *ear* without finding it embedded in words like *research*, *linear*, or *pear*. You could also avoid this by searching for *(space)ear(space)*, but then you wouldn't find *ear.* or *ear,* or *ear:*. If you tell Word to search for whole words only, it looks for a match that has a space, tab, or punctuation mark before and after it.

No is the proposed response. If you were searching for *telecommunications*, it would be faster and easier to type *telecom* in the *text* field instead of typing the whole word. So Word assumes that the text you're looking for is not necessarily a whole word. This enables you to find a word by searching for part of it. The shorter your search string, the less chance you have of making a mistake when typing it.

Typing part of a word and choosing *No* in the *whole word* field also lets you find various forms of a word without having to search for each form. For example, if you wanted to locate all the references in this book to deleting text, you could search for *delet*, choose *No* in the *whole word* field, and you would find *delete*, *deletes*, *deleted*, *deleting*, *deletion*, and *deletions*.

After the Search Is Over

If you see the message:

```
Searching...
```

it means that Word is still busy searching. If it finds the text, Word moves the cursor to highlight it and switches you back to type-in mode; you can immediately start to edit, format, or just look at what you found.

If Word doesn't find the text, you hear a beep and see the message:

```
Search text not found
```

and the cursor stays where it was when you started the search.

Canceling the Search

To cancel the Search command before you carry it out:

Press  Esc   *or*   Point anywhere in the
command area and Click-LR

To cancel the Search command after you carry it out, but before it finds the text:

Press Esc

You cannot undo the Search command with the Undo command because Search doesn't change any text.

Repeating the Search

The Search command finds the first occurrence of the text you're looking for. To find the next occurrence using the keyboard:

Press  ⇧ Shift   F4

Shift-F4 repeats the last search, with all the same options. (However, if the last search was done with the Replace command, Shift-F4 searches for the text specified in that command.)

If you want to repeat the Search command using the mouse, choose and carry out the Search command again:

Search
Click-L   SEARCH text:
Click-L

To search for the next occurrence with different options or to start the search all over again with different options, choose the Search command again and change only the options you want changed. You do not have to type in the search text or set all the options again. Word retains your last answers to the command fields until you change them (with either the Search command or the Replace command), quit the program (with the Quit command), or clear your entire work area (with the Transfer Clear All command).

Searching for Special Characters

When you press the Tab key or the Enter key, you are entering a special nonprinting character into your document. Special characters are neither letters nor numbers nor symbols: They are usually either invisible or visible only as blank space. They can be deleted, copied, or moved like any other character. They can also be searched for, but you need to use a special code when you ask Word to search for them.

The table in Figure 7-1 lists the special characters, the keys pressed to generate them, and their search codes. Most of the special characters are probably unfamiliar to you. You'll learn when and why they are used when you learn about formatting in Chapter 9, because they are formatting tools.

Special Character	*Keys Pressed*	*Search Code*
Nonbreak space	Ctrl-Space	^s
Tab character	Tab	^t
Paragraph mark	Return	^p
New-line mark	Shift-Return	^n
Division mark	Ctrl-Return	^d
Page break	Ctrl-Shift-Return	^d
Nonrequired hyphen	Ctrl-Hyphen (or automatically inserted with the Library Hyphenate command)	^-
White space (any amount of blank space)	Any combination or number of these keys: Space, Ctrl-Space, Tab, Return, Shift-Return, Ctrl-Return, Ctrl-Shift-Return	^w

Figure 7-1. *Special-character search codes.*

All search codes (except ^w) have a one-to-one correspondence to a special character. For example, embedding ^t in a search string tells Word to search for a string of text with a single tab character embedded in it. Searching for:

1^t2

will find:

1   2

if the space between 1 and 2 was made by pressing the Tab key once.

Searching for white space

The search code ^w corresponds to any combination or number of characters that appears as blank space. (But ^w does not find blank space, such as indents and line spacing, created by formatting commands.) It helps you search for space without specifying what kind of space it is.

You might, for example, be looking for a string of text that has a block of space in it, but you're not sure whether the space was created by the Spacebar or the Tab key. Even if you know what key you pressed, you might not be sure how many times you pressed it. Searching for:

1^w2

will find:

1   2

regardless of whether the space was created by pressing the Spacebar several times, or the Tab key once, or the Tab key twice, or some combination of both the Tab key and the Spacebar.

Searching for hyphenated words

The way you search for a hyphenated word depends on which kind of hyphen it contains. Word has three kinds of hyphen: normal, nonbreaking, and nonrequired. Examples of each are shown in Figure 7-2. (See Chapter 9 for a complete description of each.)

Type of Hyphen	*Example*	*Keys Pressed*
Normal	cross-country	
Nonbreaking	Cooper-Smith, -30F	
Nonrequired	mul-ti-tude	

Figure 7-2. *The three kinds of hyphen.*

Normal hyphens are typed with the normal Hyphen key, so search for a word with a normal hyphen by typing a hyphen in the search text.

Nonbreaking hyphens are typed with the Minus-sign key on the numeric keypad, so search for a word with a nonbreaking hyphen by typing a minus sign in the search text. If you're not sure whether the Hyphen key or the Minus-sign key was used to hyphenate a word, type a question mark in place of the hyphen in the search text.

Nonrequired hyphens, also called *optional hyphens*, are automatically inserted with the Library Hyphenate command, or you can type them with the Control key plus the Hyphen key. To search for a word that might have a nonrequired hyphen in it, type the word without any hyphen. Although there is a special search code for nonrequired hyphens (^-), don't use it unless you want to find *only* those occurrences of words that have nonrequired hyphens in them. For example, when you type *keyboard* as the search text, you will find both *keyboard* and *key-board* if the hyphen is a nonrequired hyphen. However, if you type *key^-board* as the search text, you will find *key-board* (with a nonrequired hyphen) but not *keyboard*.

Searching for unspecified characters

You don't have to specify every single character that you're searching for. You can put a question mark (?) in a search string and Word will interpret the question mark to mean any single character.

You might use this option, for example, if you're not sure how to spell the word you want to find. Suppose you want to find all mentions of Allan Reid in a document, but you can't remember how his name was spelled. You can search for *All?n R??d* to find *Allan Reed, Allen Reed, Allan Reid, Allen Reid, Allan Ried,* or *Allen Ried.* (This search would not find *Alan.*)

One very useful application of this feature is its ability to locate all the dates, or some other set of numbers of equal length, that fall into a certain range. If, for example, you want to locate all the references to the 1960s, search for the whole word *196?.*

Searching for hidden text

You can also search for text that has been marked with Alt-E or the Format Character command so that it can be hidden on the screen or when printing. (See Chapter 9 for a discussion of hidden text.) You must first be sure the hidden text is visible on the screen before you choose the Search command.

To make hidden text visible on the screen:

1. Choose the Options command:

Press ☐ Esc ☐ O Options
or Click-L

2. Choose *Yes* in the *show hidden text* command field:

show hidden text: **Yes** No

3. Press the Enter key to carry out the command.

You can now choose the Search command and type the hidden text in the *text* field as you would type any other text.

REPLACING

The Replace command finds a string of text, deletes it, and inserts another string in its place. It looks for text the same way the Search command does and has the same options for letter case and whole words.

Unlike the Search command, the Replace command searches in one direction only—forward from the cursor or down to the end of a document—until *every* occurrence has been found. If the cursor is highlighting a single character, it searches text from (and including) that character to the end of the document. But if the cursor is highlighting more than one character, it searches only within the highlighted text—from the first character to the last character in the selection.

If you want to confine a Replace command to a certain part of a document (a part that doesn't extend to the end of the document), highlight that part before you choose the Replace command. If you want to replace throughout the entire document, move the cursor to the beginning of the document before you choose the Replace command.

To start searching and replacing, choose the Replace command from the command menu:

Press ☐ Esc ☐ R Replace
or Click-L

Word responds with this display:

REPLACE text: ▮   with text:
        confirm:(Yes)No case: Yes(No) whole word: Yes(No)

Fill in the *text* field by typing in the text you want to find and delete. You can search for a string up to 254 characters long, including special characters and unspecified characters. Because *?* and *^* are reserved for coding, type *^?* to find *?* and type *^^* to find *^*.

The *with text* command field asks you what you want to replace it with. This text will be inserted in place of the text you're searching for.

```
REPLACE text:                          with text: █
        confirm:(Yes)No   case: Yes(No) whole word: Yes(No)
```

You can specify up to 255 characters, including special characters like tabs, but not (understandably) unspecified characters. Recall that unspecified characters are those designated with a *?* for any single character or *^w* for any amount of white space. Do not, therefore, use *?* or *^w* in the *with text* field. Because *^* is reserved for coding special characters, type *^^* if you want to put *^* in the replacement text. Type nothing in the *with text* field if you only want to find and delete some text without replacing it.

The other command fields—*confirm*, *case*, and *whole word*—provide you with options that help prevent unwanted replacements. The proposed responses, shown in parentheses, assume that you want to see the text Word finds before it's replaced, that you want to ignore whether letters are uppercase or lowercase when looking for a match, and that the text you're looking for is not necessarily a whole word. If these choices are acceptable, carry out the command right after you type in the replacement text. Otherwise, change the responses before you carry out the command. When you're ready to carry out the command, you can:

Press   [←┘Enter]   *or*   REPLACE text: Click-L

Asking for Confirmation

The *confirm* field asks if you want to approve replacements before they take place.

```
REPLACE text:                          with text:
        confirm: Yes No   case: Yes(No) whole word: Yes(No)
```

Always choose *Yes* to confirm replacements until you get a feel for what the computer finds when you ask it to search for something. (You might be surprised when you find out how exacting and literal-minded a computer can be.) If you choose *Yes,* Word stops to highlight each occurrence of the text it finds and displays the message:

```
Enter Y to replace, N to skip and continue, or Esc to cancel █
```

Press Y to replace the highlighted text and search for the next occurrence. Press N to leave the highlighted text in place and search for the next occurrence. To cancel the Replace command, press the Esc key.

If you choose *No* in the *confirm* field, Word performs the replacements without asking for your approval. This speeds up the process but might cost you time later if you haven't been careful in defining your search string.

Matching or Ignoring Case

Choose *Yes* in the *case* field when you want to find and replace only those occurrences of text that have the same uppercase and lowercase letters as the search text. For example, if you ask Word to replace *China* with *Hong Kong,* it will only replace *China*—not *china*—so you won't end up with something like *Our fine Hong Kong was damaged in transit.*

```
REPLACE text:                        with text:
        confirm:(Yes)No  case: Yes No  whole word: Yes(No)
```

Choose *No* when you want to replace all occurrences of a string, regardless of its letter case. When replacing text, Word retains the case of the text being replaced if it is all lowercase, all uppercase, or initial caps (first letter of each word capitalized). For example, if you ask Word to search for *chaos* and replace it with *order,* it will replace *chaos* with *order, Chaos* with *Order,* and *CHAOS* with *ORDER.* But if it finds *cHAos,* it will replace it with *order.*

Replacing Whole Words

The *whole word* field in the Replace command works as it does in the Search command. Having the option to search for whole words only is particularly important for the Replace command.

```
REPLACE text:                        with text:
        confirm:(Yes)No  case: Yes(No)  whole word: Yes No
```

For example, if you try to change every *man* to *person* without specifying whole words only, you could end up with gibberish like: *persony, personu-scripts, personifest, hupersonistic,* and *personner.*

138

After the Search and Replace Is Over

If you see the message:

    Searching...

the search isn't over yet; Word is still busy searching for the text you want to replace. After all replacements are made, the cursor returns to where it was when you chose the Replace command. A report in the message line tells you how many replacements were made.

If the search text isn't found, you hear a beep and see the message:

    Search text not found

Changing Your Mind

You can cancel the Replace command before you carry it out, while Word is searching, or after it replaces text.

To cancel the Replace command before you carry it out:

Press | Esc | *or*   Point anywhere in the
                      command area and Click-LR

To cancel the Replace command after you carry it out, but before it replaces the text:

Press | Esc |

To cancel the Replace command after it replaces the text, select the Undo command:

Press | Esc | | U | *or*   Undo
                          Click-L

When you undo a Replace command, everything changed by the command is restored to what it was.

Repeating the Replace Command

To repeat the last Replace command, choose the Replace command again and change any options you want changed. You don't have to type in the text or set all of the options again. Except for the *confirm* field, Word retains your last answers to the command fields until you change them (with either the Search or the Replace command), quit the program (with the Quit command), or clear your entire work area (with the Transfer Clear All command). For safety's sake, Word resets the answer to the *confirm* field to *Yes* after a Replace command is carried out.

Chapter 8

Glossaries

Glossaries let you make up your own shorthand for words, phrases, and even whole paragraphs that you type over and over again. While working on this book, I found it tedious and time-consuming to repeatedly type long command names, such as *Window Split Horizontal*. Using a glossary, I was able to type a few letters (*wsh*, for example) wherever I wanted a command name to appear. Word then spelled out the entire name for me—without a single typing error.

A glossary is a storage place for pieces of text. (You can also store sequences of commands, or macros, in a glossary. Macros are covered in Chapter 16.) Once you store a piece of text in a glossary, you can get a copy of it at any time to insert anywhere in a document or in any number of documents any number of times.

A glossary provides a convenient way to copy anything you type repeatedly. Copying text instead of retyping it speeds up document preparation, reduces your chances of making errors, and enables you to easily match the exact wording, spelling, capitalization, and often the format of recurring items that require consistent treatment and precise wording.

You can also use a glossary, instead of the scrap, to copy or move text when you don't want to take the time to find the new location right away. You can store text only temporarily in the scrap, but you can store it in a glossary for as long as you want.

You can store many pieces of text in a glossary. To keep track of them, you give each glossary entry a unique name. You can also have more than one glossary and give each saved glossary a unique filename. You might, for example, create one glossary for business correspondence, one for scientific terms, and one to help you prepare legal contracts. The only limit to the length of your glossaries and the number of glossaries you can make is your available disk space.

Glossaries can be edited, saved on disk, and printed on paper. Samples of the kinds of text you might include in a glossary are shown in Figure 8-1.

Usage	*Name*	*Text*
Parts of a Letter		
return addresses	return	National Health Organization Department of Nutrition 1500 Holgrain Lane Washington, D.C. 20107
closings	close	Yours in Good Health, Evelyn Eatwell, Ph.D. Chair, Department of Nutrition
stock paragraphs	sorry	Thank you for your order. Unfortunately, we cannot send you any merchandise without advance payment until you clear your account with us.

Figure 8-1. *Sample glossary entries.*
(continued)

Figure 8-1. *continued*

Usage	Name	Text
Parts of a Letter, *continued*		
stock sentences	help	If I can be of any further help to you, please don't hesitate to call me.
Legal Phrasing		
copyright notices	copyright	Copyright 1990 by Metaphors Unlimited. All rights reserved.
trademark notices	ibmtrade	IBM is a registered trademark of International Business Machines Corporation.
Miscellaneous Words and Phrases		
company names	ns	National Semiconductor Corporation
organization names	ioof	Independent Order of Odd Fellows
product names	mw	Microsoft Word
phrases	rda	Recommended Daily Allowance
words	hip	hippopotamus

BUILDING YOUR MAIN GLOSSARY

In this section, we'll work with the main glossary—NORMAL.GLY. We'll walk through the steps of adding entries to it, retrieving text from it, and saving it. NORMAL.GLY is the glossary you'll use most frequently. For many of you, it will be your only glossary because you won't need more than one.

Adding Entries to NORMAL.GLY

Let's start building your main glossary by adding a few useful items to NORMAL.GLY. If you used the Setup Program described in Appendix B, NORMAL.GLY already exists on your copy of the Word Program Disk (or in the same directory as the Word program on your fixed disk) and is loaded into memory each time that you start Word. NORMAL.GLY already contains some glossary entries that Word supplies. They are described later in this chapter in a section called "Using Supplied Glossary Entries."

For now, let's create your own glossary entries. You must have the text window and the main menu on the screen to start. (It doesn't matter whether you have a document in the window or not.) First, let's store your most frequently used closing to a letter in the glossary.

1. Type in the closing, exactly as you would in a letter. (It doesn't matter where you type the closing because you'll be deleting it right away.) For example:

Yours in Good Health,

Evelyn Eatwell, Ph.D.
Chair, Department of Nutrition

2. Highlight the entire closing. Choose the Delete command:

Press   Esc   D   *or*   Delete Click-L

Word responds with a proposal to delete the highlighted text to the scrap:

DELETE to: {}

3. Tell Word to delete the text to the glossary, instead of to the scrap, by typing a name for the text. (As soon as you start typing, the symbol for the scrap, ⟨⟩, disappears.) The name you type is an *entry name*. It identifies the piece of text being put in the glossary—not the whole glossary. In this case, type *close*. You should now see:

DELETE to: close

4. Press the Enter key to carry out the command.

The highlighted text disappears from the text window and is placed in the glossary.

You can also use the Copy command to store text in a glossary. The Copy command works like the Delete command—except that it leaves the highlighted text in the document. The Copy command puts a copy of the highlighted text in the glossary and assigns it the name you type in the *COPY to* command field.

Using either the Delete command or the Copy command, add a few more entries to the glossary—things that you type frequently, like your company name, phone number, or address. Give each a short entry name, such as *phone* or *address*. For now, use only letters and numbers for the entry name—no spaces or symbols. (More options for naming glossary entries are described later in this chapter.)

Using NORMAL.GLY

Let's say you've just finished typing a letter and you're ready to close it. Move the cursor to where you want the closing to appear, and type *close*. Then:

Press

Presto. It appears. The closing you stored in the glossary replaces the entry name, *close*.

You can also use the Insert command, instead of the F3 key, to retrieve glossary text. If you use the Insert command, you won't even have to type the entry name because you can select it from a list. To use the Insert command:

1. Position the cursor where you want to insert a glossary entry.

2. Choose the Insert command:

3. When you see:

INSERT from: ▉

press the F1 key (or point to the *from* field and Click-R) to tell Word to show you a list.

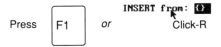

At the top of the screen, you now see a complete list of entry names currently in your glossary. (In addition to the names you entered, you see the names of glossary entries supplied by Word: *page*, *nextpage*, *date*, *dateprint*, *time*, *timeprint*, *footnote*, and—if you are using Microsoft Windows—*clipboard*.)

4. Select a name from the list to insert the corresponding glossary text in your document. (Use the direction keys to highlight the name, and press the Enter key to carry out the command. With the mouse, point to the entry name and Click-R.)

Instead of selecting from the list, you can type the entry name in the *from* field and then press the Enter key. If you type a name that isn't in the glossary that's currently in the computer's memory, you see the message:

```
Glossary entry does not exist
```

Saving NORMAL.GLY

Now save the entries you've added to NORMAL.GLY so that they don't disappear when you quit. To save NORMAL.GLY:

1. Choose the Transfer Glossary Save command:

Word responds with:

```
TRANSFER GLOSSARY SAVE filename: C:\WORDIR\NORMAL.GLY
```

The proposed response is *NORMAL.GLY*.

2. Press the Enter key to accept the proposed response and carry out the command (or, with the mouse, point to *TRANSFER GLOSSARY SAVE* and Click-L).

Word loads NORMAL.GLY each time you start Word so that it is immediately available. You can add more entries to it, retrieve text from it, or change existing entries at any time.

STORING TEXT IN A GLOSSARY

If you want to store text in a glossary, you must first type it in a document or in a blank text window. Then you can move or copy it to a temporary storage place in memory. You can save the glossary entries that accumulate in memory in a more permanent storage place—in a glossary file on a disk.

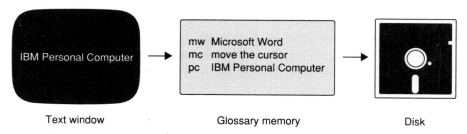

| Text window | Glossary memory | Disk |

The Delete command *moves* highlighted text from a document to glossary memory, and the Copy command *copies* highlighted text from a document to glossary memory. Both the Copy command and the Delete command prompt you to name the glossary entry. A complete glossary entry consists of an entry name and entry text:

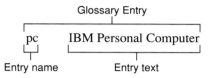

Naming Glossary Entries

Word gives you a lot of flexibility in choosing glossary entry names. They can be up to 31 characters long and can include any letters and numbers, but not spaces. You can use uppercase letters, underscore characters (_), periods (.), and hyphens (-) to make multiple-word names more readable. For example, *Property_Lease_Refund_Terms* is preferable to *propertyleaserefundterms*.

❑ NOTE: *You cannot use underscores, periods, or hyphens at the beginning or end of a glossary entry name.*

When choosing a name for a glossary entry, balance brevity with clarity. A name should be short enough to type easily yet long enough to clearly indicate what it stands for. (In addition to the entry name, you can assign glossary entries a "nickname" in the form of a control code. See the section called "Faster Glossary Retrieval" later in this chapter.)

If you try to give the same name to two different glossary entries in the same glossary, Word displays the message:

```
Enter Y to replace glossary entry, N to retype name, or Esc to cancel █
```

Press N to avoid replacing an existing glossary entry and to assign another name to the new entry. If you press Y, Word replaces the existing entry with the new one. For example, if you use the name *pc* to stand for *IBM Personal Computer* and then assign *pc* to *peanut clusters*, Word replaces *IBM Personal Computer* with *peanut clusters*.

RETRIEVING TEXT FROM A GLOSSARY

You can retrieve copies of glossary entries to insert in any document that's visible on the screen. To retrieve text stored in a glossary, the glossary must be in memory. If you have only one glossary, and that glossary is called NORMAL.GLY, you can be sure that it is available in memory. If you have more than one glossary and you're not sure which glossary is in memory, see the sections called "How to Tell What's Where" and "Loading a Glossary" later in this chapter.

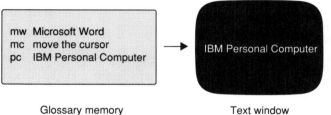

Glossary memory   Text window

The Insert command and the F3 key are the main tools for retrieving text from a glossary. Both do the same job: Which one you use depends on your preference and on what you are doing when you want to insert glossary text.

When you're typing new text, type the glossary entry name where you want the glossary text inserted and press the F3 key. Word immediately deletes the name and replaces it with the glossary text. If you don't remember the name of a glossary entry, or if it's a long, descriptive name that's difficult to type, use the Insert command and the F1 key to see and select from a list of entry names.

You can go back to a previously typed document at any time and insert glossary text. Just position the cursor where you want to insert the text and use the Insert command, or type the entry name in the document and press the F3 key.

If the entry name has already been typed in the document, move the cursor to the right of the name and press F3. Make sure the cursor is highlighting a single character or space when you press F3. If the entry name is longer than one character, you can highlight the entry name and press F3.

How the F3 Key Works

Pressing the F3 key tells Word to look for a glossary entry name and to replace it with glossary text. If a single character is highlighted, Word looks immediately to the left of the cursor for an entry name. (A space, symbol, or punctuation mark must precede the name to mark its beginning.) If more than one character is highlighted, Word expects the highlighted text to be an entry name. If Word doesn't find an entry name when you press F3, your computer beeps. If this happens, check your cursor position and try it again. If it still doesn't work, use the Insert command to see and select from a list of entry names.

Faster Glossary Retrieval

You might want to assign a control code to your most frequently used glossary entries. A control code consists of the Control key plus one or two additional characters that you choose, for example: Ctrl-C, Ctrl-CL, or Ctrl-1. Instead of using the Insert command or the F3 key to insert glossary text, you can press the control code. This speeds up glossary retrieval—if you're good at remembering key codes. For example, you might prefer to type Ctrl-C, instead of typing *close* and then pressing the F3 key, to insert a standard closing to a letter.

You can assign a control code when you create or change a glossary entry with the Copy or Delete commands. When you see:

COPY to: {}   *or*   **DELETE to: {}**

type the entry name as usual. Type a caret (^) after the name, then hold down the Ctrl key while you type the character(s) you want in the code. For example, hold down the Ctrl key while you type *C* to assign the code Ctrl-C to a glossary entry. The control code in angle brackets appears after the name, like this: *close^<Ctrl-C>*. After typing the entry name and control code, carry out the command as usual.

You can also assign a function key (like F3) or function-key combination (like Shift-F3 or Alt-F3) to a glossary entry instead of a control-key sequence. Do this only with a function key or combination that you don't use much, because all function keys and almost all of their combinations have already been assigned functions. You can still use the function key for its original purpose, but to do this you have to press Ctrl-X before you press the function key. For example, if you assign the F1 key to a glossary entry, you would have to press Ctrl-X and then F1 each time you want to use the F1 key to move the cursor to another window.

Using Supplied Glossary Entries

Word supplies some glossary entries that are always available (and cannot be deleted), no matter what glossary file is in memory: *page*, *nextpage*, *date*, *dateprint*, *time*, *timeprint*, *footnote*, and—if you are using Microsoft Windows—*clipboard*.

Page is used to include page numbers in running heads. (See the Format Running-Head command in Chapter 10.) *Nextpage* is used to include the page number of the following page.

Date and *dateprint* are handy for instantly inserting the current date in a document. Try it out: Type *date* and then press the F3 key. Today's date appears. Word uses the standard letter style format, as in: January 18, 1990. You can change the format so that the day precedes the month, as in: 18 January 1990. To do this, choose the Options command and then change the *date format* field to *DMY*.

Use *dateprint*, instead of *date*, if you want the current date printed each time you print the document. This is useful for form letters and other dated documents that are sent out more than once. *Dateprint* also helps you keep track of various versions of documents that go through several revisions. After you type *dateprint* and press the F3 key, Word displays *(dateprint)* on the screen and substitutes the current date at printing time.

Time and *timeprint* work like *date* and *dateprint*, but they allow you to insert the current time (in the form 8:10 AM) in a document. You can change to a 24-hour clock format so that 8:05 PM appears as 20:05 by setting the *time format* command field of the Options command to 24.

Word gets the current date and time from DOS, so the date and time it inserts are only as accurate as the information DOS has. DOS can get the date and time from a built-in battery-operated calendar/clock, if your computer has one. If it doesn't, DOS relies on your answers to the date and time questions it presents when you start DOS.

Footnote is used to automatically number footnotes. (See the Format Footnote command in Chapter 10.)

Clipboard is used only if you run Word under the Microsoft Windows program. Similar to the scrap, *clipboard* allows you to pass text or data between Word and other application programs run with Microsoft Windows. Instead of sending or retrieving text to the scrap, you send or retrieve text to and from the entry name *clipboard*.

EDITING A GLOSSARY

You can make changes to a glossary that's in memory by adding new entries, changing existing entries, and deleting entries. Remember that when you're editing a glossary, you're only changing the copy in memory. You must save an edited glossary, using the original filename, to replace the original glossary on disk with the new edited version.

If you want to review an entire glossary before or after you edit it, you can print it with the Print Glossary command, which is explained later in this chapter in "Printing a Glossary."

Adding New Entries

You've already walked through the steps of adding new entries to an existing glossary: You type the text in a document, highlight it with the cursor, and then either move it to the glossary with the Delete command or copy it to the glossary with the Copy command.

Changing Existing Entries

Suppose you want to change the text of the glossary entry named *pc* from *IBM Personal Computer* to *IBM PC*. You can type the new text, *IBM PC*, in your document and then copy or delete it to the old entry name, *pc*. Recall that by using an existing entry name in the Delete or Copy command, you replace the existing glossary text. Before replacing the existing text, Word prompts you to confirm that you want it replaced.

Instead of retyping the entire text, you might find it easier to retrieve the old text and edit it. For example, suppose you type the wrong zip code in an address you've stored in the glossary. You can retrieve the address with either the F3 key or the Insert command, correct the zip code, highlight the entire address, and then delete or copy it to the original entry name. After you confirm that you want to overwrite the existing glossary text, Word replaces the incorrect address with the new, corrected address.

Deleting Entries

To delete entries from a glossary, choose the Transfer Glossary Clear command. Word displays:

```
TRANSFER GLOSSARY CLEAR names: █
```

Type the name of the glossary entry you want to delete. Instead of typing an entry name, you can, as usual, refer to and select from a list of names. You can type in several names and separate them with commas to delete more than one entry at a time. After you type or select the name or names of the glossary entries you want to delete, press the Enter key to carry out the command. Word asks you to confirm that you want to erase the entry or entries by displaying the message:

```
Enter Y to clear glossary names ▮
```

Press Y if you're sure that you've typed the correct names and that you do want to delete them.

If you type a name that doesn't exist, you see the message:

```
Glossary entry does not exist
```

Word then highlights the undefined name and waits for you to change it. To change it, type the corrected name. If you originally entered only one name, it disappears as soon as you start typing; otherwise, use the Delete key to delete undefined names.

If you execute the command without typing in any names, Word thinks that you want to erase *all* entry names. If you then press Y to confirm that you want to "erase glossary names," the *entire* glossary is cleared or deleted from memory. You can press the Esc key to cancel the command when you see the confirmation message.

❑ NOTE: *If you accidentally delete an entire glossary or the wrong glossary entries, don't save your glossary. Remember that changes aren't permanently made to a glossary until you save it using the previous glossary filename.*

SAVING A GLOSSARY

Glossaries or changes made to glossaries are not automatically saved. Once you quit Word, or clear Word's memory, the contents of glossary memory disappear. This makes it easy to discard a glossary that only has short-term value to you. But in most cases, you want to save a glossary so that you can use it again.

Word makes it difficult to accidentally lose a glossary that you do want to keep. It warns you whenever a newly created or edited glossary hasn't been saved and is about to be discarded. With the warning, you get another chance to save it. For example, if you have an unsaved glossary in memory when you try to quit Word, you see the message:

```
Enter Y to save changes to glossary, N to lose changes, or Esc to cancel █
```

The Transfer Glossary Save command transfers a copy of whatever has accumulated in glossary memory onto a disk. The entire contents of glossary memory—all glossary entries and changes—are written on disk and filed away under a filename of your choice.

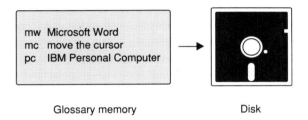

Glossary memory   Disk

After you choose the Transfer Glossary Save command, Word prompts you for a filename:

```
TRANSFER GLOSSARY SAVE filename: C:\WORDIR\NORMAL.GLY
```

The proposed response is the name of the glossary file currently in memory (usually NORMAL.GLY). If you're updating the current glossary, leave the proposed filename as is. If, instead, you're creating a new glossary file, type a new filename.

Choosing a Glossary Filename

Choose the filename NORMAL.GLY for the glossary you'll be using most frequently. If you're saving an additional, special-purpose glossary, give it a name of up to eight characters. (The same rules that apply to document filenames apply to glossary filenames. See Appendix A for details.)

    You need not type a filename extension: Word assigns the extension .GLY to glossary files unless you type in a different extension. If you give the file a different extension, you must specify both the filename and the extension each time you load it into memory.

    If you type a filename that has already been used for a glossary file, Word displays the message:

```
File already exists. Enter Y to replace or Esc to cancel █
```

This is a warning to you that the glossary being saved will replace—that is, be written over—an existing glossary of the same name. If you don't want this to happen, press the Esc key to cancel the command, and start again, using a new name this time.

A copy of the glossary stays in memory after it's saved so that you still have access to it until you quit Word or clear the memory.

WORKING WITH MORE THAN ONE GLOSSARY

As long as you have only one glossary, named NORMAL.GLY, you have immediate access to it whenever you want to add to it, change it, or retrieve text from it. In order to create and have access to other glossaries, however, you need to use commands that control what goes into and what comes out of glossary memory.

Creating a New Glossary

If you want to create a new glossary that includes some entries from the glossary that's already in memory, use the Transfer Glossary Clear command to delete those entries you don't want. Then add new entries with the Delete command or Copy command, and save the glossary under a new name with the Transfer Glossary Save command.

If, instead, you want to make a new glossary from scratch, you first need to clear the entire glossary memory.

Clearing the glossary memory

You need to clear the glossary memory before you build a new, separate glossary. Otherwise, the new glossary will include everything that's currently in glossary memory. (Always save the contents of memory before clearing it if there are any unsaved changes that you don't want to lose.)

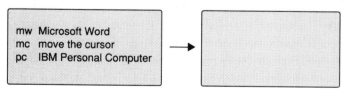

Glossary memory with entries   Glossary memory empty   Disk copy unchanged

To clear glossary memory, choose the Transfer Glossary Clear command. When you see:

`TRANSFER GLOSSARY CLEAR names: █`

carry out the command without typing anything to indicate that you want all entry names and text associated with the names cleared from memory.

Word asks for a confirmation even if the contents of memory have been saved:

`Enter Y to clear glossary names █`

Press Y to erase all glossary entries in memory. But if you want to cancel the command at this point, press the Esc key, or Click-LR when the mouse pointer is anywhere in the command area.

Loading a Glossary

If you quit Word or clear the glossary memory, you need to load or retrieve a glossary that has been saved on a disk in order to have access to it. (Remember: NORMAL.GLY is automatically loaded when you start Word.) To load a glossary means to transfer a copy of it from the disk to glossary memory, where it can be used and edited.

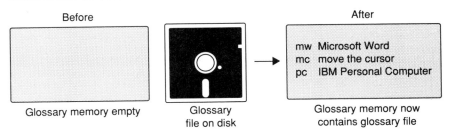

Before		After
Glossary memory empty	Glossary file on disk	mw Microsoft Word mc move the cursor pc IBM Personal Computer Glossary memory now contains glossary file

To load a glossary, choose the Transfer Glossary Load command. When you see:

`TRANSFER GLOSSARY LOAD filename: █`

type the filename of the glossary you want to load, or press the F1 key to call up the list of glossary filenames and select from it. Word only looks for filenames with the extension *.GLY*; if the glossary you're loading has a different extension, you must enter both the filename and its extension. Carry out the command after you specify the filename.

If Word can't find the file, you see the message:

```
File does not exist
```

Check to be sure you gave the correct filename, and include the drive and directory where the glossary can be found if it's not in the current document drive and directory.

Merging Glossaries

Merging glossaries allows you to retrieve text from more than one glossary at a time. As long as you don't save what is merged in memory, the glossaries remain separate and distinct files on the disk.

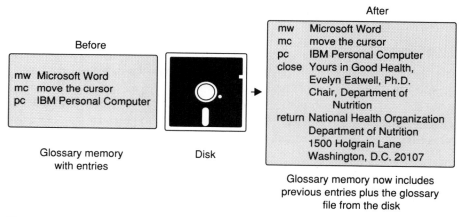

Before

```
mw  Microsoft Word
mc  move the cursor
pc  IBM Personal Computer
```

Glossary memory
with entries

Disk

After

```
mw     Microsoft Word
mc     move the cursor
pc     IBM Personal Computer
close  Yours in Good Health,
       Evelyn Eatwell, Ph.D.
       Chair, Department of
         Nutrition
return National Health Organization
       Department of Nutrition
       1500 Holgrain Lane
       Washington, D.C. 20107
```

Glossary memory now includes
previous entries plus the glossary
file from the disk

To merge two glossaries, use the Transfer Glossary Load command to load one glossary into memory (if it's not already there). Then use the Transfer Glossary Merge command to load the next one into memory. When you see:

```
TRANSFER GLOSSARY MERGE filename: █
```

type in the filename of the second glossary, or press the F1 key to see the list of glossary filenames, exactly as you did with the Transfer Glossary Load command. Carry out the command as before.

You can merge a whole series of glossary files by repeatedly executing the Transfer Glossary Merge command. To permanently join merged glossaries, save the contents of the glossary memory after merging with the Transfer Glossary Save command.

❑ CAUTION: *If a glossary entry in the file being added to memory has the same name as a glossary entry already in memory, the glossary entry already in memory will be replaced with no warning.*

Printing a Glossary

You can check the contents of an entire glossary by printing it with the Print Glossary command. This command prints whatever glossary is in memory when you choose and carry out the command. To print a glossary:

1. Load the glossary into memory.

2. Choose the Print Glossary command.

Press [Esc] [P] [G] *or* Print Click-L Glossary Click-L

HOW TO TELL WHAT'S WHERE

Glossaries stay behind the scenes until you use them. The glossary you're working with isn't visible on the screen as is a document. If you're working with more than one glossary, it's easy to lose track of which glossary is in memory and what text is stored in a glossary. Aside from printing the entire contents of a glossary with the Print Glossary command, an easy way to find out what's where is to choose a command that shows you what you want to see. If you want to use a command only to get information, you can cancel the command instead of carrying it out. Or, in the case of the Insert command, you can undo the command after you carry it out.

- To see a list of all glossary files on disk, choose the Transfer Glossary Load command and press the F1 key.

- To find out the name of the glossary file currently in memory, choose the Transfer Glossary Save command. If you have a previously saved glossary file in memory, Word shows you its filename as the proposed response in the *filename* field.

- To find out what individual glossary entries are in memory, choose the Insert command and then press the F1 key to see a list of the glossary entry names.

- To see the text attached to a specific glossary name, insert it anywhere in your document using the Insert command. You can always delete it or undo the command after you look at the text.

Chapter 9

Formatting

Formatting is packaging. It's the visual presentation of words. It affects the appearance of your documents rather than the content. However, formatting can influence the way the content is perceived. To make a document look interesting, you can vary the amount of white space surrounding the text. In addition, you can break the monotony of line after line of letters that look the same by varying (if your printer is able) the size, thickness, and shape of the letters so that some stand out more than others.

THE ELEMENTS OF DESIGN

Three basic elements make up the visual design of a printed document: page format, line format, and typeface.

The overall appearance of a printed page is called *page format*. Page format determines which areas of the page the text is printed on. When designing page format, the questions that need to be addressed are: What is the page size? How large are the margins? Should the page be divided into columns, newspaper-style? If so, how many columns? And how much space should be between columns? Should the pages be numbered? If so, where should the page numbers be placed? If footnotes and running heads are included, where should they be placed? (Running heads are titles or headings that are printed on every page to indicate the subject matter of a group of pages. In this book, the running heads tell you what part of the book you're reading and what chapter you're in.)

The appearance of individual lines on a page of text is called *line format*. Line format determines the horizontal and vertical placement of lines within the boundaries set by the page format. Should the first characters of lines be placed at the left margin? Should the last characters of lines land at the right margin? Should some of the lines be indented more than others? How much space should appear between lines? How much space should appear between columns of a table? How should entries in a table column be aligned?

Typeface questions address the appearance of individual characters. What type style (font) should be used? What size should the characters be? Should some of the characters appear darker or lighter than the rest of the document? Should some characters be uppercase or underlined?

To help you design the format of a document in a systematic way, Word asks you to view a document as being made up of three kinds of units: divisions, paragraphs, and characters. Word ties the elements of design to these three units. As you will see, *divisions* are linked to page format, *paragraphs* to line format, and *characters* to typeface.

MEASURING PAGES AND LINES

Word initially uses *lines* to measure space above or below lines and uses *inches* to measure other attributes, such as page size, margins, and indents. Instead of inches or lines, you can specify measurements in *centimeters, points, p10s* (tenths of an inch), or *p12s* (twelfths of an inch).

Points are a special unit of measure used in the printing industry; 72 points equal one inch. They let you pinpoint the size of characters or the measurements of space with much greater accuracy than the other units of measure listed here.

The *p10* and *p12* (*p* for *pitch*) units of measure let you think in terms of a number of characters or columns, rather than a measurement of space. If you're printing with a 10-pitch font, which has 10 characters per inch, one p10 equals the width of one character. If you're printing with a 12-pitch font, which has 12 characters per inch, one p12 equals the width of one character.

Use the unit of measure you're most familiar and comfortable with. When you're typing a measurement, type the number followed by an abbreviation for the unit of measure. You do not need to include the abbreviation if you are using the preset units of measure, which are, initially, inches and lines.

To indicate fractions of a unit, use decimals. For example, type *1.25* to represent 1¼, and type *1.5* for 1½. The abbreviation for the unit of measure must be one of the following:

in *or* "	for inches
cm	for centimeters
p10	for ¹/₁₀ inch, or for the number of characters if you're printing with a 10-pitch font
p12	for ¹/₁₂ inch, or for the number of characters if you're printing with a 12-pitch font
pt	for points (1 inch = 72 points; 1 line = 12 points)
li	for lines (1 line = ¹/₆ inch or 12 points)

If, for most of your work, you prefer a unit of measure other than *inches*, you can change the preset unit of measure. To change the preset unit of measure, select your preferred unit of measure in the *measure* field of the Options command. Changing the preset unit of measure eliminates the need to repeatedly type in abbreviations. (You cannot change the preset unit of measure for space above and below lines—which is *lines*—but you can individually specify units other than *lines* by typing in other unit abbreviations.)

DIVISIONS AND PAGE FORMAT

Page format is usually assigned to an entire document. To enable you to have more than one page format in a document, Word lets you divide a document into divisions and assign a different page format to each division. A *division* is the smallest unit in a document to which you can assign a particular page format. When you start a new division, you automatically start a new paragraph, and you usually start a new page as well. A division is usually made up of several consecutive pages that have the same page-format requirements. Because most documents have only one page format, most documents have only one division. The Format Division command controls the page format of divisions.

Starting a New Division

To end one division and to start a new one:

1. Move the cursor to the place where you want the new division to begin.

2. Press Ctrl-Enter.

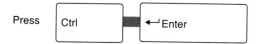

Ctrl-Enter inserts a special character, called a *division mark*, to the left of the cursor. It shows on the screen as two dotted lines (a row of colons):

:::

A division mark is a single character that can be deleted, copied, moved, or searched for like any other character. All the page-format instructions for a division are stored with the division mark at the end of the division. If you delete the division mark at the end of a division, you delete the page-format specifications for that division. The division then takes on the page-format attributes that are stored in the next division mark that occurs in the document.

The page-format instructions for the last division in a document (or for the entire document if you have only one division) are stored with the division mark that appears right above the end mark (♦). This final (or only) division mark appears in a document after you use one of the Format Division commands to change or check the proposed page format.

Starting a New Page

Word starts a new page at the beginning of each division (unless you instruct it not to with the Format Division Layout command). Within a division, Word starts a new page as it's printing whenever it reaches the bottom margin. You can tell Word to end a page and start a new one at a particular place, regardless of how far that place is from the bottom margin or from the end of a division. To end one page and start a new one:

1. Move the cursor to the place where you want the new page to start.

2. Press: Ctrl-Shift-Enter

Pressing Ctrl-Shift-Enter inserts a special character, called a *hard page break*, to the left of the cursor. A hard page break shows on the screen as a single dotted line (a row of periods):

....

A hard page break is a single character that can be deleted, copied, moved, or searched for like any other character.

Formatting Divisions: Changing Page Format

Word starts you out with a conventional page format that is suitable for many documents. The margins form a border of white space around the text on each page, with 1 inch at the top and bottom and 1¼ inches at each side. The preset (default) page size is 8½ by 11 inches, so the maximum length of each line of text is 6 inches, which is a comfortable reading length. Page numbers are not printed. That suits most business correspondence because most business letters are one page long. This initial page format is shown in Figure 9-1 on the following page.

For documents that are longer than one page, you'll probably want to number the pages. If you're preparing a legal document, you might want to number the lines. To number the pages or lines or to change any aspect of page format, use the Format Division command. It branches out into four subcommands: Margins, Page-numbers, Layout, and line-Numbers.

FORMAT DIVISION: `Margins` Page-numbers Layout line-Numbers

With the Format Division Margins command, you can:

- Change the margins.

- Change the page size.

- Allow extra space on a page for binding.

- Change the position of running heads within the margins.

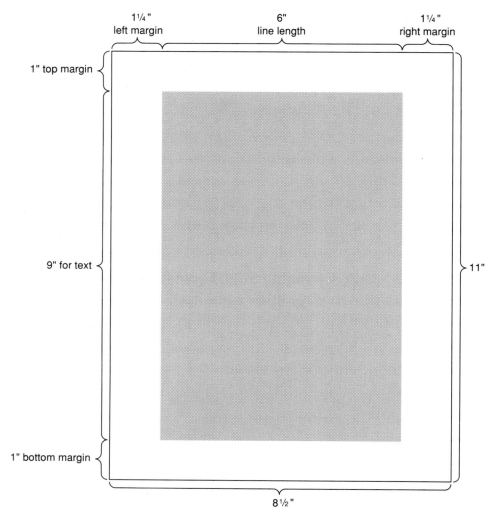

Figure 9-1. *Word's initial page format: Text is printed in shaded area.*

Use the Format Division Page-numbers command to:

■ Tell Word to print page numbers.

■ Change placement, starting point, and format of page numbers.

The Format Division Layout command lets you:

■ Specify whether a new division should start a new page.

■ Change the placement of footnotes.

■ Divide the page into multiple columns. (Usually, the text is printed in one column that extends from the left margin to the right margin, but you can choose a multiple-column format similar to that in newspapers and magazines.)

With the Format Division line-Numbers command, you can:

■ Tell Word to print line numbers in the left margin.

■ Control placement, starting point, and increments of line numbers.

Formatting running heads, footnotes, or multiple columns are not everyday tasks for most people, so they are explained separately in Chapter 10. The other formatting tasks listed above are described in this chapter.

How to Use the Format Division Commands

The Format Division commands apply to entire divisions. If a document has only one division, a Format Division command affects the entire document, regardless of where the cursor is when you choose the command. If there is more than one division, a Format Division command affects the division(s) in which the cursor is highlighting some text when the command is chosen. If you have more than one division but you want a particular page format—for example, margins or page numbers—to apply to all divisions, select the entire document (press Shift-F10) before you choose and carry out the command.

If you want to format text as you type, choose the appropriate Format Division command(s) before you start typing. The formats you choose will be applied to whatever you type until you start a new division and choose new page formats for that division.

To use any of the Format Division commands:

1. With the cursor in the division(s) you want to format, choose the appropriate Format Division command. For example, to print page numbers, choose the Format Division Page-numbers command:

2. Change the response(s) in the appropriate command field(s).

3. Carry out the command.

The sections that follow explain how and why you change responses in the command fields of the various Format Division commands.

Changing the margins or the page size

Use the Format Division Margins command to change the margins or the page-size settings. Because changing the margins is a frequently desired formatting change, you can use the Click-R shortcut for choosing the Format Division Margins command:

Format
Click-L   Division
                 Click-R

After you choose the Format Division Margins command, you see the following command fields:

```
FORMAT DIVISION MARGINS
     top: 1"                    bottom: 1"
     left: 1.25"                 right: 1.25"
     page length: 11"           width: 8.5"      gutter margin: 0"
     running-head position from top: 0.5"        from bottom: 0.5"
     mirror margins: Yes(No)                     use as default: Yes(No)
```

A printed page of text has four margins—top, bottom, left, and right—and each has its own command field.

The *top* and *bottom* margins are initially set at 1" (1 inch). The *left* and *right* margins are set at 1.25" (1¼ inches). The margins, together with the page size and the gutter margin, determine how much space is available for text on a page. If you have a small amount of text, you might want to increase the margins so that the text is centered on the page. If you're trying to fit a lot of text in as few pages as possible, you can decrease the margins. To change any one of the margins, simply type in a new measurement in the appropriate command field.

A *gutter* is an extra margin of space that allows you to bind a document that has been printed, or duplicated, on both sides of the paper. Gutter margins are added to the right margin of even-numbered pages and to the left margin of odd-numbered pages, as shown in Figure 9-2. If you're printing or duplicating on only one side of the paper, don't use the *gutter margin* field to allow for extra binding space. Instead, make the left margin bigger because, in this case, the extra binding space should always be on the left side of a page, regardless of whether the page is odd- or even-numbered.

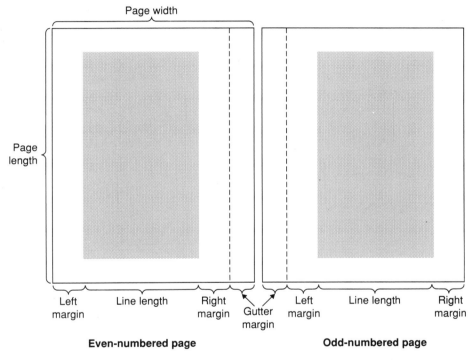

Figure 9-2. *Gutters on even-numbered and odd-numbered pages.*

You can *mirror* the margins on opposite pages of your document by changing the response in the *mirror margins* field from *No* to *Yes*. Word will then interchange the left and right margins on every even-numbered page. If, for example, you wanted to have a large space for notes along the outside edge of every page, you might set the right margin to 3 inches. With mirror margins set to *Yes*, the 3-inch margin would appear on the right side of every odd-numbered page and on the left side of every even-numbered page.

If you regularly use margins different from the ones Word initially sets, you can set the *use as default* field to *Yes* after setting new margins. Word will then use your margins as its preset margins whenever you start a new document.

Word lets you print on paper up to 22 inches wide and 22 inches long. If you're not using 8½-by-11-inch paper, type in new measurements in the *page length* field or *width* field or both of the Format Division Margins command.

```
FORMAT DIVISION MARGINS
      top: 1"                  bottom: 1"
      left: 1.25"               right: 1.25"
      page length: 11"          width: 8.5"        gutter margin: 0"
      running-head position from top: 0.5"         from bottom: 0.5"
      mirror margins: Yes(No)                      use as default: Yes(No)
```

You can use any unit of measure except lines for page width. When you're measuring the width of your paper, don't include the tear-off strips that are used to feed continuous paper through a printer.

The remaining command fields in the Format Division Margins command, *running-head position from top* and *from bottom*, control where running heads are positioned with respect to the margins. You'll learn about using these command fields to format running heads in Chapter 10.

Numbering pages

Word does not print page numbers unless you tell it to. After you choose the Format Division Page-numbers command, you see these command fields:

```
FORMAT DIVISION PAGE-NUMBERS: Yes No      from top: 0.5"      from left: 7.25"
      numbering:(Continuous)Start       at:          number format:(1)I i A a
```

To print page numbers, change the response in the first field from *No* to *Yes*. An alternative way to print page numbers is to make the page number a part of a running head. If you do put the page number in a running head, be sure to leave the first command field set at *No* so that the page number won't print twice. (See Chapter 10 for more information on running heads.)

The command fields *from top* and *from left* determine where the page number is printed. The page-number position is measured from the top and left edges of the paper. The measurement from the top must be at least ⅙ inch (one line) less than the top margin measurement (in the Format Division Margins command). You can have the page numbers printed at the bottom of the page if you type in a measurement that puts the page number somewhere in the bottom margin. (Subtract the bottom margin from the length of the paper and add at least ⅙ inch.)

Page numbers usually start with 1 for the first page of a document and continue in sequence to the end of the document. You can start numbering the pages of a document or a division with any number if you change the response in the *numbering* field from *Continuous* to *Start*. Type the number you want to start with in the *at* field.

```
FORMAT DIVISION PAGE-NUMBERS: Yes(No)    from top: 0.5"    from left: 7.25"
        numbering: Continuous Start      at:          number format:(1)I i A a
```

Pages are usually numbered with Arabic numbers (1, 2, 3, 4, and so on). To change to Roman or to alphabetic numbering, choose the response to the *number format* field that matches the style you want:

1	for Arabic (1, 2, 3, 4, . . .)
I	for Roman uppercase (I, II, III, IV, . . .)
i	for Roman lowercase (i, ii, iii, iv, . . .)
A	for alphabetic uppercase (A, B, C, D, . . .)
a	for alphabetic lowercase (a, b, c, d, . . .)

Specifying where to start printing a new division

The Format Division Layout command lets you specify where to start printing a new division. After you choose the Format Division Layout command, you see:

```
FORMAT DIVISION LAYOUT footnotes:(Same-page)End
        number of columns: 1        space between columns: 0.5"
            division break: Page Continuous Column Even Odd
```

The first two rows of command fields in the Format Division Layout command control the layout of specially formatted text: footnotes and multiple columns. Formatting footnotes and printing in multiple columns are explained in Chapter 10.

If you have only one division in your document, you don't need to worry about specifying how new divisions start. Even if you have more than one division, the proposed response to the *division break* command field, *Page*, will probably meet your needs.

Because you start a new division in order to change the page format, you usually want to start printing a new division on a new page. The *division break* command field needs your attention only if you don't want a new division to start on a new page, or if you want to specify that it start on an odd-numbered or an even-numbered page.

Choose *Page* to start printing the new division on a new page. Choose *Continuous* if you want to start printing the new division on the same page as the previous division. (Note that the page format associated with the new division won't take effect until the next page if you're using Word 4.0.) Choose *Column* if you're printing the document in more than one column on a page and if you want the new division to start in a new column, rather than on a new page. Choose *Even* to start printing the new division on the next even-numbered page. Choose *Odd* to start printing the new division on the next odd-numbered page.

Adding line numbers to a document

For legal documents such as contracts, *line numbers* make it easy to refer to specific sections of the document. To print line numbers in the left margin of a document, choose the Format Division line-Numbers command. Word displays these command fields:

```
FORMAT DIVISION LINE-NUMBERS: Yes No          from text: 0.4"
              restart at:(Page)Division Continuous    increments: 1
```

A *Yes* in the first command field tells Word to print line numbers. The *from text* field determines how far from the left edge of the text the number will be placed. The default is 0.4 inches. If you enter a measurement larger than the left margin, the line numbers won't print. If you enter a measurement that doesn't allow enough room for the longest line number, line numbers that don't fit will be truncated from the left.

Word restarts line numbering with number 1 at the beginning of each page unless you specify *Division* or *Continuous* in the *restart at* field. If you choose *Division*, line numbering starts with number 1 at the beginning of the currently selected division and continues to the end of the division. (If you have more than one division highlighted, line numbering restarts at 1 at the beginning of each division.) To guarantee consecutive line numbering throughout the entire document, highlight the entire document before you choose the Format Division line-Numbers command and choose *Continuous*.

Word normally prints every line number, but you can specify any increment of line numbers to print. For example, you can tell Word to print every fifth line number (5, 10, 15, 20, and so on) by changing the response in the *increments* field to *5*.

PARAGRAPHS AND LINE FORMAT

You can assign a particular line format to an entire document, to any group of paragraphs in a document (even if they are not in the same division), or to a single paragraph. A *paragraph* is the smallest unit in a document to which you can assign a particular line format.

Starting a New Paragraph

To end one paragraph and start a new one:

1. Move the cursor to the place where you want the new paragraph to begin.

2. Press the Enter key.

Pressing the Enter key inserts a special nonprinting character, called a *paragraph mark*, to the left of the cursor. A paragraph mark indicates the end of one paragraph and the beginning of the next paragraph. Although they are normally invisible, you can make the paragraph marks visible on the screen: Choose the Options command from the main command menu and change the response in the *show non-printing symbols* command field from *None* to *Partial* or *All*. When they are visible, you see a paragraph mark (¶) at the end of each paragraph.

A paragraph mark can be deleted, copied, moved, or searched for like any other character. All line-formatting instructions for a paragraph are stored with the paragraph mark at the end of the paragraph. If you delete the paragraph mark at the end of a paragraph, you delete the line-format specifications for that paragraph. The paragraph is then joined to the next paragraph and takes on the line-formatting instructions stored with that paragraph.

Starting a New Line

As you would expect, Word starts each new paragraph on a new line. Within a paragraph, Word automatically starts a new line when it reaches the right margin. You can tell Word to end a line and start a new one at a particular place, regardless of how far that place is from the right margin or from the end of a paragraph. To end a line and start a new one without starting a new paragraph:

1. Move the cursor to the place where you want the new line to start.

2. Press Shift-Enter.

Press ⇧ Shift ←Enter

Pressing Shift-Enter inserts a special nonprinting character, called a *newline mark*, to the left of the cursor. A newline mark marks the end of one line and the beginning of the next line. Newline marks are normally invisible; they look like spaces. But you can move the cursor to them and you can delete, copy, move, or search for them.

To make newline marks visible, choose the Options command and change the response in the *show non-printing symbols* command field from *None* to *Partial* or *All*. When newline marks are visible, they look like this: ↓.

Use Shift-Enter, instead of Enter, to end each line in a block of closely related text, such as an address, a poem, or a table of information. By doing this, the entire address, poem, or table will be treated as one paragraph and can easily be formatted as one unit. If you don't use Shift-Enter to separate the lines in a table, for example, and you decide to use a command that puts extra space between each paragraph in the document, you will end up with unwanted space between each line in the table.

Line Breaks

If you have the Special Edition with disk included, consult the Introduction

If you don't start a new line with the Shift-Enter keys, Word starts one for you when you reach the right margin. Word breaks a line after the nearest space or hyphen only—not in the middle of a word or number.

When you don't want a line to break after a particular space or hyphen, you can insert a *nonbreak space* instead of a normal space, or a *nonbreak hyphen* instead of a normal hyphen. For example, names, phrases, numbers, and expressions like the following are best kept on one line:

Chapter 1	Rand–McNally
A. M. Rinaldi, Jr.	$a^2 - b^2 = c^2$
1024 bytes	$-23°$ F

To keep them on one line:

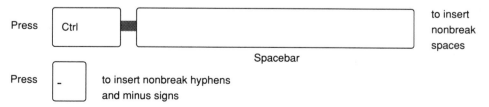

Press Ctrl [Spacebar] to insert nonbreak spaces

Press - to insert nonbreak hyphens and minus signs

These keys produce spaces, hyphens, and minus signs that look like normal spaces, hyphens, and minus signs—but are treated differently if they land at the end of a line.

In addition to nonbreak hyphens, there are two other kinds of hyphen—normal and nonrequired.

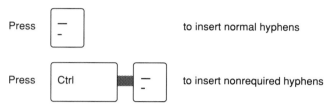

Press [—] to insert normal hyphens

Press [Ctrl]—[—] to insert nonrequired hyphens

Use *normal hyphens* for compound words that can be broken if they occur at the end of a line, such as the following:

cross-country
lickety-split
high-spirited

Notice that you would want the hyphens in these compound words to print whether the word needs to be split between two lines or not.

Use *nonrequired hyphens* when you want a hyphen to appear in a word *only* if the word needs to be split between two lines. For example, the words:

communication
keyboard
organization

could be hyphenated if they land at the end of a line and don't quite fit. But if these words appeared elsewhere on a line, you wouldn't want them hyphenated. Nonrequired hyphens don't show up on either the screen or the printed copy unless they are needed. If the cursor lands on a nonrequired hyphen, it disappears until you move it off the invisible hyphen. To make nonrequired hyphens visible so that you can easily delete or move them, choose *Partial* or *All* in the *show non-printing symbols* command field of the Options command.

You can automatically hyphenate words in a document with the Library Hyphenate command. The Library Hyphenate command inserts nonrequired hyphens where needed and is described in Chapter 14.

Formatting Paragraphs: Changing Line Format

If you type a document using Word's initial (default) line format, it will be single-spaced and will have no indents at the beginning or end of any line (unless you pressed the Tab key to indent them). Each line in a paragraph will start at the left margin so that the left edge of the text forms a straight line. If a line doesn't fill the space allowed by the margins, the extra space will appear at the end of the line and the right edge of the text will be uneven. When the left edge of the text is straight and the right edge is ragged, the text is described as being aligned *flush left*.

To change the initial line format, use the Format Paragraph command, or use formatting keys to change some paragraph formatting. Formatting keys are a combination of the Alternate key and a letter or number key. With the Format Paragraph command or the formatting keys, you can:

- Position lines flush left or flush right, justify lines, or center lines.

- Indent the first line of a paragraph.

- Indent an entire paragraph.

- Change the line spacing.

- Add blank lines between paragraphs.

- Prevent a page break from occurring within a specific paragraph or between two specific paragraphs.

- Print two or more paragraphs side by side.

Except for printing paragraphs side by side, all the formatting feats listed above are explained in this chapter. You can change the format of paragraphs as you type them, or you can go back to previously typed paragraphs and reformat them.

To format a paragraph while you're typing:

1. Start typing the paragraph.

2. Choose the Format Paragraph command.

3. Change the response(s) to the appropriate command field(s).

4. Carry out the command.

5. Continue typing the paragraph.

Instead of choosing and carrying out the Format Paragraph command, you can press an Alt-key combination to format the paragraph you're typing. The paragraph formats that you choose are immediately applied to the paragraph you're typing as well as to any succeeding paragraphs you might type. To format a paragraph after it's been typed:

1. Move the cursor to any place in the paragraph you want to format. If you want to format more than one paragraph at the same time, highlight some text in each of the paragraphs. If you want to apply a particular paragraph format to all paragraphs in a document, press Shift-F10 to select the entire document.

2. Choose the Format Paragraph command.

3. Change the response(s) to the appropriate command field(s).

4. Carry out the command.

Word assigns paragraph formats to the paragraph (or paragraphs) the cursor is in, regardless of whether the cursor is highlighting a single character or the entire paragraph.

❏ NOTE: *If you have a style sheet attached to the document you're formatting, you must press X before you press the letter(s) of an Alt-key command. For example, press Alt-XC to center lines.*

Paragraph alignment

The first command field in the Format Paragraph command, *alignment*, determines the horizontal placement of lines within margins. (If you extend the margins with indents, the alignment determines the horizontal placement of lines within the indents.) Word normally aligns paragraphs flush left. But, you can align them flush right, center them, or justify them (flush with both margins), as illustrated in Figure 9-3 on the following page.

```
FORMAT PARAGRAPH alignment: Left Centered Right Justified
        left indent: 0"            first line: 0"          right indent: 0"
        line spacing: 1 li         space before: 0 li      space after: 0 li
        keep together: Yes(No)     keep follow: Yes(No)    side by side: Yes(No)
```

When paragraphs are *flush left*, the left edge of the text looks straight and the right edge looks ragged. Any extra space in a line is put at the end of the line. Left-aligned text is the easiest to read.

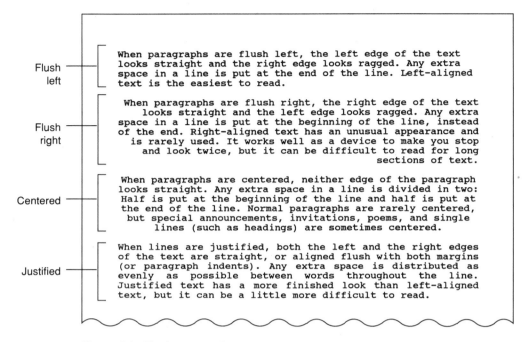

Figure 9-3. *The four types of text alignment.*

When paragraphs are *flush right*, the right edge of the text looks straight and the left edge looks ragged. Any extra space in a line is put at the beginning of the line, instead of the end. Right-aligned text has an unusual appearance and is rarely used. It works well as a device to make you stop and look twice, but it can be difficult to read for long sections of text.

When paragraphs are *centered*, neither edge of the paragraph looks straight. Any extra space in a line is divided in two: Half is put at the beginning of the line and half is put at the end of the line. Normal paragraphs are rarely centered, but special announcements, invitations, poems, and single lines (such as headings) are sometimes centered.

When lines are *justified*, both the left and the right edges of the text are straight, or aligned flush with both margins (or paragraph indents). Any extra space is distributed as evenly as possible between words throughout the line. Justified text has a more finished look than left-aligned text, but it can be a little more difficult to read. When you justify text, you might end up spending a lot of time hyphenating words at the ends of lines (so that each line is filled with as many characters as possible). Otherwise, you might end up with big gaps of space between the words in some lines.

You can change the alignment of paragraphs with Alt-key commands, instead of the Format Paragraph command:

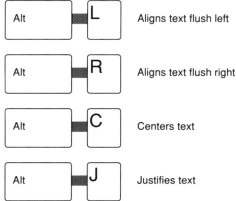

Alt	L	Aligns text flush left
Alt	R	Aligns text flush right
Alt	C	Centers text
Alt	J	Justifies text

Indenting

The second row of command fields in the Format Paragraph command lets you indent text without changing the margins or repeatedly pressing the Tab key. Indents make lines shorter than the length allowed by the margins. You can indent an entire paragraph, the first line of a paragraph, or all lines except the first line. Use indents to emphasize whole blocks of text or to set them apart from surrounding text. Rather than starting a new division and using the Format Division Margins command, use the indent command fields when you want to temporarily increase the margins.

```
FORMAT PARAGRAPH alignment:(Left)Centered Right Justified
    left indent: 0"         first line: 0"        right indent: 0"
    line spacing: 1 li      space before: 0 li    space after: 0 li
    keep together: Yes(No)  keep follow: Yes(No)  side by side: Yes(No)
```

Indenting entire paragraphs. The *left indent* is the distance from the left margin to the start of the line and is usually set to zero inches. If you assign a left indent to a paragraph, the left margin for that paragraph will be increased by the amount of the left indent. For example, if your *left margin* is set at 1¼ inches in the Format Division Margins command and the *left indent* is set at 1 inch, the left margin becomes, in effect, 2¼ inches. Lines will start 2¼ inches from the left edge of the paper.

If you assign a *right indent* to a paragraph, the right margin for that paragraph will be increased by the amount of the right indent. For example, if your *right margin* is set at 1 inch and the *right indent* is set at 1 inch, the right margin becomes, in effect, 2 inches. Lines will end 2 inches from the right edge of the paper. See Figure 9-4 for examples of entire paragraphs set off from the surrounding text with indents.

```
When paragraphs are flush left, the left edge of the text
looks straight and the right edge looks ragged. Any extra
space in a line is put at the end of the line. Left-aligned
text is the easiest to read.
            When paragraphs are flush right, the right edge of
            the text looks straight and the left edge looks
            ragged. Any extra space in a line is put at the
            beginning of the line, instead of the end. Right-
            aligned text has an unusual appearance and is
            rarely used. It works well as a device to make you
            stop and look twice, but it can be difficult to
            read for long sections of text.
When paragraphs are centered, neither edge of the paragraph
looks straight. Any extra space in a line is divided in two:
Half is put at the beginning of the line and half is put at
the end of the line. Normal paragraphs are rarely centered,
but special announcements, invitations, poems, and single
lines (such as headings) are sometimes centered.
```

```
FORMAT PARAGRAPH alignment: Left Centered Right(Justified)
   left indent: 1"              first line: 0"        right indent: 0"
   line spacing: 1 li           space before: 0 li    space after: 0 li
   keep together: Yes(No)       keep follow: Yes(No)  side by side: Yes(No)
```

```
When paragraphs are flush left, the left edge of the text
looks straight and the right edge looks ragged. Any extra
space in a line is put at the end of the line. Left-aligned
text is the easiest to read.
            When paragraphs are flush right, the
            right edge of the text looks straight
            and the left edge looks ragged. Any
            extra space in a line is put at the
            beginning of the line, instead of the
            end. Right-aligned text has an unusual
            appearance and is rarely used. It works
            well as a device to make you stop and
            look twice, but it can be difficult to
            read for long sections of text.
When paragraphs are centered, neither edge of the paragraph
looks straight. Any extra space in a line is divided in two:
Half is put at the beginning of the line and half is put at
the end of the line. Normal paragraphs are rarely centered,
but special announcements, invitations, poems, and single
lines (such as headings) are sometimes centered.
```

```
FORMAT PARAGRAPH alignment: Left Centered Right(Justified)
   left indent: 1"              first line: 0"        right indent: 1"
   line spacing: 1 li           space before: 0 li    space after: 0 li
   keep together: Yes(No)       keep follow: Yes(No)  side by side: Yes(No)
```

Figure 9-4. *Whole paragraph indents.*

Indenting the first lines of paragraphs. In a printed document, there are two standard ways to visually indicate when a new paragraph starts. One way is to indent the first line of each paragraph. The other way is to put a blank line between each paragraph. With Word, you can indent the first lines of paragraphs without pressing the Tab key each time you start a new paragraph. Or, as you'll see later in this chapter, you can insert extra lines of space between paragraphs without pressing the Enter key twice after each paragraph.

The *first line* command field indents only the first line of a paragraph. To automatically indent the first line of each paragraph as you're typing, choose the Format Paragraph command before you start typing and then enter a measurement in the *first line* field. For example, if you want to indent the first line ½ inch, type *0.5"* in the *first line* field. The first line of each paragraph you type from then on will start ½ inch from the left edge of the rest of the paragraph, as shown in Figure 9-5.

If you're reformatting paragraphs that you've already typed, the first lines of any paragraphs that are highlighted when you carry out the Format Paragraph command are instantly indented.

While the left indent is measured from the left margin, the first-line indent is measured from the left indent. First-line indents are always added to the left indent of a paragraph. So, if the left indent is 1 inch and the first line of the paragraph is indented ½ inch, the text on the first line will be indented a total of 1½ inches from the left margin and ½ inch from the rest of the paragraph.

```
            When paragraphs are flush left, the left edge of the
       text looks straight and the right edge looks ragged. Any
       extra space in a line is put at the end of the line. Left-
       aligned text is the easiest to read.
            When paragraphs are flush right, the right edge of the
       text looks straight and the left edge looks ragged. Any
       extra space in a line is put at the beginning of the line,
       instead of the end. Right-aligned text has an unusual
       appearance and is rarely used. It works well as a device to
       make you stop and look twice, but it can be difficult to
       read for long sections of text.
```

```
FORMAT PARAGRAPH alignment: Left Centered Right(Justified)
     left indent: 0"        first line: 0.5"       right indent: 0"
     line spacing: 1 li     space before: 0 li     space after: 0 li
     keep together: Yes(No) keep follow: Yes(No)   side by side: Yes(No)
```

Figure 9-5. *First-line indents.*

You can use the Alt-F command, instead of the Format Paragraph command, to indent the first line of each selected paragraph:

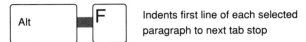 Indents first line of each selected paragraph to next tab stop

The amount of the indent depends on the tab stops set for the paragraph. If you haven't changed the default tab stops, the first line will be indented ½ inch. Otherwise, it will be indented to the first tab stop that you have set. Alt-F is cumulative: Each time you press it, the first line is indented to the next tab stop (another ½ inch, in most cases).

Hanging indents. Instead of indenting the first line of each paragraph, you can "outdent" it to produce a *hanging indent*. To produce hanging indents, type in a negative measurement in the *first line* field and a positive measurement in the *left indent* field. (Remember that first-line indents are measured from the left indent.) When you "outdent" the first line of a paragraph, you must *indent* the entire paragraph, because Word will not print outside the margins. The amount of the left indent must equal or exceed the amount of the first-line outdent.

For example, set the *first line* indent to *−0.5"* and the *left indent* to *0.5"* to make the first line stick out ½ inch from the rest of the paragraph. The first line will start at the left margin, and the remainder of the paragraph will be indented ½ inch from the left margin, as shown in Figure 9-6.

```
                        Bibliography

    Andrews, Nancy. Microsoft Word. Command Performance Series.
        Redmond, WA: Microsoft Press, 1987.

    Rampa, Janet Marian. Learn Word Now. Redmond, WA: Microsoft
        Press, 1988.

    Rinearson, Peter. Word Processing Power with Microsoft Word.
        3d ed. Redmond, WA: Microsoft Press, 1989.

    Rinearson, Peter, and Woodcock, JoAnne. Microsoft Word Style
        Sheets. Redmond, WA: Microsoft Press, 1987.
```

```
FORMAT PARAGRAPH alignment: Left Centered Right(Justified)
    left indent: 0.5"         first line: -0.5"        right indent: 0"
    line spacing: 1 li        space before: 0 li       space after: 0 li
    keep together: Yes(No)    keep follow: Yes(No)     side by side: Yes(No)
```

Figure 9-6. *Hanging indent in a bibliography.*

Using Alt-T is an easier and quicker way to create hanging indents:

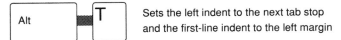 Sets the left indent to the next tab stop and the first-line indent to the left margin

To type a numbered or bulleted list, press Alt-T and type the number or a bullet. Then press the Tab key to align the text that immediately follows with the text in the remaining lines. (See Figure 9-7 for an example.) Alt-T, like Alt-F, is cumulative: To increase the hanging indent, simply press the Alt-T combination again.

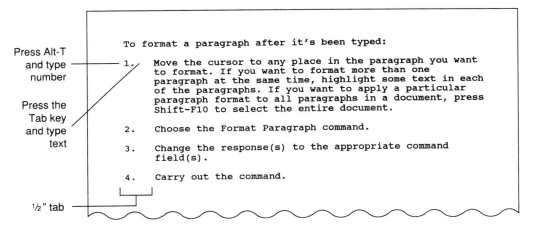

Figure 9-7. *Hanging indent in a numbered list.*

To undo the effect of an Alt-F or Alt-T command, use the Undo command, or use the Format Paragraph command and reset the indents.

Nested indents. Two other Alt-key commands let you easily nest paragraphs underneath each other in outline fashion by increasing or decreasing the left indent.

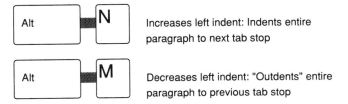 Increases left indent: Indents entire paragraph to next tab stop

Decreases left indent: "Outdents" entire paragraph to previous tab stop

Indents created by Alt-N are cumulative. Each time you press Alt-N, the paragraph is indented to the next tab stop. If your tab stops are set at ½-inch increments, press Alt-N twice to indent a paragraph 1 inch, as shown in Figure 9-8.

You can reduce the left indents assigned by Alt-N (or by the *left indent* command field) by pressing Alt-M. Each time you press Alt-M, the left indent for the selected paragraphs is reduced as shown in Figure 9-8.

```
                  When paragraphs are flush left, the left edge of the text
                  looks straight and the right edge looks ragged. Any extra
                  space in a line is put at the end of the line. Left-aligned
                  text is the easiest to read.
Press                  When paragraphs are flush right, the right edge of the
Alt-N                  text looks straight and the left edge looks ragged. Any
                       extra space in a line is put at the beginning of the
                       line, instead of the end. Right-aligned text has an
                       unusual appearance and is rarely used. It works well as
                       a device to make you stop and look twice, but it can be
                       difficult to read for long sections of text.
Press                      When paragraphs are centered, neither edge of the
Alt-N                      paragraph looks straight. Any extra space in a
again                      line is divided in two: Half is put at the
                           beginning of the line and half is put at the end
                           of the line. Normal paragraphs are rarely
                           centered, but special announcements, invitations,
                           poems, and single lines (such as headings) are
                           sometimes centered.
Press                  When lines are justified, both the left and the right
Alt-M                  edges of the text are straight, or aligned flush with
                       both margins (or paragraph indents). Any extra space is
                       distributed as evenly as possible between words
                       throughout the line. Justified text has a more finished
                       look than left-aligned text, but it can be a little
                       more difficult to read.
Press             When you justify text, you might end up spending a lot of
Alt-M             time hyphenating words at the ends of lines (so that each
again             line is filled with as many characters as possible).
                  Otherwise, you might end up with big gaps of space between
                  the words in some lines.
```

Figure 9-8. *Indenting and "outdenting" using Alt-N and Alt-M.*

Line spacing and paragraph spacing

The third row of command fields in the Format Paragraph command allows you to add additional space between lines in a paragraph and between paragraphs.

```
FORMAT PARAGRAPH alignment:(Left)Centered Right Justified
     left indent: 0"          first line: 0"          right indent: 0"
     line spacing: 1 li       space before: 0 li      space after: 0 li
     keep together: Yes(No)   keep follow: Yes(No)    side by side: Yes(No)
```

182

The *line spacing* command field is initially set at *1 li* (one line, which is ⅙ inch or 12 points). This gives you single-spaced text for standard 12-point characters. To get double-spaced text, type *2* in the *line spacing* field. With double spacing, you get one blank line above each line in a paragraph, as shown in Figure 9-9. You can increase the line spacing by a fraction of a line. For example, to set the line spacing at 1½ lines, type *1.5* in the *line spacing* field.

If you're using fonts smaller than 12 points or ⅙ inch and if you want more than 6 lines per inch, type a measurement smaller than 1 line in the *line spacing* field. For example, if you want 8 lines per inch, type *9 pt* (72 points/8) or *0.125"* (1 inch/8). Your printer might not cooperate if it requires a minimum amount of space between lines. If you're using fonts larger than 12 points or ⅙ inch, you can type *auto* in the *line spacing* field to make Word adjust line spacing to accommodate the font.

```
    When paragraphs are flush left, the left edge of the text
    looks  straight  and  the  right  edge  looks  ragged.  Any  extra
    space in a line is put at the end of the line. Left-aligned
    text is the easiest to read.
```

```
FORMAT PARAGRAPH alignment: Left Centered Right(Justified)
       left indent: 0            first line: 0          right indent: 0"
       line spacing: 1 li        space before: 0 li     space after: 0 li
       keep together: Yes(No)    keep follow: Yes(No)   side by side: Yes(No)
```

```
    When paragraphs are flush left, the left edge of the text

    looks straight and the right edge looks ragged. Any extra

    space in a line is put at the end of the line. Left-aligned

    text is the easiest to read.
```

```
FORMAT PARAGRAPH alignment: Left Centered Right(Justified)
       left indent: 0"           first line: 0"         right indent: 0"
       line spacing: 2 li        space before: 0 li     space after: 0 li
       keep together: Yes(No)    keep follow: Yes(No)   side by side: Yes(No)
```

Figure 9-9. *Single-spaced and double-spaced text.*

The *space before* and *space after* fields let you put additional vertical space between paragraphs, as shown in Figures 9-10 and 9-11. The total space between two paragraphs is the sum of the line spacing, the space after the first paragraph, and the space before the second paragraph. To avoid confusion, use only the *space before* field to put extra space between normal paragraphs. (Word deletes extra space before a paragraph that starts a page.)

If you want to add extra space before or after a special paragraph (such as a heading, list, or indented quotation), attach the extra space to the special paragraph, rather than to the normal paragraphs that come before or after it. Then, if you move the special paragraph to a new location, the extra space will move with it.

```
      When paragraphs are flush left, the left edge of the text
      looks straight and the right edge looks ragged. Any extra
      space in a line is put at the end of the line. Left-aligned
      text is the easiest to read.

      When paragraphs are flush right, the right edge of the text
      looks straight and the left edge looks ragged. Any extra
      space in a line is put at the beginning of the line, instead
      of the end. Right-aligned text has an unusual appearance and
      is rarely used. It works well as a device to make you stop
      and look twice, but it can be difficult to read for long
      sections of text.

      When paragraphs are centered, neither edge of the paragraph
      looks straight. Any extra space in a line is divided in two:
      Half is put at the beginning of the line and half is put at
      the end of the line. Normal paragraphs are rarely centered,
      but special announcements, invitations, poems, and single
      lines (such as headings) are sometimes centered.

      When lines are justified, both the left and the right edges
      of the text are straight, or aligned flush with both margins
      (or paragraph indents). Any extra space is distributed as
      evenly as possible between words throughout the line.
      Justified text has a more finished look than left-aligned
      text, but it can be a little more difficult to read.

      When you justify text, you might end up spending a lot of
      time hyphenating words at the ends of lines (so that each
      line is filled with as many characters as possible).
      Otherwise, you might end up with big gaps of space between
      the words in some lines.


FORMAT PARAGRAPH alignment: Left Centered Right(Justified)
     left indent: 0"          first line: 0"          right indent: 0"
     line spacing: 1 li       space before: 1 li      space after: 0 li
     keep together: Yes(No)   keep follow: Yes(No)    side by side: Yes(No)
```

Figure 9-10. *Adding a blank line between paragraphs.*

```
        When paragraphs are flush left, the left edge of the
   text looks straight and the right edge looks ragged. Any
   extra space in a line is put at the end of the line. Left-
   aligned text is the easiest to read.
        When paragraphs are flush right, the right edge of the
   text looks straight and the left edge looks ragged. Any
   extra space in a line is put at the beginning of the line,
   instead of the end. Right-aligned text has an unusual
   appearance and is rarely used. It works well as a device to
   make you stop and look twice, but it can be difficult to
   read for long sections of text.


   Centering Paragraphs

        When paragraphs are centered, neither edge of the
   paragraph looks straight. Any extra space in a line is
   divided in two: Half is put at the beginning of the line and
   half is put at the end of the line. Normal paragraphs are
   rarely centered, but special announcements, invitations,
   poems, and single lines (such as headings) are sometimes
   centered.
        When lines are justified, both the left and the right
   edges of the text are straight, or aligned flush with both
   margins (or paragraph indents). Any extra space is
   distributed as evenly as possible between words throughout
   the line. Justified text has a more finished look than left-
   aligned text, but it can be a little more difficult to read.
```

```
FORMAT PARAGRAPH alignment: Left Centered Right(Justified)
     left indent: 0"          first line: 0"          right indent: 0"
     line spacing: 1 li        space before: 2 li      space after: 1 li
     keep together: Yes(No)    keep follow: Yes(No)    side by side: Yes(No)
```

Figure 9-11. *Adding extra space above and below a heading.*

Two Alt-key commands let you adjust the line or paragraph spacing without using the Format Paragraph command:

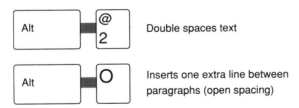

Alt + @ 2 — Double spaces text

Alt + O — Inserts one extra line between paragraphs (open spacing)

Using the Alt-O command is equivalent to setting the *space before* command field to one line.

Keeping paragraphs together

The *keep together* and *keep follow* command fields in the Format Paragraph are tools for controlling where page breaks occur. Use them to prevent special paragraphs from being divided between two pages or to prevent a heading from being separated from the text it identifies.

```
FORMAT PARAGRAPH alignment:(Left)Centered Right Justified
    left indent: 0"          first line: 0"          right indent: 0"
    line spacing: 1 li       space before: 0 li      space after: 0 li
    keep together: Yes No    keep follow: Yes(No)     side by side: Yes(No)
```

Choose *Yes* in response to the *keep together* field to prevent a page break from occurring within a particular paragraph. If a paragraph that has been assigned the *keep together* attribute lands at the bottom of a page (or column) but won't quite fit, Word moves the entire paragraph to the next page (or column).

With the usual *No* response to this field, Word would print part of the paragraph on one page and the rest on the next page. Word, however, will not ordinarily break a paragraph after the first line or before the last line of the paragraph. If only the first line of a paragraph fits at the bottom of a page, Word moves it to the next page so that it won't be isolated from the rest of the paragraph. If all except the last line of a paragraph fits at the bottom of a page, Word moves the last two lines of the paragraph to the next page. (Single lines left alone at the top or bottom of pages are called *widows* and *orphans* and are traditionally avoided. You can tell Word to abandon this tradition by choosing *No* in the *widow/orphan control* field of the Print Options command.)

The *keep follow* option prevents a heading for a section of text or for a table from landing on the bottom of a page without any text following it. The last two lines of a paragraph that has been assigned the *keep follow* attribute will be kept on (or moved to) the same page as the beginning of the paragraph that follows it. The second paragraph can be broken after the second line (unless it has been given the *keep together* attribute), but a page break cannot occur between the two paragraphs.

CHARACTERS AND TYPEFACE

A character is the smallest unit to which you can assign a particular typeface. You will usually want to assign a particular typeface to an entire document or to whole words or phrases, rather than single characters. However, Word allows you to assign a typeface to any amount of text from one character to the entire document.

Formatting Characters: Changing the Typeface

You can change the appearance of characters to emphasize certain words or parts of the text. For example, you can print characters in **boldface**, in *italics*, or with an underline. (If your printer isn't capable of printing special character formats, Word substitutes something similar.) You can raise or lower characters to produce superscripts and subscripts. If your printer offers more than one type style or font, you can specify the font and the size of characters that you want. When you want to insert comments and notes to yourself without having them printed, you can mark the characters as hidden text.

You can use the Format Character command or Alt-key commands to format characters. You can set the format of characters before you type them, or you can go back to previously typed characters and reformat them.

To choose the format for characters before you type them, press the appropriate Alt-key command (or choose and carry out the Format Character command). The character formats you choose are applied to any characters you type from then on. When you want to return to the character format that your printer normally uses, press Alt-Spacebar.

To format characters after they've been typed:

1. Highlight the characters you want to format.

2. Press an Alt-key command, or choose the Format Character command and change the responses to the appropriate command fields.

3. Carry out the command if you've chosen the Format Character command.

The format(s) you choose are applied only to the characters that are highlighted. If you have only one character highlighted, you must press an Alt-key command *twice* to indicate that you want the single, highlighted character formatted rather than the text that you type from then on.

Special printing effects

The first seven command fields of the Format Character command offer you a variety of special printing effects that can enhance your documents. To assign special printing effects, change the response to any of these command fields from *No* to *Yes*.

```
FORMAT CHARACTER bold: Yes No    italic: Yes(No)      underline: Yes(No)
        strikethrough: Yes(No)   uppercase: Yes(No)   small caps: Yes(No)
        double underline: Yes(No)  position:(Normal)Superscript Subscript
        font name: Pica          font size: 12        font color: Black
        hidden: Yes(No)
```

If you're preparing a legal document, you might want to cross out text without deleting it so that the interested parties know what was deleted from the original document. You can use the ~~strikethrough~~ feature to print a dash through selected characters. (You can also use the Format revision-Marks command to automatically mark text you add, move, copy, and replace, as well as text you delete.)

The *uppercase* field lets you change lowercase letters to UPPERCASE without retyping them. If you decide you don't want uppercase letters after all, you can switch back to lowercase letters by resetting the response in the *uppercase* field to *No*.

One form of emphasis that you might not be familiar with is called SMALL CAPS. Small caps are capital letters printed in a smaller or a condensed size. Small capital letters are often used in combination with large capital letters in titles or headings. They can also be used for acronyms. The small caps format does not change uppercase letters; text must be typed in lowercase letters to be formatted in small caps.

In addition to underlining text with a <u>single line</u>, you can <u>double underline</u> for added emphasis. A double underline is the conventional way to draw attention to the totals in an accounting or financial statement.

You can use Alt-key commands, instead of the Format Character command, to assign any of the special printing effects (except uppercase) to characters. The equivalent Alt-key combinations are:

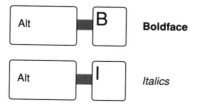

Boldface

Italics

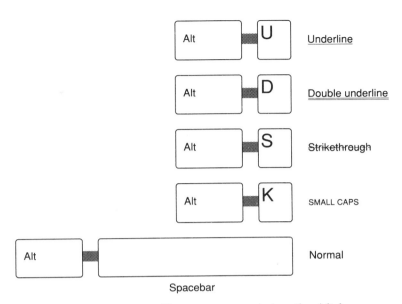

Whether you use the Format Character command or the Alt-key commands, you can assign more than one special printing effect to a character or group of characters. Here are some examples of possible combinations:

boldface italics

boldface italics underlined

boldface double-underlined

italics underlined

BOLDFACE SMALL CAPS DOUBLE-UNDERLINED

ITALIC CAPS UNDERLINED

When you're using the Alt-key commands, the character attributes accumulate until you use Alt-Spacebar to return to normal type. For example, if you make a word boldface and then assign the italics attribute, the word will be both boldfaced and italicized. If you want to change from boldface to italics, you must first return the word to normal format with Alt-Spacebar and then assign italics with Alt-I.

You can combine Alt-key commands to apply more than one character format at the same time. For example, you can press Alt-BI to make *boldface-italic* characters.

Subscripts and superscripts

When you're typing footnote references, mathematical equations, or chemical formulas, you can raise characters to produce superscripts, as in:

Cakes are round, but πr^2.

or you can lower characters to produce subscripts, as in:

$$\frac{bridge}{troubled\ H_2O}$$

```
FORMAT CHARACTER bold: Yes(No)      italic: Yes(No)         underline: Yes(No)
           strikethrough: Yes(No)   uppercase: Yes(No)      small caps: Yes(No)
           double underline: Yes(No)  position: Normal Superscript Subscript
           font name: Pica          font size: 12           font color: Black
           hidden: Yes(No)
```

Choosing the *Superscript* or *Subscript* response to the *position* command field only changes the vertical position of a character (except on some printers, such as Epson FX printers, which also reduce the size of the characters). If your printer doesn't automatically reduce the size of subscripts and superscripts and is capable of printing more than one size, you can reduce the size with the *font size* command field.

The equivalent Alt-key combinations for superscripts and subscripts are:

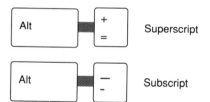

Changing fonts, font sizes, and font colors

Laser printers and many dot-matrix printers are designed with the built-in capacity to reproduce the alphabet in a variety of shapes (fonts) and sizes. Some printers even print in more than one color. If Word has access to the printer description file for your printer, you can see and select from a list of the font names, font sizes, and font colors that are available with your printer.

```
FORMAT CHARACTER bold: Yes(No)      italic: Yes(No)       underline: Yes(No)
          strikethrough: Yes(No)    uppercase: Yes(No)    small caps: Yes(No)
          double underline: Yes(No) position:(Normal)Superscript Subscript
          font name: Pica           font size: 12         font color: Black
          hidden: Yes(No)
```

To see a list of the font names for your printer, move the highlight to the *font name* command field and press the F1 key. (Word shows you a list of fonts for the printer currently specified in the *printer* field of the Print Options command. See Chapter 12.) To find out what a particular font looks like without printing it yourself, look for sample printouts in the documentation that came with your printer.

In Word, font size is a measure of the character height and must be specified in points. Don't try to measure characters to determine their size. Instead, select a size from the list of available sizes for your printer. To see a list of font sizes, press the F1 key when the highlight is in the *font size* field.

With impact printers, such as daisy-wheel or thimble printers, different fonts are generated by different printing elements. You must manually change the daisy wheel or thimble when you want to change fonts. When Word encounters a change of fonts for impact printers, it stops printing, reminds you to change printing elements:

```
Enter Y after mounting <font name> ▮
```

and waits for you to tell it when to resume printing. (For <font name>, Word substitutes the name of the font you typed in the *font name* field.)

Printing elements usually specify character size in pitch, which is the number of characters per inch. To convert pitch sizes to font sizes in points, use this table.

Pitch Size	Point Size
10	12
12	10
15	8

Proportionally spaced printing elements, which do not have a fixed number of characters per inch, usually correspond to 12-point type.

If your printer can print in more than one color, press the F1 key when the highlight is in the *font color* field to see a list of available colors.

Hiding characters

You can hide comments, questions, notes, reminders, or instructions in a document so that they don't appear in the printed copy. You have the option of printing them as well as the option of making them invisible on the screen.

```
FORMAT CHARACTER bold: Yes(No)      italic: Yes(No)            underline: Yes(No)
               strikethrough: Yes(No)      uppercase: Yes(No)     small caps: Yes(No)
               double underline: Yes(No)   position:(Normal)Superscript Subscript
               font name: Pica             font size: 12          font color: Black
               hidden: Yes No
```

Choose *Yes* in the *hidden* command field of the Format Character command to apply the hidden-text format to selected characters. The Alt-key command for hiding text is:

Word normally displays hidden text on the screen but does not print it. Word marks hidden text on the screen with a solid underline, a dotted underline, or a different color, depending on your system.

To make hidden text invisible on the screen, choose the Options command and select *No* in the *show hidden text* field. You can have Word display a two-headed arrow (↔) to indicate the location of the invisible hidden text. To do this, set the *show non-printing symbols* field of the Options command to *Partial* or *All*. If you want to print hidden text, choose *Yes* in the *hidden text* field of the Print Options command.

SEARCHING FOR AND REPLACING FORMATS

Word provides you with an easy way to find and change most formatting instructions. With the Format sEarch and Format repLace commands, you can search for and replace character and paragraph formatting instructions. You cannot search for or replace division or tab formats unless they have been assigned by a style sheet.

Both the Format sEarch and Format repLace commands branch out into three subcommands: Character, Paragraph, and Style. If you want to search for or replace a format assigned with the Format Character command, the Format Paragraph command, or an Alt-key command, choose the Character or Paragraph subcommand. And if you want to search for or replace any format assigned by a style sheet, choose the Style subcommand.

For example, to search for boldfaced words that have been formatted with either the Format Character command or the Alt-B command, first choose the Format sEarch Character command:

Now you see the following command fields:

```
FORMAT SEARCH CHARACTER direction: Up Down
         bold: Yes No              italic: Yes No           underline: Yes No
         strikethrough: Yes No     uppercase: Yes No        small caps: Yes No
         double underline: Yes No  position: Normal Superscript Subscript
         font name:                font size:               font color: Black
         hidden: Yes No
```

Choose *Up* in the *direction* field to search toward the beginning of the document or *Down* to search toward the end of the document. Use the remaining command fields to specify the format you're looking for. For example, to search for boldfaced text, you would choose *Yes* in the *bold* field. Suppose, in your search, you don't want to find text that is both bold and italic. In that case, you would specify *No* in the *italic* field. After you carry out the command, Word searches (from the cursor's location) to find the first occurrence of the specified format.

As another example, suppose you want to replace a boldface-italic format with an underline format. First choose the Format repLace Character command:

After choosing the Format repLace Character command, you first see these command fields:

```
FORMAT REPLACE CHARACTER confirm: Yes No
         bold: Yes No              italic: Yes No           underline: Yes No
         strikethrough: Yes No     uppercase: Yes No        small caps: Yes No
         double underline: Yes No  position: Normal Superscript Subscript
         font name:                font size:               font color: Black
         hidden: Yes No
```

The first command field, *confirm,* gives you the option of viewing and approving each replacement before it occurs. The remaining command fields specify the character format that you want to replace. For example, to search for and replace a boldface-italic format, choose *Yes* in the *bold* and *italic* command fields and press the Enter key. Now you see a new command field display:

```
REPLACE WITH CHARACTER FORMAT
     bold: Yes No              italic: Yes No           underline: Yes No
     strikethrough: Yes No     uppercase: Yes No        small caps: Yes No
     double underline: Yes No  position: Normal Superscript Subscript
     font name:                font size:               font color: Black
     hidden: Yes No
```

Use these command fields to specify the format you want to substitute in place of the searched-for format—in this example, bold italics. To replace with an underline format, choose *No* in the *bold* field, *No* in the *italic* field, and *Yes* in the *underline* field; then carry out the command.

Where Word searches depends on what the cursor is highlighting when you choose the Format repLace command. If the cursor is highlighting a single character, it searches forward from the cursor to the end of the document until every occurrence has been found. If the cursor is highlighting more than one character, it searches only within the selected text.

The Format sEarch Paragraph and Format repLace Paragraph commands work like the Format sEarch Character and Format repLace Character commands—except that the command fields correspond to paragraph formats. The commands for searching and replacing styles ask you to specify formats by typing in the two-character code assigned to the style you want to search for or replace with.

STRATEGY FOR FORMATTING

With Word, you can format a document at any time: before you begin typing, during the typing session, or after you've typed the entire document. You might prefer to take advantage of Word's on-screen formatting capabilities and see the final format as you type. Or you might want to type the document without interruption and then format it.

I recommend a strategy that lets you see as much formatting as possible while you're typing, with as few interruptions as possible. With this strategy, you'll use fewer formatting commands and you'll find it easier to keep track of what formatting instructions are being applied to what text.

Format Most of the Document as You're Typing

When you're designing a document, think about what most of the document will look like. Most, if not all, of a document will have the same division, paragraph, and character formats. Before you start typing, define the formats that apply to most of the document. Once the basic formatting instructions have been specified, type your document. The division, paragraph, and character formats you've chosen will be applied to the entire document.

To define the formatting for most of the document before you start typing:

1. Choose the Format Division Margins command. Check to see that the page length, page width, and margins are set the way you want before you carry out the command.

2. If you want page numbers printed, choose the Format Division Page-numbers command. Be sure the first command field is set to *Yes* and change any fields that control placement, numbering, or page-number format that need changing before you carry out the command.

3. If you want to set up multiple columns or place footnotes at the end of the document, use the Format Division Layout command. If you want line numbers printed in the left margin of your document, use the Format Division line-Numbers command.

4. Choose the Format Paragraph command. Check to see that the *alignment*, *first line* indent, *line spacing*, and *space before* command fields are set to give you the format you want. (The *left indent*, *right indent*, *space after*, *keep together*, *keep follow*, and *side by side* fields usually apply only to special paragraphs and can be ignored for now.)

5. Choose the Format Character command only if you want to change the font, font size, or font color for most of the characters in the document.

When you assign the line format that applies to most of the document, remember to take advantage of Word's ability to automatically indent the first line of each paragraph and to put extra space between paragraphs. Set the *first line* indent at something like *0.5"*, or set the *space before* each paragraph to *1 li* (one line). By using one or both of these features, you can save yourself some typing time and the document will be easier to read as you type and edit it.

If you change your mind about any of the formatting instructions that you've given:

1. Press Shift-F10 to highlight the entire document.
2. Choose and carry out the formatting command that lets you make the desired change.

The new formatting instructions are applied to the entire document and to whatever you type from then on.

If some divisions, paragraphs, or characters require special treatment, you can go back and change them after you finish typing. If you try to format a special section as you type it, you have to interrupt your typing twice: once to format that section before you finish typing it, and once again to change the formatting instructions back to their normal settings after you finish.

Format the Rest of the Document After You Type It

If a division needs a different page format from the rest of the document, move the cursor to any place in that division and use the Format Division command. The new page-format instructions you give are applied only to that division, as long as the beginning and end of the division are properly marked.

If a single paragraph needs a different line format from the rest of the document, move the cursor to any place in that paragraph and use the Format Paragraph command (or the equivalent Alt-key commands). The new line-format instructions are applied only to that paragraph.

If you want to change two or more paragraphs in sequence, highlight some text in each paragraph and use the Format Paragraph command (or the equivalent Alt-key commands). The new line-format instructions are applied only to those paragraphs that contain highlighted text.

If you want to assign a special typeface to any sequence of characters in the document, highlight the characters you want to change and use the Format Character command (or the equivalent Alt-key commands). The new character formats are applied only to the highlighted characters.

You can review the formatting instructions that are in effect at a particular place by moving the cursor there and choosing the appropriate Format Division, Format Paragraph, and Format Character commands. Should you decide to add text at the point where the cursor is, the format instructions you reviewed will also affect your additional words.

THERE'S MORE

In this chapter, we've looked at two ways to format text *directly*. One way is to use the Format command and the other is to use predefined Alt-key commands. Word offers still another method to format documents—by creating and using style sheets, which is called *indirect* formatting.

Similar to glossaries, which are used to store often-used words, style sheets are separate files that store often-used formatting instructions. When you want to use text that you stored in a glossary, you type a code that you assigned to the text instead of retyping it. When you want to use formatting instructions that you stored in a style sheet, you type a code that you assigned to the instructions instead of redefining them.

If you find yourself repeatedly defining the same formats for a number of different documents, style sheets can save you a lot of time. They let you re-use formatting instructions without recreating them. They also let you make formatting changes throughout a document or throughout several documents, without having to go into the documents to find the text that needs reformatting. You simply change the style sheet—and the documents linked to the style sheet automatically change.

Chapter 17 introduces you to the power of style sheets, showing you how to use ready-made style sheets that Word provides and how to change style sheets to suit your particular needs.

Chapter 10

Formatting Special Text

With conventional typewriters or word processors, formatting special text can require more effort than it's worth. Typing a document in multiple columns, placing footnotes at the bottoms of the pages where they are referenced, centering headings over columns in a table, or aligning the decimal points of numbers in a column are painstaking tasks that require skill and patience. Adding finishing touches like running heads on each page is easy to do, but time-consuming.

With Word, you don't have to be a skilled or a patient typist to do special formatting and to make your documents look professionally prepared. Word does the formatting for you. In this chapter, you will learn how to instruct Word to format special text, such as tables, multiple columns, footnotes, and running heads.

FORMATTING TABLES

When you want to arrange facts or figures in columns, you can use the Tab key as you do on a typewriter. Word initially sets tab stops at ½-inch increments across the page. However, you can reset the tab stops with the Options command by changing the *default tab width* field from 0.5" to some other measurement, or you can reset them with the Format Tab command.

Tab stops are considered a part of line layout and can be changed from paragraph to paragraph. Word remembers the tab stops for each paragraph from one editing session to the next. You can also use the Format Tab Set command to draw vertical lines between columns of text in a table.

Tips for Typing Tables

Because tabs and vertical lines are a part of paragraph formatting, treat a table as one paragraph when you type it. End each line of text in a table (except for the last line) by pressing Shift-Enter to start a new line rather than a new paragraph. Press the Enter key at the end of the last line to mark the end of the table paragraph. If you want the column headings in the table centered over the columns, make the heading line(s) a separate paragraph from the rest of the table so that you can set different tabs for the heading.

It's often easier to type the text for a table before you set the tabs or draw vertical lines between columns of the table. As you're typing, press the Tab key once between column entries. After the text is typed, you can determine where to set the tab stops and where to draw vertical lines. Although column entries won't be aligned as you're typing, they instantly fall into place once the tab stops are set to accommodate the longest entry in each column.

The All-Purpose Tab Command

You can set, clear, or move any number of tab stops using one command— the Format Tab Set command. You can assign tab stops to individual paragraphs, to a series of two or more paragraphs, to an entire division, or to an entire document.

After you choose the Format Tab Set command, you will see:

```
FORMAT TAB SET position: █
        alignment:(Left)Center Right Decimal Vertical    leader char:(Blank). - _
```

You'll also see a ruler in the top border of the window you're working in:

```
█═[·········1·········2·········3········4········5·········]········7····█
```

The ruler starts at the left margin and continues across the width of the
screen. It initially displays only the indents that you set for the selected para-
graph(s). It does not display the tabs that Word sets at ½-inch increments.
Symbols you initially see on this ruler are:

[Left indent (and left margin if the left indent is 0)

]   Right indent (and right margin if the right indent is 0)

¦   First-line indent

After you set tab stops or draw vertical lines, the ruler also shows the position
of the tab stops and vertical lines, and indicates the kind of tab stops that
you've set.

Tab positions and the ruler

You specify where you want to set a tab or draw a vertical line in the *position*
command field of the Format Tab Set command.

```
FORMAT TAB SET position: █
        alignment:(Left)Center Right Decimal Vertical    leader char:(Blank). - _
```

Tab stop and line positions are measured from the left margin. They are measured in inches unless you type a measurement that includes a different unit
of measure in the *position* field, or unless you change the default unit of measure in the *measure* field of the Options command.

   Although you can type a measurement in the *position* command field, it's
easier to move a highlight or the mouse pointer along the ruler to the position
where you want to set a tab or draw a vertical line. By using the ruler, you
can forget about measurements and just point to the position where you want
to set a tab or draw a vertical line. Each tick on the ruler corresponds to one
character position on the screen.

Tab stop alignment

When you set a tab stop, the *alignment* command field determines how text
will be aligned around the tab stop. The alignment options are: left, centered,
right, and decimal.

```
FORMAT TAB SET position:
        alignment: Left Center Right Decimal Vertical    leader char:(Blank). - _
```

The proposed response is left alignment. With *Left* alignment, the text is aligned flush left with the tab stop. With *Center* alignment, the text is centered around the tab stop. With *Right* alignment, the text is aligned flush right with the tab stop. *Decimal* alignment can be used to align the decimal points of a column of numbers with the tab stop. (If the text has no decimal point, it is aligned flush right with the tab stop.)

The *Vertical* option of the *alignment* field has nothing to do with aligning text around a tab stop. Use it to specify that you want to draw a vertical line rather than set a tab. When *Vertical* is chosen, Word draws a vertical line throughout the selected paragraph at the location specified in the *position* command field.

The table in Figure 10-1 illustrates each kind of tab alignment, as well as vertical lines drawn by the Format Tab Set command.

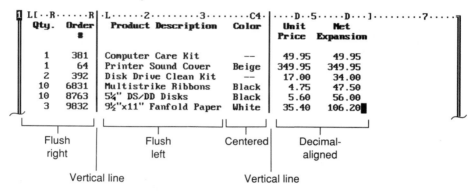

Figure 10-1. *Samples of different kinds of tab-stop alignment.*

Leader characters

Leader characters are characters that are used to fill up tabbed space. They lead your eyes from one column to the next so that you don't lose track of which line you're on. Dot leaders, for example, are commonly used in a table of contents to connect chapter or section names with the corresponding page numbers, as shown in Figure 10-2.

```
                        Table of Contents

Chapter  1:  Day is Dawning..................................1
Chapter  2:  Hot Coffee and Cold Croissants.................23
Chapter  3:  The Silent Commute.............................35
Chapter  4:  Conversations in the Elevator..................61
Chapter  5:  Exploring the In-Basket........................83
Chapter  6:  Lunch on a Rooftop.............................97
Chapter  7:  Fulfilling the Out-Basket.....................113
Chapter  8:  Homeward Bound................................117
Chapter  9:  Dinner at Dusk................................135
Chapter 10:  Night Motions and Love Potions................159
```

Right-justified tab
with dot leader

Figure 10-2. *Sample table of contents with dot leaders.*

Instead of dots, you can choose the hyphen (-) or the underscore (_) as the leader character. (Hyphens will form a broken line across the page; underscores will create a solid line.) If you don't want a leader character, choose *Blank* as the response to the *leader char* field.

```
FORMAT TAB SET position:
       alignment:(Left)Center Right Decimal Vertical   leader char: Blank . - _
```

When you assign a leader character to a tab stop, the leader appears on the ruler to the left of that tab stop.

After you set your own tab stops, the following markers appear on the ruler to indicate where you set tab stops or draw vertical lines. The markers also show what kind of alignment and leader character you assigned to each tab stop:

L	Left-aligned tab stop
R	Right-aligned tab stop
C	Centered tab stop
D	Decimal tab stop
.	Dot leader
-	Hyphen leader (broken line)
_	Underscore leader (solid line)
|	Vertical line position

For example:

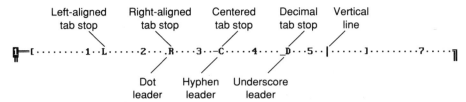

Setting, Clearing, and Moving Tabs and Vertical Lines

The easiest way to define tab stops or vertical lines with either the keyboard or the mouse is to choose the Format Tab Set command and then indicate on the ruler where you want to set, clear, or move tab stops or vertical lines. By using the ruler, you can set, clear, or move as many tabs or vertical lines as you like before you carry out the Format Tab Set command.

The position of a highlight or the mouse pointer on the ruler determines *where* you set a tab or draw a line and *which* tab stop or vertical line you clear or move. The keys that you press, or the mouse buttons that you click, determine the *action* taken—that is, whether you set, clear, or move a tab stop or vertical line.

If you're using the keyboard, you press the F1 key to make the highlight appear on the ruler. Then you use the direction keys to move the highlight along the ruler. The Left and Right direction keys move the highlight from one tick on the ruler to another. After you set your own tabs, you can use the Up and Down direction keys to quickly move the highlight from one tab stop to another.

Pressing the Insert key *sets* a tab or vertical line at the highlighted position. Pressing the Delete key *clears* a tab or vertical line at the highlighted position. You can *move* tab stops and vertical lines by holding down the Control key and pressing the Left or Right direction keys when the highlight is on the tab or vertical line that you want to move.

If you're using the mouse, you move the mouse pointer along the ruler. Clicking the left mouse button sets a tab or vertical line at the position of the pointer, and clicking both buttons removes a tab or vertical line at the position of the pointer. You can also move tab stops or vertical lines with the mouse using a hold-and-release technique similar to that used for extending the cursor.

As you move the highlight or the mouse pointer along the ruler, the measurement in the *position* command field changes to correspond to the highlight's (or mouse pointer's) position.

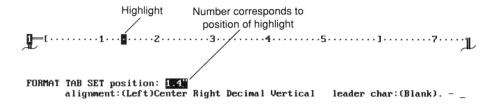

How to set tabs and draw vertical lines

To set a tab stop or draw a vertical line:

1. Move the cursor to the paragraph (or highlight some text in a group of paragraphs) where you want to set tabs or draw vertical lines.

2. Choose the Format Tab Set command:

Press Esc F T S or Format Click-L Tab Click-R

3. Change the responses in the *alignment* and *leader char* command fields, if necessary. If you're drawing a line, choose *Vertical* in the *alignment* field.

4. If you're using the keyboard, press the F1 key and use the Left and Right direction keys to move the highlight to the position on the ruler where you want to set the tab or draw the line. Then press the Ins key. If you're using the mouse, point to the position on the ruler where you want to set the tab or draw the line, and then Click-L.

You can set up to 19 tab stops or vertical lines in each paragraph. It's usually easier to insert vertical lines that separate columns of text after you've set the tab stops. Each tab you set will have the alignment and leader character specified in the command fields at the time you press the Insert key or the left mouse button. You can change the alignment or leader character for a particular tab stop by changing the command field before you set that tab. With the keyboard, you must press the F1 key or the Tab key to move the highlight from the ruler to the command fields so that you can change the alignment or leader character.

When you set a tab, the preset tabs to the left of it are automatically cleared. For example, if you set a tab at 1.8 inches, the preset tabs at 0.5, 1, and 1.5 inches are removed. The first tab stop will be 1.8 inches from the left margin. If you want to retain any of those preset tab stops, you have to set tabs at those locations. You can use this feature to your advantage. For example, if you want your first tab stop to be at 3 inches, set a tab stop at 3 inches even though there is already a preset tab at that position. By setting the 3-inch tab stop, you automatically clear all preceding preset tab stops with one quick move.

The tab stops or vertical lines you insert become fixed when you carry out the Format Tab Set command. But before you carry out the command, you might want to remove or move some tabs or vertical lines (as explained in the next two sections).

How to remove tabs and vertical lines

To remove a tab stop or vertical line after choosing the Format Tab Set command

With the keyboard:

1. Press the F1 key and use the direction keys to highlight the tab or vertical line that you want to remove. Then press the Del key.

With the mouse:

1. Point to the marker for the tab or vertical line that you want to remove, and Click-LR.

If you want to remove all tab stops that you set, and restore all the ones that Word assigns, use the Format Tab Reset-all command. As soon as you choose this command, all tabs are cleared and reset to their initial positions at ½-inch increments across the page (or to the positions defined by the *default tab width* field of the Options command).

How to move tabs and vertical lines

Moving a tab stop lets you change its position without changing (or having to redefine) its alignment or leader-character attributes. To move a tab stop or a vertical line after choosing the Format Tab Set command

With the keyboard:

1. Press the F1 key and use the direction keys to highlight the tab or vertical line that you want to move. Then press and hold the Ctrl key.

2. Use the direction keys to move the highlight to the new position. Then release the Ctrl key.

With the mouse:

1. Point to the tab or vertical line that you want to move, and Hold-L.

2. Point to the new position and Rel-L.

❑ MOUSE NOTE: *Using the techniques described above for the mouse, you can also set, clear, and move tab stops after choosing the Format Paragraph command. Being able to adjust tab stops while you are in the Format Paragraph command can be a real convenience: You can set tab stops at the same time you set other formatting instructions for a paragraph or a group of paragraphs.*

Viewing Tab Stops

Using either the keyboard or the mouse, you can turn on the ruler display at any time to view tab stops or indents. The ruler stays on until you turn it off.

To turn the ruler on or off with the keyboard:

1. Choose the Options command.

Press

2. Choose the *Yes* response in the *show ruler* command field to turn the ruler on, or choose *No* to turn it off.

```
WINDOW OPTIONS for window number: 1          show hidden text:(Yes)No
            show ruler: Yes No       show non-printing symbols:(None)Partial All
          show layout: Yes(No)            show line breaks: Yes(No)
         show outline: Yes(No)             show style bar: Yes(No)
```

3. Press Enter to carry out the command.

To turn the ruler on or off with the mouse:

1. Move the mouse pointer to the upper right corner of the window.

2. Click-L to turn the ruler on. Click-LR to turn it off.

Mouse Shortcut

Whenever the ruler is displayed and you are working in the text area, you can use the mouse to set, clear, and move tab stops and vertical lines. Use the same technique you learned for the Format Tab Set command.

The two characters between the window number and the ruler display the currently selected leader character and alignment. Move the mouse pointer to the leader character, and Click-L to change to the next character in sequence: blank, dot (.), hyphen (-), underscore (_), and back to blank. Move the mouse pointer to the alignment character, and Click-L to change to the next alignment in sequence: left (L), centered (C), right (R), decimal (D), vertical line (|), and back to left alignment.

❏ NOTE: *This shortcut does not work in versions of Word earlier than 5.0.*

FORMATTING MULTIPLE COLUMNS

Word normally prints a document in one column that extends from the left margin to the right margin. But you can tell Word to print more than one column on a page by changing the page layout with the Format Division command.

With a multiple-column format, you can put more text on each page. Because the length of each line is shorter, you can use a smaller font without detracting from the readability. Newspapers, magazines, and some books use a multiple-column format—partly to keep down printing costs, but also because it makes for attractive, easy-to-read pages. If you prepare newsletters, brochures, or manuals, or if you want to give a professional touch to any document that lends itself to multiple columns, you'll want to try this feature.

Word puts no restrictions on the number of columns you can have on a page, but the width of your paper imposes some practical limits. For 8½-by-11-inch paper, it would be difficult to print more than three columns because you have to allow for some space between columns and some space for the left and right margins.

When you divide a page into multiple columns, decide how wide the columns will be, how much space will be between columns, and how wide the margins will be. In most cases, you should reduce the left and right margins to allow more space for text. The total width of the columns, the space between the columns, and the left and right margins should equal the page width shown in the *width* command field of the Format Division Margins command.

For example, a very readable three-column format on 8½-by-11-inch paper would have three 2-inch columns of text with a ½-inch space between columns and with ¾-inch left and right margins, as shown in Figure 10-3.

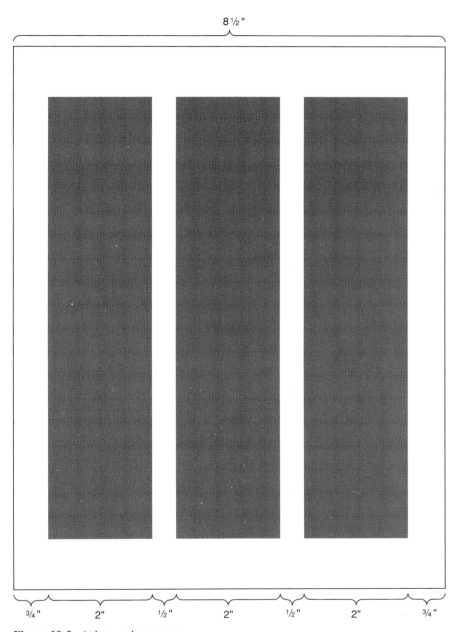

Figure 10-3. *A three-column page.*

To format a document into more than one column:

1. Choose the Format Division Layout command.

Press [Esc] [F] [D] [L] *or* Format Click-L Division Click-L Layout Click-L

2. Specify the number of columns you want on each page in the *number of columns* field.

```
FORMAT DIVISION LAYOUT footnotes:(Same-page)End
    number of columns: 1        space between columns: 0.5"
        division break:(Page)Continuous Column Even Odd
```

3. If necessary, change the amount of space between columns in the *space between columns* field.

4. Carry out the command.

If desired, you can use the Format Division Margins command to change the left and right margins by typing in new measurements in the *left* and *right* command fields.

You don't see the text arranged in more than one column on the screen; you see the text formatted in one long column. To see where each new column starts, choose the Options command and change the response to the *show layout* field to *Yes*. Word will display the columns side by side and allow you to edit them. Because Word must do more work when *show layout* is set to *Yes*, you might find that editing is somewhat slower than usual.

When Word lays out text in multiple columns, it fills each column before it starts putting text in a new column. If you want a new column to start at a particular place in the text, move the highlight to that place and press Ctrl-Enter to start a new division. Then use the Format Division Layout command, choosing *Column* in the *division break* field to specify that the new division starts in a new column.

If you divide a page into multiple columns, it's usually not practical to justify the lines of text, unless you use a small font size. The shorter your lines, the more difficult it is to avoid the unsightly gaps of space that are inserted between words to fill the lines.

To get an idea of what the pages will look like when printed, use the Print preView command described in Chapter 12. You might not be able to read the text displayed by Print preView, but you will see the column layout on the screen.

FORMATTING FOOTNOTES

Word makes it easy to create and format footnotes. You can insert them as you're typing, or you can add them later. If you instruct Word to number the footnotes for you, Word automatically renumbers them if you delete, insert, or change their order. When you create footnotes, you type them at the end of the document, but you have the option of printing each footnote on the same page as its reference mark.

A footnote has two parts: the *footnote reference mark* and the *footnote text*. The footnote reference mark is usually a superscript number, but it can also be a symbol, such as *, or a letter. It appears in two places: embedded in the document where the footnote is referenced and next to the footnote text.

Four commands come into play when you're working with footnotes:

- The Format Footnote command

- The Jump Footnote command

- The Window Split Footnote command

- The Format Division Layout command

The Format Footnote command is used to create footnotes and to change their reference marks. The Jump Footnote command lets you jump back and forth between a footnote reference and the corresponding footnote text; it also helps you find the footnote reference marks in a document. The Window Split Footnote command lets you open a special window so that you can see a footnote and the text it's associated with at the same time. The Format Division Layout command gives you the option of printing all footnotes at the end of the document or of printing each footnote on the same page as its reference mark.

The Footnote Window

When you create a footnote, the text for it is stored at the end of the document. You can open a special footnote window so that you can see the footnote text without having to scroll to the end of the document. To distinguish a footnote window from an ordinary text window, Word makes the top border of a footnote window a dashed line.

Document window

Footnote window

You can open and close footnote windows with either the keyboard or the mouse. You do not have to open a footnote window to create and edit footnotes, but it is often helpful to see the part of the document where the footnote reference mark is inserted and the footnote text simultaneously. As you scroll the text window, Word scrolls the footnote window to display any footnotes referenced in the text window.

To open a footnote window with the keyboard:

1. Choose the Window Split Footnote command.

Press [Esc] [W] [S] [F]

2. When you see:

WINDOW SPLIT FOOTNOTE at line: 3

type the line number where you want the window to start. (Line numbers start at 1 for the first line of text currently in the window being split; the smallest number you can enter is 2.) Instead of typing in the line number, you can press F1 and then press the Up or Down direction keys to move a highlight in the selection bar to the line where you want the window to start. (The selection bar is the blank column to the left of the text.)

3. Press Enter to carry out the command.

To open a footnote window with the mouse:

1. Position the mouse pointer on the right window bar next to the line where you want the footnote window opened.

2. Hold down the Shift key and Click-L or Click-R.

You close footnote windows in the same way as you close other windows: Using the F1 key, move the highlight to the window you want to close and then use the Window Close command. With the mouse, you can move the mouse pointer to the right border of the window and Click-LR.

Creating Footnotes

Use the Format Footnote command to create footnotes. If you want to see the footnote reference mark and the footnote text at the same time, open a footnote window first. Then:

1. Move the cursor to the place in the text where you want the reference mark to appear. (The reference mark is inserted to the left of the cursor.)

2. Choose the Format Footnote command:

3. You'll see a single command field, labeled *reference mark*. Type in a symbol, letter, or even a word (such as *Note*) to refer to the footnote. If you want Word to number the footnotes for you, leave the command field blank.

4. Carry out the command. Word jumps to the footnote window or to the end of the document if you haven't opened a footnote window.

5. Type the text of the footnote. The footnote text can be any length.

Editing Footnotes

Once you've created a footnote, you can go back and change either the reference mark or the footnote text. Instead of scrolling through the document to find footnote reference marks or footnote text, you can use the Jump Footnote command.

If the cursor is not on a reference mark or in the footnote text, the Jump Footnote command finds the next reference mark in the document. If the cursor is on a reference mark, the Jump Footnote command moves you to the footnote text for that reference mark. And if the cursor is in the footnote text, the Jump Footnote command moves you to the reference mark for that footnote.

To change a footnote reference mark:

1. Highlight the footnote reference mark that you want to change.

2. Choose the Format Footnote command and type the new reference mark in the *reference mark* command field. If you want automatically numbered footnotes, leave the field empty.

3. Carry out the command.

Word changes both occurrences of the reference mark—the one embedded in the document and the one next to the footnote text.

To change the footnote text:

1. Highlight the reference mark for the footnote you want to change.

2. Choose the Jump Footnote command to move to the footnote text:

Press [Esc] [J] [F] *or* Jump Click-L Footnote Click-L

3. Edit the footnote text as you would edit any other text in the document. If you accidentally delete an automatic footnote reference number adjacent to footnote text, move the cursor to where the number should be, type the glossary name *footnote*, and press the F3 key.

4. If you want to move back to the reference mark for the footnote, use the Jump Footnote command again.

To delete a footnote:

1. Highlight the footnote reference mark.

2. Press the Del key or use the Delete command to delete it.

Word deletes both the reference mark and the footnote text associated with it.

To move a footnote, just move the reference mark that's embedded in the document as you would move any other text; Word moves the footnote text for you. If you let Word number the footnotes for you, Word renumbers them after you delete or move them or after you insert new footnotes.

Printing Footnotes

Use the Format Division Layout command to specify where you want the footnotes printed. As mentioned earlier, the text for footnotes is stored at the end of the document. But you can print each footnote on the same page as its reference mark by choosing *Same-page* in the *footnotes* command field.

```
FORMAT DIVISION LAYOUT footnotes: Same-page End
        number of columns: 1        space between columns: 0.5"
            division break:(Page)Continuous Column Even Odd
```

If you choose the *End* response, all footnotes for a division print together at the end of the division. If you have only one division, all footnotes print at the end of the document.

FORMATTING RUNNING HEADS

Running heads appear in the top or bottom margin of the page, separate from the main body of text. A reader can glance at running heads to find out, for example, the subject matter for the work as a whole or for individual chapters or major sections.

You can put one running head at the top of a page and a different running head at the bottom of a page. You can put one on the first page and a different one on subsequent pages. If you're printing or duplicating the document on both sides of the page and fastening the pages together, book style, you might want to put one running head on left (even-numbered) pages and a different running head on right (odd-numbered) pages.

Three commands come into play when you're creating and formatting running heads:

- The Format Running-head command

- The Format Division Margins command

- The Format Paragraph command

The Format Running-head command lets you create a running head and assign it a general position on the page, such as the top or bottom of the page. The Format Division Margins command lets you specify the exact vertical position from the top or bottom of the page for all running heads in a document or a division. The Format Paragraph command controls the horizontal position of the running head from the left and right edges of the page. It lets you indent or center running heads, or align them flush left or flush right.

Planning Running-Head Positions

When you create a running head, you can specify its general position on the page. After you choose the Format Running-head command, you find these choices:

```
FORMAT RUNNING-HEAD position: Top Bottom None
             odd pages:(Yes)No  even pages:(Yes)No  first page: Yes(No)
             alignment:(Left-margin)Edge-of-paper
```

Word lets you specify running heads for six different positions:

- Top of first page

- Bottom of first page

- Top of even-numbered pages

- Bottom of even-numbered pages

- Top of odd-numbered pages (excluding the first page)

- Bottom of odd-numbered pages (excluding the first page)

This gives you a lot of flexibility in planning running-head positions, but all these options can be confusing.

To plan which running heads go where, visualize or sketch the first three pages of a document and decide how you want those pages labeled with running heads and page numbers. With this sketch in mind, it will be easy to answer the command fields for the Format Running-head command.

When you're printing on one side of the paper

Most word-processed documents are printed on only one side of the page, so usually you won't need to make the running heads for odd-numbered pages different from the running heads for even-numbered pages. If you're printing on one side of the page, you need to consider only four positions: the top and bottom of the first page and the top and bottom of subsequent pages (both odd- and even-numbered).

Suppose you want two running heads, one at the top of each page and the other at the bottom of each page. The top running head might tell what the document is about and the bottom head might show the page number. (See the section called "Putting page numbers in running heads" later in this chapter.) Type the two running heads as separate paragraphs and format them separately with the Format Running-head command. When formatting the running head that you want at the top of each page, choose *Top* in the *position* field and *Yes* in response to the next three fields: *odd pages*, *even pages*, and *first page*. For the running head that you want at the bottom of each page, choose *Bottom* in the *position* field and *Yes* in each of the page fields.

Notice that the proposed response to the *first page* command field is *No*. Running heads are frequently omitted from the first page, because the first page is often a title page and needs no further identification.

When you're printing on both sides of the paper

If you plan to print or duplicate a document on both sides of the paper, you might want to take advantage of Word's ability to print different running heads on odd-numbered and even-numbered pages. This feature is especially useful if you bind the document—whether you attach the pages with staples, fix the pages in a three-ring binder, or use more permanent binding. With bound documents, it's often desirable to put the page numbers and running heads on the left side of left (even-numbered) pages and on the right side of right (odd-numbered) pages.

Suppose you want a report title to appear at the top of left pages and a section title to appear at the top of right pages (except the first page), with page numbers at the bottom of each page (except the first). Further suppose that you want the page numbers in the outer corners of the pages (on the left side of left pages and the right side of right pages). You would type and format a separate running head for each position:

- *top even* for the report title on left pages

- *top odd* for the section title on right pages

- *bottom even* for left-aligned page numbers on left pages

- *bottom odd* for right-aligned page numbers on right pages

Creating Running Heads

Type running heads at the beginning of the document, at the beginning of the division to which they apply, or at the beginning of a new page.

To create a running head:

1. Type the running head as a paragraph, or as a series of paragraphs. (Running heads can be of any length.)

2. Move the cursor to the running-head paragraph. In those rare instances when the running head is more than one paragraph long, highlight some text in each paragraph.

3. Choose the Format Running-head command.

4. Assign a general position by changing the response to the *position* field from *None* to *Top* or *Bottom*.

5. Indicate whether or not you want the heading to appear on *odd pages*, *even pages*, and the *first page* of the division.

6. Carry out the command.

A paragraph that has been formatted as a running head is printed at the position assigned in the Format Running-head command, not at the position where it was typed and appears on the screen. Word marks any paragraphs that have been formatted as running heads with a caret (^) to the left of the first line of the paragraph. A running head remains in effect from the point in the document where it is typed to the end of the document, to the end of the division (if there is more than one division), or until it is replaced by a new running head that has been assigned the same position.

Vertical positioning of running heads

Word normally prints running heads that are assigned a top-of-page position $1/2$ inch from the top of the page. Running heads assigned the bottom-of-page position are printed $1/2$ inch from the bottom of the page. You can change these measurements with the Format Division Margins command. The *running-head position from top* and *from bottom* command fields control the exact vertical position of all running heads in the document, or in a particular division if you have more than one division.

```
FORMAT DIVISION MARGINS
        top: 1"                 bottom: 1"
        left: 1.25"              right: 1.25"
        page length: 11"        width: 8.5"          gutter margin: 0"
        running-head position from top: 0.5"   from bottom: 0.5"
        mirror margins: Yes(No)              use as default: Yes(No)
```

The *from top* field applies only to running heads that are assigned the *Top* position with the Format Running-head command. The *from bottom* field applies only to running heads assigned the *Bottom* position with the Format Running-head command.

When choosing a measurement for these fields, take into consideration the measurement for the top and bottom margins and the number of lines in the running head. Enter a measurement smaller than the top margin in the *from top* field and a measurement smaller than the bottom margin in the *from bottom* field. If you have a running head that is several lines long, you might have to change the top or bottom margins to accommodate the heads. Allow some space (at least one line, or $1/6$ inch) between the running head and the main body of text.

Horizontal positioning of running heads

Running heads normally are printed with the same margins as the division in which they appear. If you want to print running heads to the left of the left margin or to the right of the right margin, choose the Format Running-head command and change the response in the *alignment* field from *Left-margin* to *Edge-of-paper*. Then use the Format Paragraph command to set left and right indents for each running head. In this case, the indents are measured from the *edges* of the paper—not from the margins. (In version 4.0 of Word, *all* running heads are positioned from the edges of the paper.)

Because running heads are typed in a document as paragraphs, you can use any of the command fields of the Format Paragraph command to format running heads. In addition to indenting them, you can make them flush left, flush right, centered, or justified. If you are printing on both sides of the paper, you might want the running heads of even-numbered pages flush left and the running heads of odd-numbered pages flush right.

Putting page numbers in running heads

Putting page numbers in running heads is the best way to coordinate the position of the page number with the running head. To put the page number in a running head:

1. Type:

   page

   in the running head at the place where you want the page number to appear.

2. Press the F3 key when the cursor is immediately to the right of the word *page*. (Word puts parentheses around *page* after you press F3.)

If you want the word *Page* to precede the number, type:

Page page

instead of *page*. The word *page* is a glossary name. When you press the F3 key, you replace the glossary name with the special glossary entry *(page)*. During printing, Word substitutes the correct page number for the glossary entry *(page)* on each page where the running head appears. If you include page numbers in running heads, be sure that the response for the first command field in the Format Division Page-numbers command is *No*. Otherwise, each page number will print twice. You can also use the Format Division Page-numbers command to choose a number format and starting number for page numbers printed in running heads.

Editing and Deleting Running Heads

You can edit and delete running heads using the same techniques that you use to edit any other paragraph in a document. You can also change running heads back to normal paragraphs that are printed exactly where they are typed in the document. To do that, choose the Format Running-head command while the cursor is in the running head, change the response in the *position* field to *None*, and carry out the command. (In version 4.0 of Word, choose the Format Paragraph command, and answer *No* to each of the command fields—*odd pages*, *even pages*, and *first page*.)

Chapter 11

Filing Documents

To understand what takes place when you're
handling electronic files, think of your computer's memory as a desk top where you work
on documents, and think of individual fixed-disk
directories and floppy disks as filing drawers
where you store documents you're not working
on. Saving a document on a disk is like placing
the document in a file folder, sticking a label on
the file, and putting it in a file cabinet. Loading
a document into memory from a disk is like
opening a file drawer, scanning the labels on
the file folders, pulling a file out, and placing
it on your desk top so that you can read it and
work on it.

With a manual filing system, filing and retrieving a document involves removing it from one place and putting it in another. With an electronic filing system, you move *copies* of documents back and forth without removing the documents from either place. Transferring a document from memory to disk does not remove it from memory. To remove a document from memory, you have to deliberately clear it or replace it with something else by loading another document in its place. Transferring a document from a disk to memory does not remove it from the disk. To remove a document from a disk, you have to deliberately delete it.

The back-and-forth transfer of copies of documents between memory and disks is done with the Transfer command. You've already worked with the three most important file-handling commands: Transfer Save to store documents on disk, Transfer Load to retrieve documents, and Transfer Options to determine where documents are filed. In addition to saving and loading documents, you can delete them from disks or clear them from memory, you can rename them, and you can merge documents by inserting an entire document in another.

Safe storage and easy retrieval of files are the most important filing concerns. Word excels in both areas: Its file-handling commands have so many built-in safeguards that you should never accidentally lose a file.

An important part of Word's filing capabilities is its document-retrieval feature. Document retrieval, based on summary information you provide, lets you search across directories for documents. You can conduct a search on the basis of a document's title, the name of the author or preparer, the creation or revision date, and text in the file. You'll learn about Word's document-retrieval commands in Chapter 15. Before you learn how to use the other file-handling commands, let's look at Word's filing system.

THE KINDS OF FILES AND HOW THEY ARE NAMED

The two main types of files are data files and program files. Data files are files that you create, and program files are the files that help you create them.

Data Files

The *data files* that you create with Word are document files to store documents, glossary files to help you create and edit documents, and style sheet files to help you format documents.

If you give each type of data file a common filename extension, it's easy to tell what kind of file you see on a directory listing by looking at its extension. If you use the extensions that Word recommends, both you and Word will know what kind of file it is. Unless you specify a different filename extension, Word assigns:

.DOC to document files.
.GLY to glossary files.
.STY to style sheet files.

Word automatically makes backup copies of any files you create: It saves the last version of a document, glossary, or style sheet file each time you save a new version, and it gives the filename extension, .BAK, to the last version.

Program Files

A number of *program files* store the Word program and accessory programs or information that Word needs in the course of processing your words. These include the Word program itself, the spelling dictionary, the thesaurus, the hyphenation file, and the help file.

As you work, Word creates temporary files, also called scratch files, with the extension .TMP, to record the editing changes you make to documents. These scratch files are erased after you save your work or end an editing session. Word also creates a file, called MW.INI (Microsoft Word INItialization), to record the name of the document you last worked on and many of the options you last selected so that they are remembered from one editing session to the next. For example, Word records responses to all command fields of the Options command in the MW.INI file.

WHERE TO STORE FILES

If you have two floppy-disk drives, it's usually more convenient to store the program files on a disk in drive A, and the data files on a separate disk in drive B. If you have a fixed disk, you can store both program and data files on the fixed disk. For both a fixed disk and higher-capacity floppy disks, it's best to organize your disk space into subdirectories with separate subdirectories for different categories of files. (See Appendix A.)

The Current Document Drive

Word stores and looks for data files on the disk in the *current document drive*, which initially is the default data drive. For a floppy-disk system, this is drive B; and for a fixed-disk system, it's drive C. If you have multiple directories,

Word stores and looks for data files in the *current document directory*. This is the directory in use in the current document drive when you start the Word program.

You can override the current document drive and directory for an individual file by specifying a different drive and directory when you give the name of the file. Or, you can change the current document drive and directory for all files by specifying a different drive and directory in the *setup* command field of the Transfer Options command. (See Chapter 4.) Word remembers the setup you specify only until you quit Word or clear all of Word's memory with the Transfer Clear All command—unless you tell Word to save your setup. To save your setup, change the response to the *save between sessions* field to *Yes*. The Transfer Options command is especially useful for keeping track of where documents are stored in a multiple-directory system.

SPECIFYING FILENAMES

When you use the file-handling commands, which are covered in the next sections, you must tell Word which file to look for or what name to give to files you're saving or renaming. If you're saving a file for the first time or renaming a file, you must type the name in the *filename* command field. If you're loading, merging, or deleting a file, you can either type in the filename or select it from a list. Whenever you have the choice, select it from a list to avoid mistyping it.

Typing Filenames

It doesn't matter whether you use uppercase letters, lowercase letters, or some combination of both when you type a filename—Word changes them all to uppercase letters. Except when deleting a file, you usually don't have to type the filename extension. When you save a document file, Word assigns the extension .DOC to the filename—unless you type in a different extension. When you retrieve a document file, Word assumes the filename extension is .DOC—unless you type in a different extension.

If you're storing or retrieving a document in the current document directory in the current document drive, you don't have to include the drive and pathname when you type a filename. If you're storing or retrieving a document that is not in the current document drive or directory, you must tell Word where to find it by specifying the drive or directory path (as explained in Chapter 4 and Appendix A).

Viewing and Selecting Filenames from a List

When you're loading, merging, or deleting files, you can ask to see a list of the files on a disk and select a filename from that list. When you're renaming a file, you can ask to see a list of existing filenames, but you can't choose a name from the list.

When the highlight is in the *filename* command field, press the F1 key or point at the command field and click the right mouse button to see a list of files on the current document disk and in the current document directory. To see a list of files in another drive or directory, type the drive and pathname, if necessary, in the command field before you request the list.

Most commands show you a list of .DOC files only. To see a complete directory of all files on the current document disk and in the current document directory, type *.* in the *filename* command field before you request the list. The asterisk (*) is called a wild card: It replaces any number of unspecified characters. You can use it, for example, to request a list of only those files that have a particular extension. Suppose you assign the extension .LET to files that store letters; you can then type *.*LET* to see a list of all .LET files.

To select a filename from a list, use the direction keys to move the highlight to your choice. Then press the F1 key again to move back to the command fields or press the Enter key to carry out the command. With the mouse, point to the filename you want to select and Click-L to select the file, or Click-R to both select the file and carry out the command.

SAVING A DOCUMENT

When Word saves a document, it transfers a copy of the document in the active window to a disk. You've already walked through the steps of saving a document in Chapter 4, but we didn't discuss the Transfer Save command in detail. You use the Transfer Save command to save document files only. (The Transfer Glossary Save command saves glossary files, and the Gallery Transfer Save command saves style sheet files.)

After you choose Transfer Save, you see two command fields:

```
TRANSFER SAVE filename: █
                 format:(Word)Text-only Text-only-with-line-breaks RTF
```

The *filename* Field

In the *filename* field, you specify the name you want to give to the document and the place where you want it saved (if other than the current document drive and directory). If it's already been saved, the proposed response will be the name and location that were used when it was last saved. If you use the proposed response, the previous version of the file is renamed with the filename extension .BAK to indicate that it's a backup copy. If a backup copy for the file already exists, the old .BAK file is deleted. (Should anything happen to the current version of the file, you can load the backup copy and rename it, giving it a .DOC extension or any other extension you choose.)

If you don't use the proposed response and you save the file under a new name or in a new location, you create a new file. The previous version of the file remains unchanged as a separate file. (In most cases, you'll want to use the Transfer Rename command to change a file's name or directory location.) If you type in a name that has already been given to another file on the same floppy disk or in the same directory, you must confirm that you want to overwrite that file.

The *format* Field

For most files, the proposed response *Word* in the *format* command field need not be changed. When you save a file, you usually want to save it as a Word file with any formatting that goes with it. However, the *format* field gives you the options to save the document as a standard ASCII file in which only the text without any formatting is saved (*Text-only*) or as a standard ASCII file in which the text and the line breaks are saved (*Text-only-with-line-breaks*). You have the option to convert the format to what is called *Rich Text Format* (*RTF*).

Saving a document without saving Word's formatting is sometimes necessary if you will be using the file with other software or transmitting the file to other equipment, such as typesetting equipment or non-IBM computers. Most other programs do not understand Word's unique formatting instructions. A standard ASCII file contains characters that are encoded in a way that is standard throughout most of the computer industry. (Pronounced *as-kee*, ASCII stands for American Standard Code for Information Interchange.) This includes printable characters such as letters, numbers, punctuation marks, and symbols, plus nonprintable characters such as spaces, tabs, carriage returns, line feeds, and form feeds. A standard ASCII file does not include any special characters or instructions that control the formatting or printing of a document.

A text-only file is a standard ASCII file that includes carriage returns only at the end of each paragraph. If you want to use a Word file with another program, such as a word-processing or a database program that does not need a carriage return at the end of each line, you can save it as a *text-only* file. If you use Word to write computer programs or to create DOS command files such as CONFIG.SYS and AUTOEXEC.BAT, save them as *text-only* files.

Choose *Text-only-with-line-breaks* in the *format* command field to create a partially formatted ASCII file that is more suitable for telecommunications and that can be printed without being reformatted. When you choose this option, Word replaces many formatting instructions with standard ASCII characters that produce the same results. For example, it replaces instructions about left indents and tabs with spaces. And it maintains the same line breaks by inserting a carriage return and line feed at the end of each line.

The Rich Text Format (RTF) was developed by Microsoft with the hope that it would become an industry standard that would enable documents to be transferred from one application to another without losing any formatting. With RTF, all formatting is converted into ASCII codes—but not all programs can interpret these codes. Before converting a file to RTF, check to see that the receiving software can accept it.

When you want to save a file without Word's standard formatting, it's a good idea to first save it under one filename with Word's usual formatting and then save it without Word's formatting under another filename or filename extension to preserve the original formatting. Simply changing the filename extension from the usual .DOC is an easy way to identify and separate copies of a file that have a nonstandard format. For example, use .TXT (for text-only format), .TLB (for text-only-with-line-breaks format), or .RTF (for Rich Text Format).

If you choose *Text-only* or *Text-only-with-line-breaks* in the *format* command field of the Transfer Save command, Word asks you to confirm your choice:

```
Enter Y to confirm loss of formatting █
```

Press N or the Esc key to cancel the command if you accidentally changed the response to the *format* field.

When to Save a Document

It's a good practice to save your work every half hour or so—more often if you're a fast typist. Then, if the power fails or if your equipment fails, your loss is minimized because you lose only what you did since you last saved. If you don't save frequently, you might run out of workspace in memory or floppy-disk space on both your working copy of Word and the document disk.

Save your work whenever you see the word *SAVE* in the status line. If saving all documents, glossaries, and style sheets doesn't restore the available memory space and turn off the *SAVE* indicator, choose the Transfer Clear All command. If you continue working while the *SAVE* indicator is on, it starts blinking. The Word program might then fail and the computer might lock up. If this happens, you will lose everything you did since you last saved, and you will have to restart the computer and Word.

As you work, Word creates temporary scratch files. If Word runs out of space for these files, it displays either of these messages:

```
Scratch file full
Word disk full
```

in the message line and does not allow any more editing. If your computer seems to lock up and you see one of the above messages while you're working, first reduce the amount of space used for scrap storage. You can do this by copying a single character to the scrap. If the message doesn't disappear, immediately save any documents, glossaries, or style sheets that you're working with. If the message still doesn't disappear after saving everything, use the Transfer Clear All command to clear all memory and to erase all scratch files. You can then reload the document you were working on.

Automatic saving

If you have the Special Edition with disk included, consult the Introduction

If you take advantage of Word's *autosave* feature, the program will back up your files as you work. Every few minutes Word will stop for a moment and save—in temporary files—all the documents, style sheets, and glossaries you are using. Although you must still save a document in a permanent file once you finish editing it, autosave can free you from worry about power failures. The autosave feature also saves your work when the *SAVE* indicator appears.

To enable autosave, choose the Options command and, in the *autosave* field, type the number of minutes you want between automatic saves. You can disable autosave by typing *0* (zero). If you want Word to notify you before doing an automatic save, change the response to the *autosave confirm* field to *Yes*.

Word uses three special filename extensions when it performs an automatic save: .SVD for documents, .SVS for style sheets, and .SVG for glossaries. Normally you never see these files because Word deletes them when you quit the program. However, if something happens to your computer while you are working in Word—for example, you accidentally turn the power off—the autosave files remain on your disk. When you start Word again, it checks for any autosave files on your disk. If it finds any, it asks you if you want to recover them. Press Y to have Word recover the autosave files and save them under their original names.

How to Save a Document

To save a document:

1. Move the cursor to the document window if it isn't already there.

2. Choose the Transfer Save command.

3. Type the name of the file in the *filename* command field if there is no proposed response or if you want to save the document under a new name or in a new location. Include the drive and pathname, if necessary.

4. Change the response to the *format* command field only if you don't want to save Word's usual formatting instructions.

5. Carry out the command.

If you're saving the document for the first time, Word displays a *Summary Information* questionnaire before completing the save. Your answers to the questions provide information for the Library Document-retrieval command. (See Chapter 15 for more information on document retrieval and filling out the summary sheet.) To bypass the summary questions, you can press the Enter key when you see them. By choosing *No* in the *summary sheet* field of the Options command, you can tell Word not to display summary questions when you save new documents.

After the document is written onto a disk, Word displays in the message line the total number of characters in the document. When you save onto a floppy disk, Word also displays, in parentheses, the number of bytes of storage remaining on the disk. The document remains in memory after it is saved. You still see a copy of it in a text window, so you can continue to edit the document or you can print it.

If you type a name that belongs to another document on the same floppy disk or in the same directory, you see the message:

```
File already exists. Enter Y to replace or Esc to cancel ▮
```

If you press Y, the document you're saving replaces the document with the same name. You can cancel the command at this point by pressing N or the Escape key.

Shortcuts for saving documents

If the document you're saving already has a name and you want to save the document under that name, you can sidestep the command fields. To save the file under its current name with Word's formatting instructions included, you can press Ctrl-F10 or, with the mouse, Click-R when you choose the Save subcommand.

If There Is No Room to Save a Document

If Word can't find enough space to save a document, it cancels the Transfer Save command and displays the message: *Document disk full.*

You can make room for the document you want to save by deleting .BAK files or files that you don't need anymore. After you delete any unnecessary files with the Transfer Delete command, try the Transfer Save command again.

If this doesn't do the trick, you can save the document onto another formatted floppy disk. (If necessary, you can format a new disk without leaving Word by using the Library Run command and the DOS Format program. See the section titled ''Running Other Programs'' at the end of this chapter.) You might need to swap disks several times, depending on the amount of memory you have and the length of the file. When Word saves a document on a new floppy disk, it needs access to both the old and the new disks, as well as to the Word program disk. Word prompts you to switch floppy disks when necessary by displaying instructions in the message line.

To save a document on a new floppy disk:

1. Choose the Transfer Save command.

2. When you see *Enter filename* in the message line, remove your current document disk, and insert the new, formatted disk.

3. Enter the filename and carry out the command as usual.

4. When you see a message similar to either of the following messages:

   ```
   Enter Y to retry access to B:\FILENAME.DOC █
   Enter Y to retry access to B:\FILENAME.BAK █
   ```

   insert the disk containing the original copy of the document and then press Y.

5. When you see a message similar to:

   ```
   Enter Y to retry access to B:\MW492280.TMP █
   ```

   insert the new document disk and then press Y.

You might have to repeat steps 4 and 5 a number of times before the save is complete.

LOADING DOCUMENTS

When Word loads a document, it transfers a copy of the document from a disk to memory. Like saving documents, loading documents is not new to you at this point. But let's go over it again so that you can compare it with the other file-handling commands.

After you choose the Transfer Load command, you see the display:

```
TRANSFER LOAD filename: █                    read only: Yes(No)
```

Although you can type in a filename, it's usually easier to select one from a list. The list of filenames shows only those with the .DOC extension in the current document drive and directory unless you specify otherwise.

To see filenames on another disk or in another directory, type the disk name and directory path in the *filename* command field before you press the F1 key to display the list. To see all filenames, regardless of their filename extensions, type *.* in the *filename* command field before you ask for a list. In addition to .DOC files, you can load .BAK files and document files that have filename extensions other than .DOC.

If you type the filename, instead of choosing it from a list, you don't need to type the filename extension if it is .DOC. If the filename has no extension, type a period (.) after the name, so Word won't assume that it has the extension .DOC. You don't need to type the drive name or directory path, unless the file isn't in the current document drive and directory.

In most cases, you won't need to change the proposed response to the *read only* command field. A *No* response lets you view and make changes to the document. A *Yes* response lets you view the document but not revise it unless you save the revised version under a different name. This option protects a file from accidental changes.

How to Load a File

To load a file:

1. If you have more than one window open, move the cursor to the window where you want to load the document.

2. Choose the Transfer Load command.

3. Type in the name of the file you want to load, or press the F1 key (or Click-R in the *filename* command field) to see a list of files and select from it.

4. Change the response to the *read only* command field only if you don't want to make changes to the file.

5. Carry out the command.

After Word loads the file, it tells you how many characters are in it. If there already is a file in the window, Word clears it from the window and memory, provided there are no unsaved changes to it. If there are unsaved changes, Word displays the message:

`Enter Y to save changes to document, N to lose changes, or Esc to cancel ▌`

Press Y to save the existing file before loading a new file. Press N to load the new file without saving changes made to the existing file. Press the Esc key to cancel the command altogether.

If Word cannot find the filename you requested, you see the message:

`File does not exist. Enter Y to create or Esc to cancel ▌`

If you don't want to create a new file, press N or the Esc key to cancel the command and choose the Transfer Load command again. This time, check the list of files in the current document directory to see if the file you want is there. Perhaps you typed the wrong filename, inserted the wrong document disk, or forgot to specify the path for a file that's not in the current directory. Press Y only if you want to create a new file.

DELETING FILES

Whenever you need to make room for new files on a full disk, you can delete unnecessary files or backup copies of files with the Transfer Delete command. You can use this command to delete any kind of file stored on disk, including document files, backup files, glossary files, and style sheet files. As a safeguard against accidental deletion, you cannot delete any files that are currently loaded in memory. If you want to delete a file visible in a window, first clear it from memory with the Transfer Clear Window command.

After you choose the Transfer Delete command, you're asked to specify the name of the file you want to delete:

`TRANSFER DELETE filename: ▌`

As with most filing commands, it's easier to select the name from a list than to type it. In the list, Word displays the names of all files stored in the current document directory and drive.

If you do type the name, instead of selecting it from a list, be sure to type it exactly as it appears in the disk's directory. Always include the filename extension—even if it's a .DOC file. As usual, include the drive and pathname if you're deleting a file that's not in the current drive and directory.

How to Delete a File

To delete a file:

1. Choose the Transfer Delete command.

2. Request a list and select the name of the file that you want to delete from the list, or type the filename in the *filename* command field.

3. Carry out the command.

Word immediately asks you to confirm that you want to delete a file:

```
Enter Y to confirm deletion of file(s) █
```

This lets you double-check the command and cancel it, if you want, by pressing N or the Escape key.

After Word deletes the file, it tells you in the message line how many bytes of storage space are now available on the disk. If you typed in a filename that Word can't find, you see the message: *File does not exist*. Choose the command again, and check the list of filenames to see if you typed in the wrong file, drive, or directory name.

If the file you're trying to delete is currently loaded in memory, you see the message: *Cannot delete file*. If you truly want to delete it, you can use the Transfer Clear Window command and then the Transfer Delete command to delete the file.

RENAMING FILES

The Transfer Rename command lets you change the name of any document file that is currently in memory. If you have more than one window open and more than one document in memory, the Transfer Rename command changes the name of the document with the cursor in it. If you have multiple directories, the Transfer Rename command also lets you change a file's location, removing it from one directory and adding it to another. (You cannot, however, move a file from one disk to another with the Transfer Rename command.)

After you choose the Transfer Rename command, you're asked to give the new name for the file:

`TRANSFER RENAME filename:` `C:\WORDIR\SAMPLE.DOC`

The name shown as the proposed response in the *filename* command field is the existing name and will be changed to the name you type.

When choosing a new filename, remember that you cannot have more than one file on the same floppy disk or in the same directory with the same name. To avoid using a name twice, you can check the filenames in use before you type the new filename. To see the list of all files on the current document disk or in the current document directory, type *.* in the *filename* field, and press the F1 key or Click-R in the field. Then type the new filename, taking care not to use one of the names on the list.

The proposed response also tells you in which drive and directory the file is located. For example, if you were changing the name of a file called OVERDUE.DOC located in the FORMLTTR directory on a fixed disk, you would see:

`TRANSFER RENAME filename:` `C:\FORMLTTR\OVERDUE.DOC`

When you type in a new filename without including a drive and directory path, Word assumes that you want the file stored in the current document drive and directory, regardless of where the file is now stored. In the above example, if FORMLTTR is not the current directory and you type only the new filename in the command field, the file will be saved in the current document drive and directory under the new name and *removed from* the FORMLTTR directory.

If you have multiple directories, you need to be careful that you don't inadvertently give documents a new location when you merely want to give them a new name. On the other hand, the Transfer Rename command is a good tool for purposefully changing a file's location. You can type in a new directory location for a file in the *filename* command field—with or without changing the file's name. When you change a file's directory path with the Transfer Rename command, Word removes the file from the directory it now resides in and stores it in the directory you choose.

How to Rename a File

To rename a file:

1. Load the file, if it isn't already loaded.

2. Move the cursor to the window containing the file you want to rename, if it isn't already there.

3. Choose the Transfer Rename command.

Press   Esc   T   R   *or*   Transfer Click-L   Rename Click-L

4. Type the new name in the *filename* command field. Include the path-name if necessary.

5. Carry out the command.

After the file is renamed, you see the new name in the lower right corner of the window. The name of the backup copy (.BAK file) is not changed. If you type a name that already exists on the disk or in the directory where the document is stored, Word cancels the command and displays the message: *Cannot rename file.* If you get this message, choose the Transfer Rename command again and type in another name.

MERGING FILES

Merging files allows you to join two separate documents. With the Transfer Merge command, you can insert an entire document at any place in another document. Merging documents affects only the contents of memory unless you save the new, merged document. You can save a merged document under a new name if you want to preserve the original documents in their original state (assuming you have enough disk space). Or you can save a merged document under the name of one of the original documents to replace that document with the merged document. You can merge a whole series of documents by repeatedly using the Transfer Merge command.

One reason for merging documents is to print two or more documents as one document with continuous page numbers or footnote numbers. If you want to temporarily merge two or more documents in order to print them as one document, use the Transfer Merge command without saving the merged documents, or use the Print Merge command. With the Print Merge command, you can save the instructions to merge the documents at print time without actually saving the results of merging. (See Chapter 13 for help with the Print Merge command.)

After you choose the Transfer Merge command, you're asked to give the name of the file you want to insert in the active document (that is, the document with the cursor in it):

TRANSFER MERGE filename: ■

If you ask to see a list, Word shows you only the names of files ending in .DOC. If you've been using other filename extensions for your document files, you can see a list of all files by typing *.* in the command field before you request the list.

How to Merge Two Files

To merge two files:

1. Load one of the files if it isn't already in memory.

2. Move the cursor to the place where you want to insert the second file.

3. Choose the Transfer Merge command.

Press | Esc | T | M | *or* | Transfer Click-L | Merge Click-L

4. Select the name of the file that you want to insert from the list of files on the current document disk and in the current document directory, or type the name of the second document in the *filename* command field. Include the pathname if the document is not in the current directory.

5. Carry out the command.

The second document will be inserted to the left of the cursor.

If you enter the name of the active document in the *filename* field, Word cancels the command and displays the message: *Cannot move text into itself.*

If you type a filename that Word can't find, Word cancels the command and displays the message: *File does not exist.* Choose the command again and check the disk's current document directory by pressing the F1 key or by pressing the right mouse button while pointing at the *filename* field.

CLEARING PART OF WORD'S MEMORY

If you have a document in a window, you must clear it from the window and from memory before you can create a new document in that window. You can clear a single document from memory with the Transfer Clear Window command. Clearing Word's memory, whether you clear part or all of it, does not affect anything that is already saved on disk. If anything being cleared from memory isn't saved, Word notifies you and gives you the chance to save it before it's erased.

Clearing a single window removes from memory the document in that window and the style sheet, if any, that has been linked to the document. (If a style sheet named NORMAL.STY is on the document disk, it is loaded into memory after the memory is cleared.) Using the Transfer Clear Window command does not affect the contents of glossary memory. To clear only the glossary from memory, use the Transfer Glossary Clear command, as described in Chapter 8.

How to Clear a Single Window

To clear the contents of one window:

1. Move the cursor to the window you want to clear, if you have more than one window open.

2. Choose the Transfer Clear Window command:

Press [Esc] [T] [C] [W] or Transfer Click-L Clear Click-L Window Click-L

Word clears the window immediately after you choose the command. If there are unsaved changes to the document, you see the message:

```
Enter Y to save changes to document, N to lose changes, or Esc to cancel █
```

Press Y to save the document before clearing the window. Press N to clear the window without saving the document. Press the Esc key to cancel the command without saving or clearing.

If there are unsaved changes to the style sheet attached to the document, you see a similar message:

```
Enter Y to save changes to style sheet, N to lose changes, or Esc to cancel █
```

CLEARING ALL OF WORD'S MEMORY

Using the Transfer Clear All command is like starting Word from scratch. Unlike most of the other Transfer commands, the Transfer Clear All command affects more than document files. It erases all documents, glossaries, and style sheets from memory, as well as temporary files that Word creates. If you have opened additional windows, they are closed. If there is a glossary file named NORMAL.GLY, and a style sheet file named NORMAL.STY on the document disk, they are loaded into memory after all memory is cleared.

The Transfer Clear All command is a quick way to close all windows and open one new, empty window in which you can create a new document or load a document from disk.

How to Clear All of Word's Memory

To clear all of Word's memory:

- Choose the Transfer Clear All command.

Press [Esc] [T] [C] [A] or **Transfer** Click-L **Clear** Click-R

If there are no unsaved changes to any documents, glossaries, or style sheets currently in memory, Word immediately removes all the contents of memory and loads NORMAL.STY and NORMAL.GLY, if those files are available on the current document disk.

If there are unsaved changes to any documents in memory, Word highlights the document and displays the message:

```
Enter Y to save changes to document, N to lose changes, or Esc to cancel █
```

If there are unsaved changes to any style sheets in memory, you see the message:

```
Enter Y to save changes to style sheet, N to lose changes, or Esc to cancel █
```

If there are unsaved changes to any glossaries in memory, you see the message:

```
Enter Y to save changes to glossary, N to lose changes, or Esc to cancel █
```

Pressing Y in response to any of these messages makes Word save the document, glossary, or style sheet indicated in the message before clearing the memory. Pressing N tells Word not to save the document, glossary, or style sheet. Pressing the Escape key cancels the Transfer Clear All command.

RUNNING OTHER PROGRAMS

The Library Run command is your key to running other programs without leaving the Word program. As discussed in Appendix A, DOS has a number of programs that help you manage files, such as COPY, DIR, FORMAT, DEL, and REN. To run these or other programs without quitting Word, first choose the Library Run command. Then type in the DOS command that starts the program. For example, to format a blank floppy disk in drive B, type:

FORMAT B:

If the Format program cannot be found, Word displays the message: *Bad command or file name.* If this happens, press any key to return to Word, insert a DOS disk in drive A that has the Format program on it, and try the command again. (If the program is not in the current document directory in the current document drive, include the correct drive and pathname when typing the program name.) After the Format program finishes, Word displays the message: *Press a key to resume Word.*

Chapter 12

Printing Documents

Word offers an assortment of printing commands and options that take care of a wide variety of printing needs. In this chapter, you'll learn how to print more than one copy of a document, print any part of a document, speed up printing by ignoring some formatting instructions, edit a document while printing one or more documents, and change printers without changing the document or permanently altering the program. In addition, you'll learn how to use your computer as a typewriter, printing characters as soon as you type them; repaginate a document without printing it; and send the printer output to a file instead of to the printer.

INTRODUCING YOUR PRINTER

The first time you print a document, you need to introduce Word to your printer. To take advantage of whatever features your printer offers, Word needs to know what kind of printer you're using, how your printer is connected to your computer, and what kind of paper feeder you have. If you used the Setup program described in Appendix B, Word already knows most of this information. If you tried printing and experienced difficulty, choose the Print Options command and check to see if the responses to the *printer*, *setup*, *model*, *graphics resolution*, and *paper feed* command fields describe your printer.

If you have the Special Edition with disk included, consult the Introduction

```
PRINT OPTIONS printer: EPSONFX              setup: LPT1:
           model: FX-286e & FX-1050          graphics resolution: 60 dpi
           copies: 1                         draft: Yes(No)
           hidden text: Yes(No)              summary sheet: Yes(No)
           range:(All)Selection Pages        page numbers:
           widow/orphan control:(Yes)No      queued: Yes(No)
           paper feed: Continuous            duplex: Yes(No)
```

If you change your printer, your paper feeder, or your printer hookup, you might need to change the printer information shown in the Print Options command.

The first command field, *printer*, should show the name of the .PRD file that matches your printer. If it doesn't, press the F1 key while the *printer* field is highlighted to see a list of printer description files on your Word program disk or in your fixed-disk directory. If you see a .PRD file that matches your printer, select it. (Use the direction keys to move the highlight to the .PRD file you want, and press the F1 key again.)

If you don't see a .PRD file that matches your printer, you can choose the TTY.PRD file as a stopgap solution. Although TTY.PRD ignores any advanced capabilities that your printer might have, it will enable almost any printer to work. Later, run the Setup program again, as described in Appendix B, to add the correct printer description file to your copy of Word.

The *setup* field tells Word where to send the printer signals by providing the DOS device name that describes the printer hookup. Valid responses are *LPT1:*, *LPT2:*, or *LPT3:* for parallel printers connected to parallel-printer adapters, and *COM1:* or *COM2:* for serial printers connected to asynchronous communications adapters.

The easiest way to find out the correct device name for your printer is to try the various names until you find the one that works. If you have only one printer connected to your computer, it is either LPT1: (for a parallel printer) or COM1: (for a serial printer). If you're not sure which kind of printer you have, first try LPT1: and then COM1:. (LPT2:, LPT3:, and COM2: are usually used only if you have more than one printer of the same type connected to your computer at the same time.)

To change the device name shown in the *setup* command field, use the direction keys to move to the field, and press the F1 key to see a list of alternatives. Use the direction keys again to move the highlight to your choice, and press the F1 key to return to the command fields.

The *model* and *graphics resolution* fields further describe your particular printer. (If you are using version 4.0 of Word, you won't see these fields.) As with the *printer* and *setup* fields, press the F1 key to see a list of possible responses and choose the model and graphics resolution that match your printer. If no list is available for the .PRD file shown in the *printer* field, Word will beep and display the message: *List is empty.*

The *paper feed* command field tells Word what kind of paper feeder your printer has and instructs Word how to make use of it. To change the response, use the direction keys to highlight the field and press the F1 key. Word will display the types of paper feeders available for the printer you selected earlier. Highlight your choice, and press the F1 key again. (In version 4.0 of Word, the command field is simply called *feed*. Move the highlight to the field, and then press the Spacebar until your choice is highlighted.)

When *Continuous* is chosen, Word expects paper to be fed continuously by either an automatic sheet feeder or tractor feed for continuous paper. *Manual* indicates that you will feed sheets of paper manually. With manual feed, Word stops after printing each page and waits for you to insert another sheet. After you press Y, it prints the next page. The *Bin1*, *Bin2*, and *Bin3* responses tell Word that you have an automatic sheet feeder with multiple bins of paper. The number (1, 2, or 3) tells Word which bin of paper to use. When you choose *Mixed*, Word takes a sheet of paper from bin 1 of a multiple-bin feeder to print the first page and takes paper from bin 2 to print subsequent pages: Use this option for documents that use letterhead stationery for the first page and blank sheets or a different letterhead for other pages.

If you change any of the responses to the *printer, setup, model, graphics resolution,* or *paper feed* command fields, you must press the Enter key (or use the mouse) to carry out your changes. Word records your responses and remembers them until you change them.

HOW TO START PRINTING

You can start printing at any time. You don't have to wait until you save the document. But the document must be in a window before you can print it. If you have more than one window open, move the cursor to the document you want to print.

Most of the time, you can start printing by simply turning on your printer and choosing the Print Printer command:

The Print Printer has no command fields. All options that control how a document is printed are found in a separate command—the Print Options command. Before you choose the Print Printer command, you might want to choose the Print Options command so that you can reset or simply review the responses to its command fields. (See the section called "The Print Options Command" later in this chapter.)

The Print Printer command is carried out as soon as you choose it. Before Word starts printing, it formats the document, determining where to break pages and adjusting the formatting instructions to suit your printer. To determine how much text will fit on each page, Word takes into consideration all division, paragraph, and character formats that you assigned while you were creating and editing the document. While it is formatting each page, you see a message that tells you which page it's formatting.

HOW TO STOP PRINTING

Once printing starts, you can temporarily interrupt it or you can cancel it altogether. To interrupt or stop printing, press the Esc key. Word stops printing and displays the message:

```
Enter Y to continue or Esc to cancel █
```

When you're ready to restart printing, continuing from where you left off, press Y. If, instead, you decide to cease printing, press the Esc key again.

THE PRINT OPTIONS COMMAND

Choose the Print Options command before you start printing if you want to:

- Change printers or the paper-feeding arrangement.

- Print more than one copy of a document.

- Speed up printing.

- Print hidden text.

- Print a summary sheet with the document.

- Print part of a document, instead of the whole document.

- Disregard widows and orphans.

- Edit a document while printing.

- Print a series of files.

- Print on both sides of the paper.

As explained earlier in this chapter, you need to change the responses to the *printer* and probably the *setup* fields of the Print Options command if you want to change printers. And if you want to change the paper-feeding arrangement, you need to change the *paper feed* command field. The other printing options are explained below.

Printing Multiple Copies

You can instruct Word to print more than one copy of a document by typing the number of copies you want in the *copies* command field of the Print Options command. This is faster and easier than repeatedly choosing the Print Printer command to generate more than one copy.

```
PRINT OPTIONS printer: EPSONFX          setup: LPT1:
       model: FX-286e & FX-1050         graphics resolution: 60 dpi
       copies: 3                        draft: Yes(No)
       hidden text: Yes(No)             summary sheet: Yes(No)
       range:(All)Selection Pages       page numbers:
       widow/orphan control:(Yes)No     queued: Yes(No)
       paper feed: Continuous           duplex: Yes(No)
```

Printing at Top Speed

If you're more interested in reviewing the content of a document than seeing it formatted, you can speed up the printing by changing the response in the *draft* field from *No* to *Yes*.

```
PRINT OPTIONS printer: EPSONFX          setup: LPT1:
       model: FX-286e & FX-1050         graphics resolution: 60 dpi
       copies: 1                        draft: Yes No
       hidden text: Yes(No)             summary sheet: Yes(No)
       range:(All)Selection Pages       page numbers:
       widow/orphan control:(Yes)No     queued: Yes(No)
       paper feed: Continuous           duplex: Yes(No)
```

When Word prints a draft, it saves printing time by ignoring special formats like boldface and italics, microspace justification on dot-matrix printers, and font changes for impact printers.

Printing Hidden Text

Text that you mark as hidden with the Format Character or Alt-E command is not usually printed. To print hidden text, whether it is visible on the screen or not, choose *Yes* in the *hidden text* field of the Print Options command.

```
PRINT OPTIONS printer: EPSONFX          setup: LPT1:
       model: FX-286e & FX-1050         graphics resolution: 60 dpi
       copies: 1                        draft: Yes(No)
       hidden text: Yes No              summary sheet: Yes(No)
       range:(All)Selection Pages       page numbers:
       widow/orphan control:(Yes)No     queued: Yes(No)
       paper feed: Continuous           duplex: Yes(No)
```

Printing Summary Sheets

When the *summary sheet* option is set to *Yes*, Word prints summary information on a separate page before printing the document.

```
PRINT OPTIONS printer: EPSONFX          setup: LPT1:
       model: FX-286e & FX-1050         graphics resolution: 60 dpi
       copies: 1                        draft: Yes(No)
       hidden text: Yes(No)             summary sheet: Yes No
       range:(All)Selection Pages       page numbers:
       widow/orphan control:(Yes)No     queued: Yes(No)
       paper feed: Continuous           duplex: Yes(No)
```

The summary that Word prints is a copy of the Summary Information questionnaire that you optionally fill out when you first save a document. By using the Library Document-retrieval command, explained in Chapter 15, you can print the summary sheet alone or along with the document.

Printing Part of a Document

If you want to print only part of a document, you can highlight the part you want to print and change the response in the *range* field from *All* to *Selection*.

```
PRINT OPTIONS printer: EPSONFX                setup: LPT1:
        model: FX-286e & FX-1050              graphics resolution: 60 dpi
        copies: 1                             draft: Yes(No)
        hidden text: Yes(No)                  summary sheet: Yes(No)
        range: All Selection Pages            page numbers:
        widow/orphan control:(Yes)No          queued: Yes(No)
        paper feed: Continuous                duplex: Yes(No)
```

If you have the Special Edition with disk included, consult the Introduction

Instead of printing a highlighted section of the document, you can print specified pages by first choosing the *Pages* response. Then you must specify the page numbers that you want to print in the *page numbers* field. To print a range of pages, type the starting page number and the ending page number, separated by either a hyphen (-) or a colon (:). For example, type:

4-7

to print pages 4, 5, 6, and 7.

If you want to print the last part of a document but you don't know the last page number, type a large number after the hyphen. For example, to print from page 20 to the end of a 52-page document, you could type:

20-100

If the pages that you want to print are not consecutive, separate the page numbers with commas, instead of hyphens. For example, type:

4,7,9

to print pages 4, 7, and 9. You can specify both consecutive and nonconsecutive page numbers at the same time. For example, type:

2-4,22,24

to print pages 2, 3, 4, 22, and 24.

Because page numbering can restart at page 1 for each division, you might have duplicate page numbers in a document. In that case, type the division number after the page number to specify the page you want to print. For example, type:

8D2

to print page eight in the second division.

Controlling Widows and Orphans

As explained in Chapter 11, Word avoids creating widows and orphans by refusing to print single lines of paragraphs at the tops and bottoms of pages. If you do not want Word to do this, choose *No* in the *widow/orphan control* field.

```
PRINT OPTIONS printer: EPSONFX        setup: LPT1:
        model: FX-286e & FX-1050      graphics resolution: 60 dpi
        copies: 1                     draft: Yes(No)
        hidden text: Yes(No)          summary sheet: Yes(No)
        range:(All)Selection Pages    page numbers:
        widow/orphan control: Yes No  queued: Yes(No)
        paper feed: Continuous        duplex: Yes(No)
```

With *widow/orphan control* off, Word fills up the page, as defined by the margins, without regard for widows and orphans. You might want to turn off *widow/orphan control* when, for example, you want the same number of lines on each page or when you're trying to print a document on as few pages as possible. You can still control where individual page breaks occur by asking to confirm page breaks with the Print Repaginate command.

Printing While Editing

Word's queued printing feature lets you continue editing while printing a document. If you change the response to the *queued* command field from *No* to *Yes*, Word prints in the background, leaving the screen free for you to continue working.

```
PRINT OPTIONS printer: EPSONFX        setup: LPT1:
        model: FX-286e & FX-1050      graphics resolution: 60 dpi
        copies: 1                     draft: Yes(No)
        hidden text: Yes(No)          summary sheet: Yes(No)
        range:(All)Selection Pages    page numbers:
        widow/orphan control:(Yes)No  queued: Yes No
        paper feed: Continuous        duplex: Yes(No)
```

Word does an admirable job of managing your computer's resources so that editing while printing is not so slow that it's impractical—as it is with many other word processors. However, the dual tasks do slow down editing, and you need room on your document disk for an extra copy of the file that you're printing. Before it starts printing a queued file, Word formats the file for printing, as usual, and temporarily stores that printer version of the file on your document disk so that most of the computer's memory is free for other tasks. This temporary printer file is deleted after it's printed.

To print while editing:

1. Load the document you want to print.

2. With the cursor in that document, choose the Print Options command. Change the response to the *queued* command field from *No* to *Yes* and carry out the command.

3. Choose the Print Printer command to start printing.

Wait for Word to format the file to be printed and to write the printer file to disk. When Word starts printing, you can start editing the document that's being printed, you can load another document to edit, or you can clear all or part of Word's memory so that you can start creating a new document.

If you want to stop printing temporarily, choose the Print Queue Pause command. When you're ready to continue printing from where you left off, choose the Print Queue Continue command. If you want to restart printing from the beginning of the document, choose the Print Queue Restart command.

If you want to cancel the queued printing altogether, choose the Print Queue Stop command.

Printing a series of files

When you use the queued option, as described in the previous section, you can put more than one file in the printing queue. This allows you to instruct Word to print a series of documents. You don't have to wait for Word to finish printing each document before you tell it to print the next one, but you do have to wait for Word to finish formatting each document before you tell it to print the next one.

Again, you must have enough space on your document disk to hold extra copies of the files you print. And again, you can edit or create documents while Word is printing.

To print a series of documents, start by following the instructions in the previous section for printing while editing. After Word finishes formatting the first document:

1. Load the next document to be printed.

2. With the cursor in that document, choose the Print Printer command.

3. Wait for Word to finish formatting that document.

4. Repeat steps 1 through 3 for each additional document that you want to print.

Each time you choose the Print Printer command, you're instructing Word to format the document that is currently in the active window and to store that document in a temporary printer file until it is printed. After Word finishes printing one temporary printer file, it deletes that file and starts printing the temporary printer file that was created next. Word starts printing each document on a new page.

Printing on Both Sides of the Paper

If your printer is capable of printing on both sides of a sheet of paper, you can set the *duplex* field to *Yes* to instruct Word to print on both sides.

```
PRINT OPTIONS printer: EPSONFX                setup: LPT1:
       model: FX-286e & FX-1050               graphics resolution: 60 dpi
       copies: 1                              draft: Yes(No)
       hidden text: Yes(No)                   summary sheet: Yes(No)
       range:(All)Selection Pages             page numbers:
       widow/orphan control:(Yes)No           queued: Yes(No)
       paper feed: Continuous                 duplex: Yes No
```

OTHER PRINT COMMANDS

All printing features covered so far are activated by changing responses to command fields in the Print Options command before choosing the Print Printer command. A few more printing commands activate other features, independent of the Print Printer command:

- The Print Repaginate command allows you to repaginate a document without printing it and to confirm page breaks before printing.

- The Print Direct command allows you to use your printer as a typewriter.

- The Print File command allows you to save the printer version of a document in a file instead of printing it.

- The Print preView command allows you to see the full-page layout of your document before you print it. (Note that the Print preView command is not available in versions of Word prior to version 5.0.)

Repaginating Without Printing

Normally, Word decides where new pages in a document start as you type. However, sometimes you might want to make changes to a document based on a previously printed copy. You can tell Word not to paginate a document until it's printed by choosing the Options command and changing the response in the *paginate* field from *Auto* to *Manual*. (Versions of Word prior to version 5.0 always use manual repagination.) The advantage of postponing pagination until a document is printed is that the page numbers that appear on the screen always match the page numbers in the last printed copy of a document—no matter how many changes you made to the document since you last printed it. As mentioned before, this is helpful when you're making changes that were marked on a printed copy; the Jump Page command always finds the page on the screen that corresponds to the printed page that you have in hand.

If you're creating or editing a document with manual repagination but you don't want to wait until you print it to see how many pages you have and where new pages will start, use the Print Repaginate command. The document won't be printed, but the page breaks and page numbers in the status line are updated as if it were printed. Pressing the Escape key during repagination cancels the command and resets all page breaks to where they were before you chose the command.

To repaginate a document without printing it, choose the Print Repaginate command:

Press ⬚Esc ⬚P ⬚R *or* Print Click-L Repaginate Click-L

Word displays a single command field:

```
PRINT REPAGINATE confirm page breaks: Yes No
```

With the proposed response of *No*, Word paginates the document for you after you carry out the command. Page breaks that Word inserts are called *soft page breaks* and are marked with a dotted line lighter than the dotted line that appears for *hard page breaks* that you insert. Soft page breaks can change if you revise a document. Hard page breaks stay in place until you delete them.

Approving page breaks

If you want to check each page break and have the opportunity to move it while Word is formatting, choose *Yes* in the *confirm page breaks* field of the Print Repaginate command. If you choose *Yes*, Word stops to highlight the first character of each new page and waits for you to confirm or move the page break. If it's a page break inserted by Word, you see the message:

```
Enter Y to confirm page break or use direction keys to reposition ▮
```

You can press Y to accept the page break, or you can press the Up direction key to move the page break up before you press Y. If you move the page break, Word inserts a hard page-break character (a heavy dotted line) instead of a soft page break.

If Word finds a page break that you inserted, it gives you the opportunity to remove it:

```
Enter Y to confirm or R to remove page break ▮
```

If you remove it, Word proposes a new break (if necessary) and gives you the opportunity to approve it or move it up.

It's a plus to have this option to control where Word breaks a document into pages, but most documents don't require such close attention to each and every page break. Remember that you have other tools to prevent undesirable page breaks—the *keep together* and *keep follow* command fields of the Format Paragraph command and the *widow/orphan control* field of the Print Options command.

Using Your Computer as a Typewriter

No matter how well versed you are in Word or any other word-processing program, sometimes you might prefer to use a typewriter. Creating, formatting, and printing a file might seem like a long route to take when you just want to type a short note or an address on an envelope.

Word attempts to solve this problem with the Print Direct command. This command makes your printer and keyboard behave somewhat like a typewriter. As you type on the keyboard, characters are sent, one at a time, directly to the printer, instead of to the screen or to memory. Unfortunately, direct printing is not without its own problems.

Printing starts at the far left edge of the paper, unless you space over to another printing position, and continues to the right edge of the paper until you press the Enter key. You can't correct mistakes (not even with the Backspace key), nor can you format the characters you type. In fact, you can't even see them on the screen: Whatever was on the screen when you started direct printing remains on the screen. The characters you type appear on the paper only, and with some printers, they are not printed until you press the Enter key to start a new line.

You can use the Print Direct command when you first start up Word or when you are in the middle of editing another document. You don't have to stop to save the document or clear the window first.

To use your printer as a typewriter:

1. Choose the Print Direct command.

2. Space over to where you want to start typing.

3. Type the text, pressing the Enter key to start new lines or to skip lines.

4. Press Esc to cancel the command when you want to go back to editing.

Printing to a File

With the Print File command, you can send the printer version of a document to a permanent file on disk, rather than to a printer. After you quit Word, you can print this file using the DOS commands COPY or PRINT (or any equivalent copy or print utility): You cannot print it using Word. You get almost the same results as if you had printed it with Word.

You might use the Print File command to create a file that can be printed by someone who has the same disk operating system (or an equivalent) but does not have the Word program.

To print a document to a file instead of to the printer:

1. Load the document.

2. With the cursor in the document, choose the Print File command:

Press Esc P F *or* Print Click-L File Click-L

3. Type a name for the new file in the *filename* command field. (Give it a filename extension, such as .PRN, that distinguishes it from ordinary document files. If you don't specify an extension, Word does not add one.)

4. Carry out the command.

Previewing Before You Print

If you have a monitor that can display graphics, you can see what your document will look like before you print it. The Print preView command displays one or two pages at a time, scaled to fit your screen. You might not be able to read everything clearly, but you can easily see the layout of the document.

To preview a document:

1. Load the document.

2. With the cursor in the document, choose the Print preView command.

3. To move forward or backward through the document, press the PgUp or PgDn key to move one page at a time. To move rapidly to another point in the document, choose the Jump subcommand or Click-LR on the vertical scroll bar (the left edge of the screen).

4. Press E (for Exit) to resume editing.

The one printing command that we haven't talked about yet is the Print Merge command. To find out about this command, as well as a host of other commands that represent Word's most advanced features, turn to Part III of this book.

PART III

SUPER WORD

Chapter 13

Merge Printing

The command that eliminates more repetitive, numbing work than any other command is the Print Merge command. With Print Merge, you have at your fingertips a most amazing duplicating machine. Not only can it churn out countless printed copies of a document, but it can alter each copy according to your instructions. Each copy can be individually tailored to suit its intended audience.

As copies of a document are being printed, Word can methodically insert selected bits and pieces of text from another file, insert an entire document from another file, or prompt you to tell it what to insert.

In this chapter, I'll cover two applications of the Print Merge command that can save you a lot of time without using a lot of disk space: mass mailings and chain printing.

MASS MAILINGS

To understand how mass mailings are generated, first imagine what you would do if you were instructing an assistant to send the same letter to a number of people—but you wanted each letter to be an original, not a copy. You would hand your assistant two things: a draft of the basic letter that goes to everyone and a list of the names and addresses of the people to whom you want to send the letter.

You might draw blank lines on the letter to indicate where the name and address go, and you might spell out exactly what goes in each blank by labeling each one, as blanks on a form are labeled. You could then instruct your assistant to type a copy of the letter for each person on the list. When typing the letters, your assistant would refer to the mailing list and substitute information from the list for each labeled blank in the letter.

With Word, you can type the letter once, provide Word with a mailing list, and then watch as Word prints a copy of the letter for each person on the list. Word plugs in names and addresses from the list as it prints the letters. The basic letter is called the *main document,* and the mailing list is called a *data document.* You must prepare both the main document and the data document in such a way that Word understands what you want to do.

Preparing the Main Document

The main document for a mass mailing is usually a letter, but it can be any kind of document that you want to mass-produce and yet personalize. You prepare the main document as you would prepare any other document, except that you include some instructions to Word and you use *field names* to represent the text that varies from one copy of the document to another. The *instructions* tell Word where to find the text to substitute for the field names.

Each instruction or field name that you type in the document must be enclosed in the special symbols « and », so that Word knows it is not to be printed as part of the text. These symbols do not appear on any of the key tops on your keyboard, so you must:

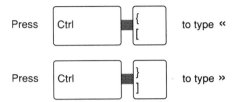

The field names

The field names tell Word *what* information from the data document goes in the document, and the positions of the names tell Word *where* to put it. The field names are similar to the labeled blanks that you see on a form. You can use any name to refer to a field (one item) of information. The name can be up to 64 characters long and should clearly identify what you're referring to. Use letters and numbers but no spaces or decimal points. Begin each field name with a letter (rather than a number or symbol).

If your main document is a letter, it might start out like this:

```
                              (dateprint)

«contact»
«company»
«street»
«city», «state»  «zip»

Dear «greeting»,

I am happy to announce that we are now the authorized
distributors for Designer Diskettes by Pierre Flopet.
```

Notice that the glossary name *dateprint* is being used in the sample letter to insert the current date in printed copies of the letter. When you're preparing documents that you plan to use for more than one mailing, it's better to instruct Word to fill in the date for you. Wherever you want the current date to appear, type *dateprint* and press the F3 key. (See Chapter 10 for more information on the use of *dateprint*.)

The DATA instruction

If you want Word to get names and addresses (or any other variable information) from a separately prepared list, or data document, you must use the DATA instruction to tell Word the filename and location of the data document.

You must type the DATA instruction at the very beginning of the main document. The instruction starts with the word *DATA* and is followed by a space and then the filename of the data document. Word needs to know the complete name of the data document, including the filename extension if it is not .DOC. For example, if the data document you want to use is called *CUSTOMER.LST*, you would type:

«DATA CUSTOMER.LST»

as the first line of your document. If the data document isn't in the current document drive or directory, include also the drive and pathname. For example, type:

«DATA C:\SALES\CUSTOMER.LST»

to tell Word that the data document called CUSTOMER.LST is in the SALES directory on the disk in drive C.

It doesn't matter to Word whether you type instructions and field names in uppercase or lowercase letters. In the sample documents here, I'll use uppercase letters for instructions to distinguish them from field names, which I'll put in lowercase letters.

Preparing the Data Document

You can prepare a data document with Word. A data document looks something like a table, with column headings and rows of information. Unlike entries in a table, however, the information in a data document is usually squeezed together to save space, rather than aligned in neat columns. Here's a short data document that might be used with the example letter in the previous section:

```
company, contact, greeting, street, city, state, zip
PreFab Bridges Corp., George Girder, Mr. Girder, 1593
Suspension Rd., Birmingham, AL, 23098
Hedgerow Enterprises, Joseph Bush, Joe, 1302 Border Lane,
Evergreen Village, NH, 10386
Gemstone Jewellers, Ruby Rhinestone, Ruby, 433 Diamond
Blvd., Wichita, KS, 49708
```

The header record

The first line of column headings is called the *header record*.

```
company, contact, greeting, street, city, state, zip
```

Notice that the field names in the sample letter match names in the header record. The field names are the key to what's in the data document, and they must appear in the first line of the data document. As in the main document, each field name can be up to 64 characters long and should describe the kind of information found in that field.

To let Word know where one field name ends and the next one begins, you must separate the names with a single comma, semicolon, or tab character. To end the header record, press the Enter key. If you use commas or semicolons to separate field names, you can also put an optional space after each comma or semicolon so that the field names are a little easier to read.

You can use tabs instead of commas or semicolons to make a much more readable data document. But in order to align the columns of information, you have to set tabs that allow for the longest entry in each column. In a long data document, this can be more trouble than it's worth. If you try it, be careful not to insert more than one tab character between columns, or Word will misread your data document.

The data records

Each row of information under the header record is called a *data record*. Data records contain the pieces of information that are inserted in place of the field names in the main document. In a data document that stores a simple mailing list, a data record would include all the mailing information that you have for one person or company. For example:

```
PreFab Bridges Corp., George Girder, Mr. Girder, 1593
Suspension Rd., Birmingham, AL, 23098
```

Each piece of information in a data record is called a *field entry*. The field entries in each data record must be in the same order as the corresponding field names in the header record. The number of field names in the header record and the number of field entries in each data record must be the same. That is, your information table must have as many columns as it has column headings. But a data document can have more fields of information than are called for by a main document.

Each field entry can be as long as you like, and you can have up to 256 separate fields for each record. As with field names, you must separate field entries with a single comma, semicolon, or tab character—whichever you use in the header record. To let Word know where one record ends and the next one begins, end each record by pressing the Enter key *once*. Be sure that you don't press the Enter key *before* you get to the end of the data record—otherwise Word will look in the wrong places to find the information that corresponds to the field names. If you press the Enter key more than once *after* a data record, Word also gets confused.

You can leave a field blank by not typing anything in the field, but don't forget to separate the blank field from the other fields with the usual comma, semicolon, or tab. For example, if the second record in the sample mailing list didn't have a street address, the record would look like this:

```
Hedgerow Enterprises, Joseph Bush, Joe,, Evergreen Village,
NH, 10386
```

If a field entry contains a comma, semicolon, or tab, you must enclose the entire field entry in double quotes to signal Word that the comma is not a field separator. For example, if Gemstone Jewellers was located in Suite 303, its record would look like this:

```
Gemstone Jewellers, Ruby Rhinestone, Ruby, "433 Diamond
Blvd., Suite 303", Wichita, KS, 49708
```

If a field entry contains double quotes, you must type each double quote twice and enclose the entire field entry in another set of double quotes. For example, if George Girder went by the nickname ''Chip'' (with quotes around it), his record would be:

```
PreFab Bridges Corp., George Girder, """"Chip"""", 1593
Suspension Rd., Birmingham, AL, 23098
```

Saving a data document

When you use the Transfer Save command to save a data document, you can give it any name you like. You might want to assign it a filename extension, such as .LST or .DAT, to indicate that it is a data document and not an ordinary document. When you save a data document created with Word, you can choose *Word* in the *format* command field.

Preparing data documents with other programs

If you create a lot of data documents, you should consider purchasing a data-management program that makes entering, editing, and sorting data easier. Most mailing-list programs, filing programs, and database programs produce data files that Word can use: ASCII files with fields separated by commas, semicolons, or tab characters and with each record terminated with a single carriage return (paragraph mark). Data files created by other programs do not include header records. So, if you create a data document with some other program, you need to create a separate document to store the header record. You must include the name of that document, along with the name of the data document, in the DATA instruction of the main document.

If you use a data-management program, you might need to experiment a little. The *Using Microsoft Word* manual offers some tips for using data documents that were not created with Word.

Merging the Main Document with the Data Document

After you prepare the main document and the data document, you're ready to merge them using the Print Merge command. The main document and the data document can be on separate disks, but both disks must be in the computer when you choose the Print Merge command. The instructions in the main document tell Word what to do, so you start by loading the main document with the Transfer Load command. Then, choose the Print Merge command:

Press [Esc] [P] [M]   or   Print Click-L   Merge Click-L

The Print Merge command branches into three subcommands:

    PRINT MERGE: Printer Document Options

The Print Merge Options command gives you the choice of merging all records in the data document with the main document or merging only selected records:

    PRINT MERGE OPTIONS range: All Records   record numbers:

All, the proposed response, prints a copy of the main document for each record in the data document. Choose *Records* if you want a copy of the main document for only some records. If you choose *Records*, indicate which records you want in the *record numbers* command field. If you want a range of records printed, separate the beginning and ending numbers of the range with a hyphen. For example, type *10-20* to merge records 10 *through* 20 with the main document. List individual record numbers by separating them with a comma. For example, type *10,20* to merge records 10 *and* 20 with the main document.

After you carry out the Print Merge Options command, Word takes you back to the Print Merge command where you can choose to send the merged information directly to a printer or to a file:

    PRINT MERGE: Printer Document Options

Choose the Printer subcommand to print the merged documents without viewing them on the screen. After choosing the Print Merge Printer command, Word prints the first copy of the document, inserting the data from the first (or first selected) record in the data document. It continues printing copies of the document until each data record specified in the Print Merge Options command is used.

Neither the data document nor the main document is altered by the merge printing. The results of the merging appear only on the printed copies of the document. Figure 13-1 shows the results of merging the sample letter (main document) and the data document that you saw in the previous sections.

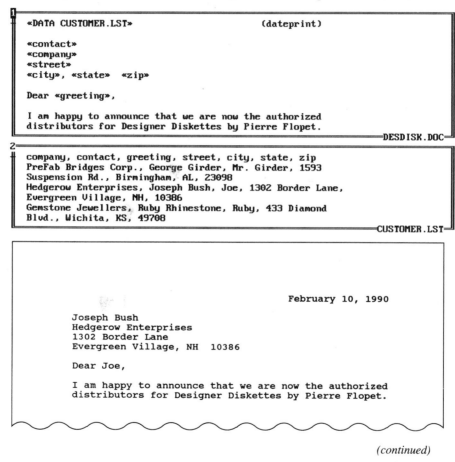

(continued)

Figure 13-1. *A sample main document and data document and the results of merge printing them.*

Figure 13-1. *continued*

```
                                        February 10, 1990

    George Girder
    PreFab Bridges Corp.
    1593 Suspension Rd.
    Birmingham, AL  23098

    Dear Mr. Girder,

    I am happy to announce that we are now the authorized
    distributors for Designer Diskettes by Pierre Flopet.
```

```
                                        February 10, 1990

    Ruby Rhinestone
    Gemstone Jewellers
    433 Diamond Blvd.
    Wichita, KS  49708

    Dear Ruby,

    I am happy to announce that we are now the authorized
    distributors for Designer Diskettes by Pierre Flopet.
```

If you want to check the merged output before printing it, you can choose the Print Merge Document command to send the merged documents to a file instead of directly to a printer. You're asked to specify a filename:

`PRINT MERGE DOCUMENT filename: █`

If you type in the name of an existing file, you're asked to confirm that you want to overwrite the file. (Word will not overwrite a file that is loaded into memory.) After Word prepares the new merged file, you can check, edit, format, and print it as you would any other file.

Some Other Print Merge Instructions

The DATA instruction tells Word to look in a data document for bits and pieces of text that are missing from a form letter or another main document. Two other Print Merge instructions, ASK and SET, tell Word to ask you to type in the missing text before it starts printing the document. All three of these instructions rely on field names embedded in the document to tell Word what text is missing and where the replacement text should be inserted. A fourth instruction, INCLUDE, works independently of field names: It tells Word to insert an entire file into the main document.

The ASK instruction

The ASK instruction is useful when you don't want to create a data document, or when the data document you have does not include all the information you want to put in the form letter or main document. When it encounters the ASK instruction, Word pauses before it starts printing each copy of the document and prompts you to type in replacement text for a particular field name.

An example of an ASK instruction is:

```
«ASK company=?Type the company name and press Enter»
```

The instruction begins with the ASK command, followed by the field name of the information you want Word to ask you for. Next comes an equal sign, and then a question mark that tells Word to prompt you to type in that information when it's ready to print the letter.

Following the question mark is the exact wording of the prompt you want to see on the screen. This is an optional part of the command. If you don't specify a prompt, Word prompts you with the uninspiring, generic message:

```
Enter text. Press Enter when done
```

which doesn't give you a clue as to what kind of text you are to enter.

Writing screen prompts for yourself or others can be fun. This is your chance to make the computer speak to you the way you'd like to be spoken to. You can be as playful or as serious as you like.

A good application for the ASK instruction is to quickly prepare customer response letters. You might, for example, want to promptly send response letters to individuals who request a catalog of your products. You might have only a few of these response letters to prepare each day. You can set up a standard-response letter that's ready to print, except for the name and address of the recipient. When Word is printing the letter, it prompts you to supply the name and address, as well as any other variable information for which you tell Word to prompt you.

Instead of starting such a letter with a DATA instruction, you would start it with an ASK instruction for each field name in the letter, as shown in the following example:

```
«ASK contact=?Type the contact name and press Enter»
«ASK company=?Type the company name and press Enter»
«ASK street=?Type the street address and press Enter»
«ASK city=?Type the city and press Enter»
«ASK state=?Type the state and press Enter»
«ASK zip=?Type the zip code and press Enter»
«ASK greeting=?Type the name for salutation and press Enter»
                                                  (dateprint)

«contact»
«company»
«street»
«city», «state»  «zip»

Dear «greeting»,

Thank you for your interest in our products. Enclosed, you
will find a catalog and price list describing our full line
of accessories designed to make your work more enjoyable.
```

When Word starts printing the first copy of the letter, it displays in the message line the prompt for the first ASK instruction:

```
Type the contact name and press Enter
```

After you type in the text (in this case, the contact name) and press the Enter key, Word displays the next screen prompt:

```
Type the company name and press Enter
```

This continues until Word has all the information it needs to print the letter.

After the first copy of the letter is printed, Word starts again, displaying the same screen prompts for the next copy of the letter. Word continues to print letters and prompt you for information until you press the Escape key to cancel the merge printing.

Using the ASK instruction is not practical for a very large mailing, because someone has to stay by the computer to answer questions for each letter and wait for the letter to print before answering the questions for the next letter. For large mailings, it's better to prepare a data document that Word can refer to as it's printing the document.

The SET instruction

The SET instruction is similar to the ASK instruction—both call for your input at print time. However, with the SET instruction, Word prompts you only once to type in text to replace a particular field name. It then uses that text for all copies of the document.

The format for the SET instruction is the same as the format for the ASK instruction. A letter to sales representatives that includes a few SET instructions for entering information about a price change might look like this:

```
«DATA SALESREP.LST»
«SET effective=?Type effective date and press Enter»
«SET product=?Type product name and press Enter»
«SET newprice=?Type new price and press Enter»
                                             (dateprint)

«contact»
«street»
«city», «state»  «zip»

Dear «greeting»,

Starting «effective», the new price for «product» will be
«newprice». Any orders for «product» prepared on or after
«effective» should include the new price. You should
personally notify customers in your territory and urge them
to order before the price change.
```

When you print the letter with the Print Merge command, Word displays the messages:

```
Type effective date and press Enter
Type product name and press Enter
Type new price and press Enter
```

one at a time, waiting for you to respond to the first one before displaying the next one. After you supply the necessary information, Word starts printing copies of the letter. The effective date, product name, and new price that you type in response to the prompts are inserted in each copy of the letter, in place of the corresponding field names. All other field names in this sample letter are replaced by information from the data document named SALESREP.LST.

The INCLUDE instruction

The INCLUDE instruction lets you insert an entire file in your main document at print time. This instruction is particularly useful when you want to insert standardized paragraphs (boilerplate) that you use in a variety of documents. By storing these standardized paragraphs in separate files, you create modules of text that you can plug into any document during printing.

To insert an entire file in your main document, type an INCLUDE instruction where you want the file inserted. The INCLUDE instruction contains the name of the file you want to insert. For example, if you want to insert a file called PRICES.DOC, which stores a price list for your products, type:

«INCLUDE PRICES.DOC»

As usual, if the filename extension is not .DOC, include the extension. If the file is not in the current document drive or directory, include the drive and pathname.

Let's take a look at the INCLUDE instruction in the context of a letter. Suppose you want to include the current price list, which is stored in a file called PRICES.DOC, in the following form letter responding to a customer inquiry:

```
Thank you for your interest in Designer Diskettes by Pierre
Flopet. I'm sending you a few samples so you can see for
yourself that floppy diskettes don't have to be ugly. Try
them out. In addition to being works of art, they work! If
that's not enough to convince you that you should be using
Designer Diskettes, take a look at our prices:

«INCLUDE PRICES.DOC»
```

When you print the letter with the Print Merge command, the price list is inserted in the letter. The letter (the main document) and the price list (the included document) can be on separate disks, but both disks must be in the computer when you choose the Print Merge command.

If you want to check the results of merging text with the INCLUDE instruction before printing, you can use the Print Merge Document command to create a file copy that you can edit before printing.

Recall that the Transfer Merge command also lets you insert one document into another. And, similarly, glossaries let you insert blocks of standardized text into documents. The Print Merge command offers some advantages over these methods. For example, if you use the INCLUDE instruction, you won't be using additional disk storage space every time you insert the text into a document. Also, you can update the inserted text without changing every document that already includes it. This is especially helpful with main documents that you use for several mailings. In the preceding letter, for example, you can update the price list by simply editing the PRICES.DOC file. You don't need to change the letter or any other document that uses the INCLUDE instruction to include the updated price list.

CHAIN PRINTING

Chain printing is the printing of a series of separate documents as one long document. Pages and footnotes are renumbered so that they are continuous from the beginning to the end of the finished document.

To chain documents together for printing, you prepare a main document that consists of INCLUDE instructions only. You then use the Print Merge command to print the main document. For example, to link the files named SECTION1.DOC, SECTION2.DOC, and SECTION3.DOC, the main document would be:

```
«INCLUDE SECTION1.DOC»
«INCLUDE SECTION2.DOC»
«INCLUDE SECTION3.DOC»
```

Chained documents are printed one after another without any page breaks. If you want to start any of the documents on a new page, you must insert a new page mark (press Ctrl-Shift-Enter) before the INCLUDE instruction for that document.

THERE'S MORE

To get you started, I've covered only the most essential merge printing operations in this book. There are a few more merge printing features you might want to explore. The most impressive of these is the use of conditional instructions, which let you insert text only if certain conditions are met. For example, you can tell Word to include a message in a letter only if the recipient lives in a particular state or orders a certain dollar volume of your product.

Chapter 14

Spelling, Hyphenation, and the Thesaurus

Despite attempts to make the spelling of English words more phonetic and efficient, our language hasn't changed much. And adherence to traditional spelling and hyphenation rules, no matter how arbitrary, is still valued.

If you have the Special Edition with disk included, consult the Introduction

Word can check your spelling, hyphenate words for you, and, with an electronic thesaurus, help you find the words that more precisely express what you want to say. But don't burn your bulky, paper dictionary or thesaurus yet. Electronic spellers, hyphenators, and word finders are not perfect; however, they can catch most of your typing and spelling errors, improve your writing, and save you time.

CHECKING SPELLING

With the Spell feature, you can proof and correct spelling in an entire document or part of a document without leaving the Word program. You have a good deal of control over how Spell works, and you can customize it to suit your needs. (The version 4.0 Spell feature differs from that of version 5.0. Refer to your version 4.0 manual for details, if you're using version 4.0.)

Proofing Documents

When Spell examines a document or part of a document, it calls your attention to any words that aren't in its dictionaries as well as to a common typing error—repeated words (such as *to to*). Neither paper nor electronic dictionaries are all-inclusive, so you'll find that some of the words that Spell doesn't recognize are correctly spelled.

After Spell shows you a word that it doesn't recognize, you can tell Spell to correct it, mark it for later correction, or leave it as it is. Whichever option you choose, you won't have to deal with the same word twice. If Spell encounters the word again, it remembers (until you leave Word) how you treated the word the first time and corrects, marks, or ignores it for you.

To begin proofing a whole document or part of a document without leaving Word:

1. Load the document you want to proof.

2. If you want the *entire* document checked for spelling, move the cursor to the beginning of the document or highlight the entire document. If you want only *part* of the document checked for spelling, move the cursor to the beginning of the part you want to check or highlight the part you want to check.

3. Choose the Library Spell command:

If you have a floppy-disk system, Word tells you to insert the Spell disk in place of the Word Program disk.

After the Spell dictionaries are loaded into memory, Spell starts checking the spelling of each word in the document. If Spell doesn't find any errors, it reports *No incorrect words found* and returns you to your document. If it finds a misspelled, repeated, or unknown word, it highlights the word and shows it in the context of surrounding words in the text window. In a new window, the Spell window, Spell explains why it stopped at the word, telling you that the word is not in the dictionary or that it is repeated in the document. You can then correct it, mark it for later correction, or choose the Ignore command to leave it as is.

If you have the Special Edition with disk included, consult the Introduction

If you start Spell while in the middle of a document, it checks your spelling from that point until it reaches the end of the document. Then it displays the message:

```
Enter Y to continue spelling from top of document or Esc to exit █
```

If you want Spell to finish checking the rest of the document, press Y; otherwise, press the Esc key.

When Spell is finished, it reports the number of words it checked and the number of words it did not recognize.

Correcting words

When Spell highlights a word, it suggests possible corrections by showing you a list of alternative words in the top part of the Spell window. For example, if it finds the word *bak* in your document, you see:

```
┌─────────────────────Spell──────────────────────┐
│                                                 │
│  bake          ba              baa              │
│  Bach          back            bah              │
│  balk          bank            bark             │
│  bask          bay             backs            │
│  balks         banks           barks            │
│                                                 │
├─────────────────────────────────────────────────┤
│  bak   Not found                                │
└─────────────────────────────────────────────────┘
SPELL: Correct Add Exit Ignore Options Undo
```

You can choose a word from the list, or you can type in the correction. To choose from the list, use the direction keys to highlight your choice and press the Enter key. With the mouse, point to your choice and Click-R.

If the word you intended is not listed, you must type in the correction. In the example above, if you meant to type *beak* instead of *bak*, you would have

*If you have the
Special Edition
with disk
included, consult
the Introduction*

to type in the correction because *beak* does not appear in the list of alternatives. To type in a correction, choose the Correct command, type the correction, and carry out the command.

Spell checks the correction you type. If it doesn't find it in the dictionary, you see the message:

```
Word not in dictionary. Enter Y to confirm or N to retype █
```

Press N if you want to retype the correction, or press Y to leave it as is.

Marking words

If Spell finds a word that you don't know how to fix, you can mark it for later correction. To do this, choose the Correct command, type the word—including a marker (such as an asterisk or other special symbol) before or after the word—and carry out the command. Later, using Word's Search command, you can search for markers and correct each marked word. The marker serves to remind you that the word needs your attention and helps you find it.

Ignoring words

Occasionally, the Spell program finds and highlights a word that you know is correct. It might be a word that is not in the dictionary that Spell is using, such as a proper noun, an acronym, a technical term, or a possessive form of a word. If you're certain it's spelled correctly, you can tell Word to pass over it by choosing the Ignore command. If Word finds the word again in the same document, it ignores it and doesn't bring it to your attention.

Interrupting and quitting Spell

As you're running Spell, you might spot some text that needs revising. Or you might encounter an error that Spell can't fix, such as an unwanted space in the middle of a word. For example, if you type *auto matically*, Spell would approve *auto* but ask you to fix *matically*. To delete the unwanted space, you need to get out of Spell and go back to the main editing menu. Word makes it easy to interrupt and restart Spell without losing your place or having to start all over.

You can interrupt or stop Spell at any time by pressing the Escape key or by choosing the Exit command when it is displayed. Spell will return you to editing mode and move the cursor to the last word in the document that it checked. If you pressed the Escape key to interrupt Spell, Spell will ask you to confirm that you want to return to editing mode. Any changes to the document that have already been made by Spell will be unaffected by the interruption. Each time you exit Spell, it tells you the number of words it checked and the number of words it didn't recognize.

To restart Spell, simply choose the Library Spell command and Spell will continue checking the document from the cursor location.

Spelling Checker Options

The Options command on the Spell menu lets you customize the way Spell works. After you choose the Options command, you see these command fields:

If you have the Special Edition with disk included, consult the Introduction

```
OPTIONS   user dictionary: SPECIALS.CMP
          lookup:(Quick)Complete            ignore all caps: Yes(No)
          alternatives:(Auto)Manual         check punctuation:(Yes)No
```

The *lookup* field, normally set to *Quick*, determines how many alternative words Spell searches for when it can't find a word in the dictionary. With *Quick* lookup, Spell assumes that the first two letters of the word are correct. (Most spelling errors do not occur in the first two letters.) This is much faster than *Complete* lookup, where Spell assumes every letter might be incorrect and therefore looks for many more possible alternatives.

Spell automatically looks for and lists alternative spellings when it finds a word it doesn't recognize. If you find that you can correct most of your errors without the help of these lists, you can save time by choosing *Manual* in the *alternatives* field. When you choose *Manual*, Spell won't take time to list alternatives unless you manually request them. To manually request a list of alternative spellings, choose the Correct subcommand when Spell displays an unknown word and press the F1 key.

Some documents include many initials, acronyms, or program commands that appear in uppercase letters and that Spell won't recognize—for example, ASCII, COD, AWOL, and DIR. You can tell Spell to ignore them from the start by choosing *Yes* in the *ignore all caps* field. (Instead of ignoring them, you might want to add them to a Spell dictionary.)

Spell normally ignores punctuation marks (. , ; : ! and ?), symbols (such as @, #, %, &), and numbers (1, 2, 3, and so on). It assumes that these characters, like spaces, simply separate words. By choosing *Yes* in the *check punctuation* field, you can have Spell check for spaces after punctuation marks. With this option, Spell also scouts for special characters and numbers accidentally embedded in words or immediately adjacent to words. Although Spell can't tell you whether you used the correct punctuation, it can help you find some common errors involving misplaced punctuation, special characters, and numbers.

If you have the Special Edition with disk included, consult the Introduction

In addition to customizing the Spell program with the Options command, you can add words to or delete words from the main dictionary. You can create a special *user dictionary* to store words unique to your work and create *document dictionaries* to store words unique to individual files. The user and document dictionaries supplement, rather than replace, the main (or standard) dictionary that comes with Word. (Consult the *Using Microsoft Word* manual for help with creating and altering dictionaries.)

AUTOMATIC HYPHENATION

If you want to avoid unsightly gaps of space in justified text or unpleasant raggedness in left- or right-aligned text, let Word add optional hyphens wherever necessary to even out the length of lines.

To hyphenate all or part of a document:

1. Load the document. If you want to hyphenate the entire document, move the cursor to the beginning of the document and be sure that the cursor is highlighting a single character. If you want to hyphenate part of the document, highlight the part that you want to hyphenate.

2. Choose the Library Hyphenate command:

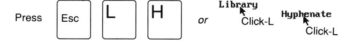

3. You see these command fields:

   `LIBRARY HYPHENATE confirm: Yes No`   `hyphenate caps:(Yes)No`

4. If you want to confirm the placement of each hyphen, choose *Yes* in the *confirm* field. If you don't want to hyphenate words that begin with uppercase letters, choose *No* in the *hyphenate caps* field.

5. Carry out the command.

After hyphens are inserted, Word tells you how many words were hyphenated. (Word inserts hyphens where they will be needed in the printed copy. Unless the *show line breaks* field of the Option command is set to *Yes*, line breaks on the screen might not match the line breaks that will occur in the printed copy and some hyphenated words might appear in the middle of lines. If an optional hyphen is not at the end of a line, you won't see it on the screen unless the *show non-printing symbols* field of the Options command is set to *Partial* or *All*.)

Confirming Hyphenation

If you choose *Yes* in the *confirm* field of the Library Hyphenate command, Word stops to highlight each proposed hyphenation so that you can approve the location before the hyphen is inserted. With each proposed hyphen, Word displays the message:

If you have the Special Edition with disk included, consult the Introduction

```
Enter Y to insert hyphen, N to skip word, or use direction keys to reposition █
```

Press Y to confirm the hyphen position. Press N only if you don't want to hyphenate the word at all.

If you want to hyphenate the word but change the location of the hyphen, use the Up and Down direction keys to find other recommended hyphen locations in the word. If you don't like any of the suggested locations, use the Left and Right direction keys to position the hyphen. When the cursor is positioned where you want to insert an optional hyphen, press Y to confirm the location.

Stopping and Undoing Automatic Hyphenation

You can interrupt and cancel the Library Hyphenate command by pressing the Escape key. Any hyphens already inserted stay in place. To remove *all* optional hyphens inserted by the Library Hyphenate command, choose the Undo command after you interrupt the Library Hyphenate command or after you let it run its course.

To remove individual hyphens that Word inserts, delete them as you would delete any other text. Optional hyphens must be visible before you can select and delete them, so first change the *show non-printing symbols* command field of the Options command to *Partial* or *All*.

USING THE THESAURUS

To extend your vocabulary and sharpen your writing, you can look up words in a thesaurus to find synonyms or alternative words. To use Word's thesaurus:

1. Highlight the word in your document that you want to look up.

2. Choose the Library thEsaurus command:

277

*If you have the
Special Edition
with disk
included, consult
the Introduction*

Word opens up a special window labeled *Word Finder Thesaurus* and displays a list of synonyms. For example, if you look up the word *spirit* in the Thesaurus, you would see a display similar to the one shown in Figure 14-1. The size and location of the Thesaurus window depends on where in your document window the word you're looking up is located. Word keeps the word and its context within the document in view while you look for a good alternative word. Reminders of what you can do while in the Thesaurus and how you can do it are highlighted in and around the borders of the Thesaurus window.

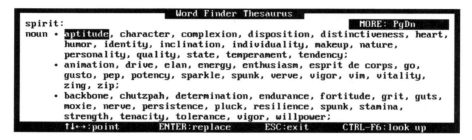

Figure 14-1. *A Thesaurus window.*

To see more of the list of synonyms, press the PgUp or PgDn key or, with the mouse, point to the left border of the Thesaurus window and Click-L or Click-R. When you're ready to select a synonym to replace the word highlighted in the document:

■ Use the direction keys to move the highlight to the synonym you want, and press the Enter key. Or, with the mouse, point to the synonym and Click-R.

After you choose a synonym, Word closes the Thesaurus window. If you want to close the Thesaurus window without choosing a synonym, press the Esc key. With the mouse, you can point to *ESC:exit*, which appears at the bottom of the window, and Click-L.

Other Thesaurus Maneuvers

Sometimes the route to the best word is not so direct. You might need to scout around the Thesaurus before you find a suitable word. You might, for example, look up synonyms for one of the synonyms listed in the Thesaurus window. Use the direction keys to move the cursor to the synonym and press Ctrl-F6. You can select a synonym from that list to replace the word highlighted in the document, or you can go back to the previous list shown. To go back to the previous synonym list shown, press Ctrl-PgUp.

To use the mouse, you can point to the words *CTRL-F6:look up* or *CTRL-PgUp:last word* at the bottom of the screen instead of pressing the Ctrl-F6 or Ctrl-PgUp keys.

If you have the Special Edition with disk included, consult the Introduction

If, while the Thesaurus window is open, you think of another word you would like to see synonyms for, simply start typing it. A little box will overlay words in the Thesaurus window so that you can see what you type:

After you type the word you want to look up, press the Enter key to see a list of synonyms for that word. Again, you can choose a synonym from that list to replace the word highlighted in the document, or you can press Ctrl-PgUp to return to the previous synonym list.

Chapter 15

Finding Files

The family of Transfer commands gives you access to a file if you can specify the filename and location. You can select files from a list, but that list can include files in only one location at a time—a single disk or directory specified in the *setup* field of the Transfer Options command. With the family of document-retrieval commands, you can access files from more than one location at a time. As with Transfer commands, you can find a file by specifying its filename and location or you can select a file from a list. The main difference is that you have more control over the list of files you see when you use document-retrieval commands.

You can instruct Word to list files from more than one directory. You can create a list of files that share common characteristics (independent of their location). For example, you can create a list of files written by the same author or prepared by the same operator. You can find files having common subject matter and files created or revised on the same date or in a specific time frame.

Word's ability to search for files rests in part on the information you provide in summary sheets.

SUMMARY SHEETS

When you first save a file, Word displays a questionnaire titled Summary Information:

```
SUMMARY INFORMATION
    title: █                          version number:
    author:                           creation date: 3/6/90
    operator:                         revision date: 3/6/90
    keywords:
    comments:
```

The information you type in the questionnaire is saved as a summary sheet with the file. You can view, revise, and print the summary sheet with the Library Document-retrieval commands. (You can also use the Print Printer command to print a summary sheet along with the document if the *summary sheet* field of the Print Options command is set to *Yes*.)

About the Fields in the Summary Sheet

Word uses some of the summary sheet fields to find and sort files; the others are for your information only.

The search and sort fields

Word can use three of the fields that you fill in—*author*, *operator*, and *keywords*—to find files. It can also use the *author* and *operator* fields to sort files. The *author* is the person who wrote or created the document, and the *operator* is the person who prepared or last saved the file. You can use up to 40 characters to specify an author or operator, and you can include more than one name in each field, separating the names with spaces or commas.

Use the *keywords* field to store words that identify the subject matter or purpose of the document. Although Word can find documents that include particular words or text by searching through the documents themselves, searching through the *keywords* field of summary sheets for words is much faster. Include any words you might want to search for later such as the main words in the title as well as key topic words from the text. Try to anticipate what in the document you might look for later as you do when you set up subject files and cross indexes for paper files. You can use up to 80 characters for keywords. Separate multiple keywords with spaces or commas.

Word fills in the *creation date* and *revision date* for you. It also includes the size of the file in characters with the summary sheet information. You can use the *creation date*, *revision date*, and size to find and sort files, whether you fill out the rest of the summary sheet or not.

The information-only fields

The other three fields—*title*, *version number*, and *comments*—help you identify a file when you view its summary sheet. Word doesn't use these fields to sort or search for files. *Title* gives you ample room (40 characters) to give the file a name that indicates its contents more clearly than the 8-character-maximum filename length that DOS allows.

The *version number* can help you distinguish between variations of what is basically the same document. You can assign a number or a word (or words) up to 10 characters. For example, you might identify a form letter used for reminding customers that their accounts are overdue with the title, "Overdue Account Form Letter." You might have separate versions of the letter for accounts that are 30 days, 60 days, or 90 days past due. Rather than assigning the different versions a nondescript number, you can type *30 days*, *60 days*, or *90 days* in the *version number* field. You can also use the *comments* field to explain what is unique about particular versions.

Use the *comments* field to include any useful information about a file, whether it is detailed summary information or reminders to yourself or others. You might, for example, include a reminder to use the document for a particular purpose or to edit the document further. Or you might keep notes on what has been done to the document so far. Has it been proofread for spelling? Has it been formatted? Who has reviewed it? You have space for up to 220 characters in the *comments* field, so use it in whatever way is helpful to you.

The table on the following page provides a summary of facts about the fields in a summary sheet.

Field of Information	Maximum Characters	Automatically Filled In	Search Key	Sort Key
title	40	No	No	No
version number	10	No	No	No
comments	220	No	No	No
author	40	No	Yes	Yes
operator	40	No	Yes	Yes
keywords	80	No	Yes	No
creation date	8	Yes	Yes	Yes
revision date	8	Yes	Yes	Yes
size	- - -	Yes	No	Yes

Filling Out a Summary Sheet

Use the direction keys to move from one field in a summary sheet to another. To correct text as you're typing responses, you can use the Backspace key to erase characters to the left. You can move the cursor with the F9 and F10 keys and then insert characters to the left of the cursor or delete highlighted characters with the Delete key. You can leave fields blank if you don't think the information is essential to your finding files. After you fill out a summary sheet, press the Enter key to save the summary sheet with the file.

Choosing Not to Fill Out Summary Sheets

Filling out summary sheets is optional. You can press the Enter key or the Escape key when you see the questionnaire to skip past it, or you can tell Word not to request summary information for new files by choosing *No* in the *summary sheet* field of the Options command. You can add information to a summary sheet or revise information later with the Library Document-retrieval Update command. (See the section titled ''Updating Summary Sheets'' later in this chapter.)

Searching for files based on the creation date, revision date, or text in the files does not depend on whether or not you fill out summary sheets. Because Word fills in the *creation date* and the *revision date*, you can always use the document-retrieval commands to search for files that were created or revised in the same time frame. Because the text contained in files is independent of summary sheets, you can always search for files that share common text, but this is slower than searching for keywords from the summary sheet.

THE DOCUMENT-RETRIEVAL COMMAND

All document-retrieval activities start with the Library Document-retrieval command. After you choose this command, the screen changes to display a list of document names at the top and the main document-retrieval menu at the bottom, as shown in Figure 15-1.

```
Path: \SALES\HARDWARE
 C:\SALES\HARDWARE\BOLTS.DOC          C:\SALES\HARDWARE\NAILS.DOC
 C:\SALES\HARDWARE\HAMMERS.DOC        C:\SALES\HARDWARE\NUTS.DOC
```

(Blank screen space for additional document names)

```
DOCUMENT-RETRIEVAL: Query Exit Load Print Update View Copy Delete

Press Spacebar to mark-unmark file, Ctrl+Spacebar to mark all, or Esc for menu
                          ?                              Microsoft Word
```

Figure 15-1. *Document-retrieval screen and menu.*

Initially, the files displayed in the top part of the screen are the .DOC files in the current document drive and directory. (That drive and directory are specified in the *setup* command field of the Transfer Options command.) The first line of the document-retrieval screen states the path (or paths) for the displayed filenames.

There are eight commands in the main document-retrieval menu:

```
DOCUMENT-RETRIEVAL: Query Exit Load Print Update View Copy Delete
```

Query is the file search command and gives you control over which documents are listed at the top of the screen. With the Query command, you can tell Word to search for documents that meet the criteria you specify and then display the names of all files matching your search criteria. You can then view or revise the summary information for the files, load the files, or print them with the other document-retrieval commands.

View also controls the document list at the top of the screen. It determines how much information about each file is shown and how files are sorted within the list.

Load lets you load a file and return to Word's main menu.

Print lets you print files appearing in the document list or their summary sheets or both. With the Print command, you can print a single file or a series of files.

Update lets you revise the summary information for a file.

Copy lets you copy one or more files to a different drive or directory.

Delete lets you erase one or more files.

Exit takes you back to Word's main editing menu and editing screen where you can view and edit document text.

SEARCHING FOR DOCUMENTS WITH THE QUERY COMMAND

The Query command determines which files appear in the document list at the top of the screen. By specifying the search criteria in the command fields of the Query command, you can tell Word to find a file or a group of files and list them in the document list. Most command fields of the Library Document-retrieval Query command mirror the fields of the summary sheet:

```
QUERY path: C:\SALES\HARDWARE
  author:
  operator:
  keywords:
  creation date:                    revision date:
  document text:
  case: Yes(No)                     marked files only: Yes(No)
```

The Path Field

The *path* field tells Word where to look for files and, optionally, which filenames to include. You can specify both locations and filenames in the *path* field. If you don't specify a path, Word looks in the current document drive and directory. You can specify more than one path, separating the paths with commas. (Spaces are optional.) For example, typing:

> *C:\SALES\HARDWARE, C:\SALES\SOFTWARE*

tells Word to look in the Hardware and Software subdirectories of the Sales directory in drive C.

If you don't specify any filenames, Word looks for all .DOC files in the specified or default path. When you specify files, you can include the wildcards ? and * in the filenames. Use a question mark (?) to stand for a single unspecified character. Use an asterisk (*) to stand for any number of unspecified characters. For example, to search for all documents with the filename extension .RPT in the Hardware and Software subdirectories, type:

C:\SALES\HARDWARE*.RPT, C:\SALES\SOFTWARE*.RPT

You can also specify individual filenames in the path field. For example, if you want to batch print a series of files and you know their filenames, simply type in the filenames and their paths (if necessary) in the *path* field. Separate multiple filenames with commas. (Spaces are optional.) For example, if you want Word to find the files named HAMMERS.DOC, NAILS.DOC, NUTS.DOC, and BOLTS.DOC, type:

HAMMERS.DOC, NAILS.DOC, NUTS.DOC, BOLTS.DOC

in the *path* field. Word assumes it can find the files in the current document drive and directory because no paths are specified. If these files are in the Hardware subdirectory and if the Hardware subdirectory is not the current document directory, you would type:

\SALES\HARDWARE\HAMMERS.DOC,
\SALES\HARDWARE\NAILS.DOC, \SALES\HARDWARE\NUTS.DOC,
\SALES\HARDWARE\BOLTS.DOC

In this case, Word assumes that all the files are in the current document drive because no drive is specified.

You can use up to 128 characters to specify filenames and paths in the *path* field. Only the files described by the *path* field are listed at the top of the document-retrieval screen.

The Other Search Fields

Most of the command fields of the Query command are used to search for files that have common characteristics. The other search command fields can be used to narrow the list of files found by the *path* field to include only those files that have specific authors, operators, creation dates, revision dates, keywords, or text. When you fill in *author*, *operator*, *keywords*, *creation date*, or *revision date* fields, Word looks for files in the specified path(s) that have matching information in their summary sheets. When you specify *document text*, Word looks for files that have matching text in the file itself. The *case* field is related to the *document text* field; it indicates whether the letter case of the specified text is matched (*Yes*) or ignored (*No*).

The Query command does not have a *whole word* option, as does the Search command on the main menu. So, when you search for authors, operators, keywords, or document text, Word finds your search string whether or not it is embedded in other text. For example, if you specify *opera* in the *document text* field, Word finds all documents that contain the words *operator*, *cooperate*, and *operation*—as well as files that include the word *opera*.

One way to avoid this problem is to make use of the *keywords* field. For example, if *opera* is entered as a keyword in the summary sheets for documents related to opera, you can search for *opera* as a keyword rather than as document text. Doing this reduces the chances of finding documents you don't want to find. When searching for an acronym like *RAM* as document text, you could choose *Yes* in the *case* field of the Query command to avoid finding *ram*, *tram*, *frame*, *bramble*, and countless other words. Another way to avoid finding embedded words is to specify what you don't want to find. Word uses the tilde symbol (~) to represent *NOT*. For example, if you're searching for documents authored by someone named Hart, you could type:

Hart~Hartford~Hartley

in the *author* field to say you want to find *Hart* but not *Hartford* or *Hartley*.

You can use up to 80 characters to specify authors, operators, keywords, or document text and up to 25 characters to specify creation or revision dates in the Query command fields.

When you have more than one entry in one field

You can search for more than one author, operator, keyword, piece of document text, creation date, or revision date. When you have multiple entries in any field, you must separate them with a comma (,), which means *OR*, or an ampersand (&), which means *AND*. For example, if you want to find documents authored by either Carlo or Larry, type:

Carlo, Larry

in the *author* field. But if you want to find documents coauthored by Carlo and Larry, type:

Carlo & Larry

in the *author* field.

You can use parentheses to clarify expressions. For example, type:

(Pete & David),(Carlo & Larry)

if you want to find documents coauthored by Pete and David or by Carlo and Larry.

Sometimes it's easier to specify what you don't want to find than to specify what you do want to find. For example, suppose you have access to the work of five authors (Carlo, Larry, Pete, David, Clyde) and you want to locate files created by all except one (Clyde). You can use the tilde (~) to specify which one you don't want rather than specifying the four you do want. In this example, type:

~Clyde

in the *author* field.

The *AND*, *OR*, and *NOT* symbols (& , ~) are called logical operators. They can be used with all fields except the path field. You can use the wildcards, * and ?, with all fields except the date fields.

When you want to search for a range of dates

You can specify an open-ended range of dates rather than single date(s) by using the greater than (>) and less than (<) symbols. These symbols are logical operators that can be used only with the *creation date* and *revision date* fields. When used with dates, the > symbol means *after* and the < symbol means *before*. For example, to find files created after December 31, 1989, type:

>12-31-89

To find files created before January 1, 1990, type:

<1-1-90

You can search for a closed range of dates by combining an ampersand (&) for *AND* with the > and < symbols. For example, to find documents revised in 1990, type:

>12-31-89 & <1-1-91

which means after 12-31-89 and before 1-1-91.

You can exclude a range of dates from a search by combining a comma (,) for *OR* with the > and < symbols. For example, to exclude documents revised during the last six months of 1989, type:

<7-1-89, >12-31-89

which means before 7-1-89 or after 12-31-89.

You cannot combine a tilde (~) for *NOT* with the > or < symbol.

When you want to search for special symbols

To include any of the symbols used to represent logical operators in a search string, enclose the entire string in quotes to signal Word that the symbol is not being used as an operator. For example, to search for references to Bluff & Blunder, Inc. in documents, type:

"Bluff & Blunder, Inc."

in the *document text* field. Otherwise, Word looks for documents that contain either ''Bluff'' and ''Blunder'' or ''Inc.''

Because quotation marks also have a special meaning to Word, you must *double* them when you want to include quotation marks in a search string. For example, searching for:

""pursuit of happiness""

finds:

"pursuit of happiness"

To include either of the symbols used for wildcards (? or *) as part of a search string, precede the symbol with a caret (^).

Putting It All Together

You use the Query command to determine which files are listed on the document-retrieval screen. After you choose the Query command, you fill in the field or fields you want to search for. The following table summarizes key facts about the command fields of the Query command that help you search for files.

Search Field	Maximum Length	Use Logical Operators? & , ~	> <	Use Wildcards? * ?
path	128	Comma only	No	In file name only
author	80	Yes	No	Yes
operator	80	Yes	No	Yes
keywords	80	Yes	No	Yes
document text	80	Yes	No	Yes
creation date	25	Yes	Yes	No
revision date	25	Yes	Yes	No

You can enter search criteria in more than one field to pinpoint the files you want to see. For example, if you want to examine all documents that are related to a customer named Huntington Industries and that were prepared in 1987, your responses to the command fields of the Query command might look like this:

```
QUERY path: \SALES\HARDWARE\*.*,\SALES\SOFTWARE\*.*,\SALES\CUSTSERV\*.*
   author:
   operator:
   keywords:
   creation date:                        revision date: >12-31-86 & <1-1-88
   document text: Huntington Industries
   case: Yes(No)                         marked files only: Yes(No)
```

Notice that although you don't need to know the filenames, you do need to specify the directories where the documents can be found. The wildcard expression *.* was used in the paths to include all filenames and filename extensions.

Once your search is defined, press the Enter key. Word responds by displaying the list of files that meet your search criteria. For example:

```
Path: \SALES\HARDWARE\*.*,\SALES\SOFTWARE\*.*,\SALES\CUSTSERV\*.*
C:\SALES\CUSTSERV\2-87-HI.LET      C:\SALES\HARDWARE\HI_8-87.LET
C:\SALES\CUSTSERV\5-87-HI.LET      C:\SALES\HARDWARE\HWCLIENT.LST
C:\SALES\CUSTSERV\9-87-HI.LET      C:\SALES\SOFTWARE\HI_7-87.LET
C:\SALES\CUSTSERV\COMPLAIN.1Q      C:\SALES\SOFTWARE\HI_9-87.LET
C:\SALES\CUSTSERV\COMPLAIN.3Q      C:\SALES\SOFTWARE\SWCLIENT.LST
C:\SALES\HARDWARE\HI_3-87.TYL
```

You can further refine the list by using the Query command again. For example, if you want to find only those documents pertaining to complaints, you could add the word *complain* in the *document text* field to find documents containing the words *complain, complaint, complained,* and other derivatives.

```
QUERY path: \SALES\HARDWARE\*.*,\SALES\SOFTWARE\*.*,\SALES\CUSTSERV\*.*
   author:
   operator:
   keywords:
   creation date:                        revision date: >12-31-86 & <1-1-88
   document text: Huntington Industries & complain
   case: Yes(No)                         marked files only: Yes(No)
```

(If you can depend on finding the client's name or the word *complain* in the *keywords* field of document summary sheets, it would be much faster to search for them as keywords.)

You can also limit the document list by marking files and specifying *Yes* in the *marked files only* field of the Query command. (See ''Marking Files'' later in this chapter.) With the View command, you can adjust the display of documents to see more summary information about the files listed. Once the list includes the files you want, you can select a file and view or update its summary sheet, load the file, copy or move the file to another disk or directory, delete the file, or print the file or its summary sheet or both. You can copy, move, delete, and print files individually or in batches.

ADJUSTING THE DISPLAY OF LISTED DOCUMENTS

After Word finds the documents that meet the search criteria given in the Query command, it lists them at the top of the document-retrieval screen. With the View command, you can control how much information is given about each file in the document list and the order in which the files are displayed. After you choose the View command from the document-retrieval menu, you see these command fields:

```
VIEW: Short Long Full
      Sort by:(Directory)Author Operator Revision_date Creation_date Size
```

The first command field controls how much information about each file is displayed. The second command field, *Sort by*, determines the order in which the files appear. The proposed responses, *Short* view sorted by *Directory*, show the drive, path, and filename of each file with the directories listed alphabetically and the files listed alphabetically within each directory. Short view sorted by directory is shown in Figure 15-2. The document list shown in Figure 15-2 results from looking for the chapters in this book that contain the document text *search*.

Figure 15-2. *Short view sorted by directory.*

With a short view, the files are listed in a two-column format that allows only 39 characters for each file. If the path and filename are too long to fit in the space, Word shortens them by replacing middle characters with an ellipsis (...).

If you choose *Long* view, you see the path and filename of each file plus the title of the file from the summary sheet and the *sort key* (that is, the field by which the files are sorted). For example, if you choose *Long* view and sort the files by *Revision_date*, you see a display like that shown in Figure 15-3.

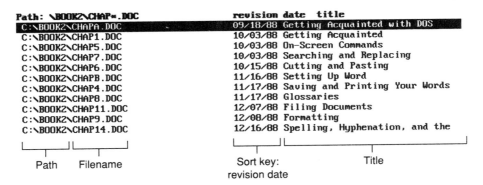

Figure 15-3. *Long view sorted by revision date.*

If the files are sorted by *Directory*, as proposed, the author's name is shown in the sort-key column of *Long* view because the directory is already shown in the first column.

When you choose *Full* view, you can see the entire summary sheet for whichever document in the list is highlighted, as shown in Figure 15-4. You can use the direction keys to move the highlight to any file on the list to see its summary sheet. If necessary, you can use the scroll keys, PgUp and PgDn, to see more of the list.

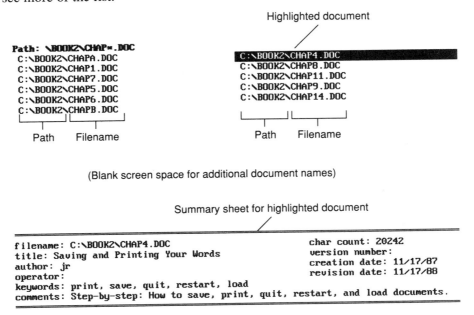

Figure 15-4. *Full view sorted by revision date.*

UPDATING SUMMARY SHEETS

Using the Update command on the document-retrieval menu, you can revise the summary sheet for any formatted Word file. (Files that were not saved with Word's formatting do not have summary sheets.)

To update a summary sheet for a file listed on the document-retrieval screen, highlight the file and choose the Update command. You see the fields of the summary sheet for the file that is highlighted. For example:

```
UPDATE SUMMARY filename: C:\BOOK2\CHAP4.DOC
   title: Saving and Printing Your Words      version number:
   author: jr                                 creation date: 11/17/87
   operator:                                  revision date: 11/17/88
   keywords: print, save, quit, restart, load
   comments: Step-by-step: How to save, print, quit, restart, and load documents
```

You can use the direction keys to move from field to field. To edit an existing entry, use the F9 and F10 keys to position the cursor where you want to insert or delete text. Press the Del key to delete characters highlighted by the cursor, and press the Backspace key to delete the character to the left of the cursor. When you finish revising the fields that need changing, press the Enter key.

To update a summary sheet for a file that isn't listed on the screen, choose the Update command from the document-retrieval menu and type the drive, path, and filename for the file in the *filename* field. Press a direction key to see the existing responses to the summary sheet fields for that file. Once the summary sheet is visible, you can edit it (as described above).

LOADING FILES

You can load any file with the Load command on the document-retrieval menu. To load a file listed on the screen, highlight it and choose the Load command. You have the same *read only* option that you have with the Transfer Load command on the main menu:

```
LOAD filename: C:\BOOK2\CHAP4.DOC                    read only: Yes(No)
```

After checking to see that the file named in the *filename* field is the one you want, press the Enter key, or point to *LOAD* and Click-L to carry out the command. After loading the file, Word returns you to the editing screen with the file and the main editing menu displayed. If the active window has a file in it with unsaved changes, Word alerts you with the now-familiar message: *Enter Y to save changes to the document, N to lose changes, or Esc to cancel.*

Whichever option you choose, you exit the document-retrieval menu and can now choose commands from the main editing menu.

To load a file that isn't displayed in the document list, type the drive, path, and filename in the *filename* field of the Load command.

MARKING FILES

The remaining commands on the document-retrieval menu—Copy, Delete, and Print—act only on files that are listed and marked on the document-retrieval screen. You must first use the Query command to list any files that you want to copy, move, delete, or print. You can perform these actions on more than one file at a time by marking each file before choosing the appropriate command. (With the mouse, you can mark files after you choose the Copy or Print command.)

To mark a file using the keyboard, highlight the filename with the direction keys and press the Spacebar. You can mark all listed files by holding down the Control key and then pressing the Spacebar. With the mouse, point to the file you want to mark and Click-R. After you mark a file, an asterisk appears to the left of its filename. (Remember that you can tell Word to display only marked files by choosing *Yes* in the *marked files only* command field of the Query command.) To unmark a file, highlight it and press the Spacebar or, with the mouse, point to it and Click-R.

COPYING, MOVING, AND DELETING FILES

The Copy command lets you copy or move files to another drive or directory, and the Delete command lets you delete files.

To copy or move files, mark the file or files you want to copy or move and choose the Copy command from the document-retrieval menu. You see these command fields:

```
COPY marked files to drive/directory: █
    delete files after copy: Yes(No)          copy style sheets: Yes(No)
```

Type the new location for the file or files in the first command field. If you are copying or moving two or more files, they will be copied or moved to the same location. Use the *delete files after copy* field to specify whether you want each marked file copied or moved: Choose *Yes* to move each file or choose *No* to copy each file. If any style sheets are attached to the marked files, the *copy style sheets* field gives you the option to copy or move them along with the files.

To delete files, mark the file or files that you want to delete and choose the Delete command from the document-retrieval menu. Word asks you to confirm that you want to delete the marked files before it deletes them. Be sure to check which files are marked before you press Y to confirm. You can press the Escape key to cancel the command if necessary.

PRINTING FILES

You can print files that are listed on the document-retrieval screen with the Print command. Word applies the settings chosen for the Print Options command from the main menu.

To print a listed file, mark the file and choose the Print command from the document-retrieval menu. (If you want to print more than one file at a time, mark each file that you want to print.) You see a single command field:

```
PRINT marked files: Summary Document Both
```

You can choose to print the summary sheet only (by choosing *Summary*); the document only (by choosing *Document*); or both the summary sheet and the document (by choosing *Both*) for each marked file. Recall that with the Print Printer command, you can print the document alone or with its summary sheet (by choosing *Yes* or *No* in the *summary sheet* field).

After you carry out the command, Word starts printing the specified documents. You can choose other commands and continue working while Word is printing. You can press the Escape key as usual to interrupt printing. Word displays the message:

```
Enter Y to continue or Esc to cancel ▌
```

Press Y when you're ready to resume printing, or press the Esc key again to cancel the Print command and return to the document-retrieval menu.

Chapter 16

Macros: Custom-made Commands

Macros are custom-made commands that speed up word processing and make it easier. The building blocks for macros are all the keys on the keyboard, the commands you find on menus and on keys, and a group of special instructions. Once a sequence of commands and keystrokes is recorded in a macro, the macro can be played back by pressing a control code made up of one to three keys. You store macros in glossaries, along with glossary entries that are made up of text only. Unlike other glossary entries, any key on your keyboard can be recorded in a macro.

With macros, you can reduce complicated tasks to a few keystrokes, combine several steps into one, remind yourself of what needs to be done, assign new tasks to function keys, customize the way Word works, or make Word imitate a word processor that you're more familiar with.

In this chapter, you'll learn how to run the ready-made macros that Word provides, how to edit macros, and how to create macros from scratch by recording them. You'll find that creating macros can save you time and does not require special knowledge or skills.

THE READY-MADE MACROS

Word supplies some ready-made macros that are waiting for you to try. To use the supplied macros, you first need to load MACRO.GLY, the glossary file in which they are stored.

If you have the Special Edition with disk included, consult the Introduction

Merging MACRO.GLY

Glossaries are loaded from disk into memory with the Transfer Glossary Merge command. If a glossary is already in memory, the newly loaded glossary is merged with it. Because NORMAL.GLY is loaded whenever you start Word, merging MACRO.GLY with NORMAL.GLY and saving the result as NORMAL.GLY makes the supplied macros readily available. You can find MACRO.GLY on either the Utilities 2 disk or the Utilities disk. If you have a fixed disk, the Setup program copied MACRO.GLY to the same directory as the Word program.

To merge the supplied macros with the glossary currently in memory:

1. If you have a floppy-disk system, insert the Utilities 2 or Utilities disk in drive B.

2. Choose the Transfer Glossary Merge command.

3. When the *filename* field appears, type:

    MACRO

   If you have a fixed disk, include the path for MACRO.GLY if it is not in the current document directory. For example, type:

    C:\WORD\MACRO

   if your Word program directory is called Word.

4. Press Enter to carry out the command.

If you want to make the supplied macros a permanent part of the glossary in memory, save the glossary with the Transfer Glossary Save command. Whether you save them or not, the supplied macros are now loaded in glossary memory and ready for you to run.

Try Some

The quickest way to find out what macros can do is to try the ready-made macros. Load any long document and begin experimenting with the macros described in the next sections. When you finish experimenting, use the Transfer Clear Window command without saving the document so that the document is not permanently altered.

To copy or move text

Let's start with a macro that copies text. Named *copy_text.mac*, it has been assigned the control code Ctrl-CT. Although you don't really save keystrokes when you use this macro, it leads you through the steps of copying text so that you don't have to remember the *Select text–Choose and carry out Copy command–Select location–Press the Insert key* sequence.

Your cursor can be anywhere in the text window when you start this macro. Simply press Ctrl-CT. (Hold down the Ctrl key while you press C. It doesn't matter whether the Control key is down when you press the second letter, T.) The message line prompts you to highlight the text you want to copy:

```
Select text to be copied, press Enter when done
```

For trial purposes, highlight any text and press the Enter key. Now the macro prompts you to move the cursor to the place where you want to insert the copy of the text:

```
Select destination point, press Enter when done
```

When you press the Enter key, a copy of the text is inserted to the left of the cursor.

A similar macro, *move_text.mac*, works in the same way to move text. Press Ctrl-MT now to see how it works. Highlight any piece of text when prompted, and follow the instructions in the message line to move the text to a new location.

To move the cursor a page at a time

If you have a document longer than one page, you can try the macros *next_page.mac* and *prev_page.mac*. As their names suggest, you can use these macros to jump to the beginning of the next or previous page. Their control codes are Ctrl-JN (Jump Next) and Ctrl-JP (Jump Previous). The macros choose the Jump command for you and determine the page number that will take you to the next or previous page. You can use Ctrl-JN and Ctrl-JP to move through documents one full page at a time.

To save part of a document in a new file

To begin to see the timesaving power of macros, try the macro called *save_selection.mac*. After you press Ctrl-SS, this macro opens and clears a new window for you, copies highlighted text to the new window, saves the text in the new window as a new file, prompts you to give it a filename, and then closes the new window. All you have to do is highlight the text you want to copy and save in a new file before you start the macro and then give the new file a name when prompted.

Try it. Select any paragraph in a document and press Ctrl-SS. You'll see commands being chosen and carried out lickety-split until Word draws a new window. When command displays stop flashing, you're asked to give the excerpt in the new window a filename. Type a name like *ERASE-ME* to remind yourself to delete this test file later, and press the Enter key. Before you know it, the process is complete, and the screen is back to what it was when you started the macro.

Viewing a List of Macros

Now that you tried using some macros, take a look at the complete list of supplied macros. If you merged the file MACRO.GLY with the glossary you now have in memory, you can see the names of all supplied macros. Choose the Insert command and press the F1 key, or, with the mouse, point to the *from* field and Click-R. The macros Word provided are identified with the *.mac* extension. Notice how each macro is followed by a control code that can be used to run the macro. For example, the control code for the macro called *save_selection.mac*, Ctrl-SS, looks like this:

```
<Ctrl S>S
```

The angle brackets around *Ctrl* and *S* indicate those two keys must be held down together. The control code and the macro name are separated with a caret so that the entire entry looks like this:

```
save_selection.mac^<Ctrl S>S
```

You can run a macro after choosing the Insert command by typing the macro name (*save_selection.mac*, for example) in the *from* field or by highlighting the macro when the list is in view and pressing the Enter key. With the mouse, you can point to your choice in a list of macros and Click-R. You can also run a macro by typing the name (without the control code) in the document and pressing the F3 key. The easiest way is to type the control code—if you remember it.

Examining a Macro

You can insert a macro in a document (without running the macro) to examine the macro's contents. Let's examine one now to see what a macro looks like. To examine a macro:

1. Choose the Insert command.

2. When you see:

   ```
   INSERT from: {}
   ```

   press the F1 key to see a list of macros.

3. Using the direction keys, move the highlight to the macro that you want to see. In this case, move the highlight to the macro named *save_selection.mac*.

4. Type a caret (^) and press the Enter key.

The macro contents are inserted in the currently active window. When inserted in a document, the macro called *save_selection.mac* looks like this:

```
<ctrl esc>c<enter><esc>wsh<tab>y<enter><ins>«set
promptmode="user"»<esc>ts«pause Enter filename to save to,
press Enter when done»<enter><esc><ctrl esc>wc<enter>
```

The individual steps of this macro are listed and explained in the table on the following page. Notice that special keys are represented by abbreviations enclosed in angle brackets (<>). The Insert key, for example, is represented by <*ins*> and the Escape key appears as <*esc*>. This macro contains two special instructions enclosed in chevrons (« »): a Set instruction and a Pause instruction. The Pause instruction tells Word to display a message that tells you what to do. The message in this Pause instruction tells you to type the filename and press Enter. (When given a Pause instruction, Word waits until you press the Enter key before it proceeds with the next step.)

Macro Step	Purpose
<ctrl esc>	Activate command menu. (The Control-Escape key combination is used instead of the Escape key in case the menu is already activated.)
c	Choose Copy command.
<enter>	Carry out command to copy selected text to the scrap.
<esc>wsh	Choose Window Split Horizontal command.
<tab>y	Move to *clear new window* field and choose *Yes* response.
<enter>	Carry out command to open and clear new window.
<ins>	Insert text from the scrap (using Insert key).
«set promptmode="user"»	Ensure user gets to see all prompts.
<esc>ts	Choose Transfer Save command.
«pause Enter filename...»	Pause, display message, and wait for operator to type the filename and to press Enter when done.
<enter>	Carry out the Save command.
<esc>	Skip the summary information.
<ctrl esc>wc	Choose the Window Close command.
<enter>	Carry out the Close command.

Editing a Macro

Once you have a macro in view on the screen, you can edit it with the tools you use to edit any other text. Every character in a macro is significant, and Word has a number of specific rules about writing macros. Minor changes can easily be made; and here you will learn how to create new macros by making minor changes to existing macros.

Let's change *save_selection.mac* so that it prompts you to highlight the text you want to copy before it copies the text. We'll also add a comment at the beginning of the macro and change the macro's name and control code when we save it. Comments explain the purpose of a macro or of individual steps in a macro. Word ignores comments when it executes a macro. You can include any text in a comment that helps you remember what a macro does.

To alter *save_selection.mac* so that it prompts you to highlight text:

1. With the macro visible on the screen, move the cursor to the first character of the macro. Insert a comment at the beginning of the macro by typing:

   «COMMENT Prompts you to select text, which it then copies and saves in a new file.»

   To type « and », press Ctrl-[[and Ctrl-]].

2. After the comment, add a Pause instruction that prompts you to highlight text. Type:

   «PAUSE Highlight the text you want to copy to a new file and press Enter»

   The macro now looks like this:

   ```
   «COMMENT Prompts you to select text, which it then copies
   and saves in a new file.»«PAUSE Highlight the text you want
   to copy to a new file and press Enter»<ctrl
   esc>c<enter><esc>wsh<tab>y<enter><ins>«set
   promptmode="user"»<esc>ts«pause Enter filename to save to,
   press Enter when done»<enter><esc><ctrl esc>wc<enter>
   ```

3. Highlight the entire macro and choose the Copy or Delete command to save the new macro.

4. When prompted with *COPY to* or *DELETE to*, type a new name to reflect the change. For example, type:

   copy-save-select.mac

   followed by a new control code, *Ctrl-CS*. To type the control code, type a caret (^) and press Ctrl-C followed by S. The control code appears on the screen after the name as follows:

   ```
   copy-save-select.mac^<ctrl C>S
   ```

   Press Enter to record the new macro.

Now press Ctrl-CS to see if the new macro works. Because you saved the edited macro under a new name, the original macro, *save_selection.mac*, remains in the glossary unchanged.

By editing the new macro, you can easily create another macro that deletes selected text and saves it in a new file—thus moving the text instead of copying it. All you have to do is change one letter so that the macro chooses the Delete command instead of the Copy command. In the first group of keystrokes following the Pause instruction, change:

```
<ctrl esc>c
```

to:

```
<ctrl esc>d
```

You should also change the word *copies* (to *deletes*) in the Command instruction and the word *copy* (to *move*) in the Pause instruction to reflect the change. Saving the newly edited version of the macro to a name such as *del-save-select.mac* with the control code Ctrl-MS (for Move Selection) clarifies the purpose of the macro and preserves the original macros. This new macro provides a fast way to break a long file into two separate files. It prompts you to highlight the part you want to move to a new file, deletes it from the existing file, and saves it in the new file.

CREATING MACROS

The easiest way to create macros from scratch is to type the actual commands and keystrokes that you want to include in the macro while Word records them. When you finish recording a macro, you give it a name and store it in a glossary.

Naming Macros

Naming a macro is similar to naming a glossary entry. Choose a name that indicates what the macro does. The name can be up to 31 characters long (including the control code) and can include any letters and numbers but no spaces and only a few symbols. You can use an underscore character (_), a hyphen (-), or a period (.) where you would normally use a space. It's helpful to distinguish macros from ordinary glossary entries by appending *.mac* to their names. For example, a macro that prints and saves a file might be called *print_save.mac*.

Assigning Control Codes

When naming macros, you can assign a control code to reduce the number of keys you have to press to use the macro. For example, when you want to use the *print_save.mac* macro described above, it would be more convenient to press Ctrl-PS than to type the macro name and press the F3 key or to select the name from a list.

Control codes can be a combination of the Control key plus one or two additional characters. For example: Ctrl-S, Ctrl-SL, or Ctrl-2.

❑ WARNING: *If you use only one character, you'll soon run out of letters that help you remember what each macro does.*

Instead of a Control-key combination, you can use a function key or a function-key combination, such as F5, Shift-F5, Ctrl-F5, or Alt-F5.

Keep in mind that Word has already assigned tasks to all function keys and almost all function-key combinations. If you assign a new task to a function key or function-key combination, you must press Ctrl-X before you press the function key or combination in order to use it for its original purpose. For example, if you assign F5 to a macro, you would have to press Ctrl-X and then F5 to turn on the overtype mode. Although Ctrl-X gives you access to original key assignments, it's best not to assign a function key or combination to macros unless you don't use the function key often or unless you want to remap the block of function keys.

Control codes are assigned by typing a caret after the macro name and then pressing the keys you want included in the code. For example, to assign the control code Ctrl-P, you would type a caret (^) and hold down the Control key while you press P. When the Control-key combination includes two characters, such as Ctrl-PS, hold down the Control key while you press the first character. You can hold down or release the Control key while you press the second character. (To allow more space for long macro names, *release* the Control key before you press the second letter. This results in an abbreviated control code, such as <Ctrl-P>S rather than <Ctrl-P><Ctrl-S>, which uses 7 more of the possible 31 characters for the macro name.)

How to Record Macros

Before you start typing what you want included in a macro, press Shift-F3 to turn the macro recorder on. When it is on, *RM* (for *Record Macro*) appears in the status line. When you're through typing the commands, press Shift-F3 again to turn off the macro recorder. After you stop recording, Word chooses the Copy command so you can copy the macro to the glossary currently in memory. When the Copy command prompts you for a macro name, type in a name and, if desired, a control code. Then carry out the command. That's all there is to it.

For example, you might want to hyphenate your entire document from any point within it. A macro that moves the cursor to the beginning of the

If you have the Special Edition with disk included, consult the Introduction

document and starts the hyphenation process without hesitating at any menus saves time and keystokes. To create this macro:

1. Press Shift-F3 to turn on the macro recorder.

2. Press the keys that move the cursor to the top of the document, and then choose and carry out the Library Hyphenate command:

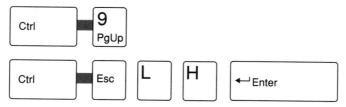

3. Press Shift-F3 to turn off the macro recorder.

4. When you see:

COPY to: █

type a macro name. For example, type:

hyphenate-all.mac

5. If desired, assign a control code to the macro. First type a caret:

∧

and press the keys you want to be the control code. For example, press:

and then press:

to assign the control code Ctrl-HA. You now see this:

hyphenate-all.mac^<ctrl H>a

Notice that when two keys are held down together, Word encloses them in angle brackets.

6. Press the Enter key to carry out the command.

If you make a mistake while recording

If you press the wrong keys while recording a macro, press Shift-F3 to stop recording. When Word prompts you to give the macro a name, press the Esc key to cancel the Copy command. You must then start all over by pressing Shift-F3 to begin recording again.

If you don't discover your error until after you save the macro, you can carefully edit the macro or delete it with the Transfer Glossary Clear command. After choosing the Transfer Glossary Clear command, enter the name of the macro you want to delete in the *names* field.

More Sample Macros to Record

The following sections describe some useful macros that you can record by using the procedure just described. When assigning control codes, whether they are function keys or Control-key combinations, don't forget to type a caret before you type the control code.

To transpose characters, words, and sentences

A common typing error is to switch the order of two letters. Sometimes you notice the error as soon as you type it, and you might want to correct it right away. The Spell program can find and correct most of these errors, but in some cases Spell can't find the error. For example, if you accidentally type *tow* instead of *two*, Spell won't detect it as an error because *tow* is a correctly spelled word.

Correcting this kind of error is not difficult with Word, but if you've been using another word processor you might be accustomed to having a special command to transpose characters. To make a macro that transposes two characters typed in the wrong order, record this sequence of keystrokes:

You can name the macro *transpose-char.mac* and assign Ctrl-TC as the control code. Then when you want to correct two letters that are switched, move the cursor to the second letter and press Ctrl-TC. Try using the macro now: type the word *form*, move the cursor to *r*, and press Ctrl-TC. The word *form* becomes *from*.

Similarly, you can make a macro to transpose two words by recording these keystrokes:

Make up your own name and control code for the macro. Before you run the macro, you need to move the cursor to any character in the second word.

You can even make a macro to transpose two sentences with these keystrokes:

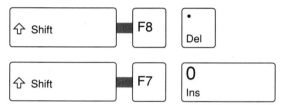

Before you run this macro, you need to move the cursor to any character in the second sentence.

To split windows

If you frequently use more than one window, a macro that splits a window at the position of the cursor is handy. Record:

and call the macro *window-split.mac* with the control code Ctrl-WS. This macro is useful when you want to look at two different parts of the same document. But if you want to create a new document in the newly opened window, you must first clear it. So why not make another macro that opens a window at the position of the cursor and clears it for you? Record:

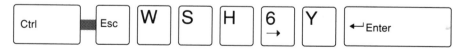

and call this macro *window-split-clr.mac* with the control code Ctrl-WC.

To make a macro that splits a window and chooses the Transfer Load command so that you can immediately load another document in a newly opened window, record:

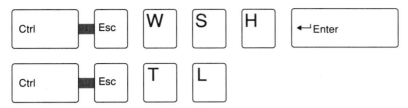

and call it *window-split-load.mac* with the control code Ctrl-WL.

In each case, using these macros reduces your keystrokes by more than half, reduces the likelihood of procedural error, and frees you from having to rethink how to accomplish these tasks.

To print what?

I often print part of a document by choosing *Selection* or *Pages* in the *range* field of the Print Options command. Then I usually forget to change the range setting back to *All*—so the next time I print, I get part of a document when I want all of it or a different part of it. Recording the following keystrokes in a macro ensures that you check the Print Options command before you print.

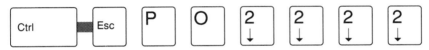

You can call this macro *print.mac* and assign Ctrl-PR as a control code. The macro chooses the Print Options command and moves the highlight to the *range* field so that you can easily change it, if necessary. If you need to change any other fields, you can do so. Once the Print Options are set, simply press the Enter key twice to start printing.

Instead of using this macro for all printing, you can make three separate macros for printing: *print-all.mac* (Ctrl-PA), *print-selection.mac* (Ctrl-PS), and *print-pages.mac* (Ctrl-PP).

The recorded keystrokes for the macro that prints all of a document would be:

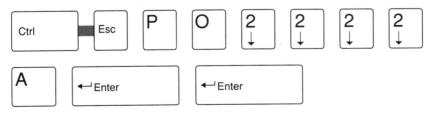

*If you have the
Special Edition
with disk
included, consult
the Introduction*

The keystrokes for printing a highlighted part of the document would be:

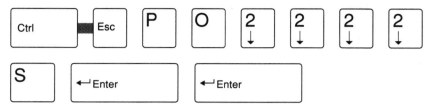

And the keystrokes for printing designated pages of a document would be:

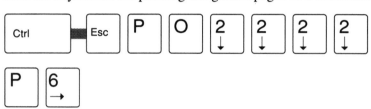

The first two macros change the response to the *range* field of the Print Options command and carry out both the Print Options and the Print Printer command to start printing. The last macro selects the Print Options command, chooses *Pages* in the *range* field, and ends by moving the cursor to the *page numbers* field, where you can type the page numbers that you want to print. You must then press the Enter key twice to start printing.

By using the techniques explained in the sections "Examining a Macro" and "Editing a Macro" earlier in this chapter, you can record this last macro and then edit it to add a Pause instruction. The Pause instruction causes the macro to wait for you to type in the page numbers and press the Enter key before it carries out the Print Options command and chooses the Printer subcommand to start printing. When edited to include the Pause instruction and the Printer subcommand, the macro looks like this:

```
<ctrl esc>po<down 4>p<right>«PAUSE»<enter><enter>
```

To imitate other word processors

Old habits are hard to break. If you've been working with another word processor, your hands might reflexively select the familiar commands and keys before you can think of the new ones that Word uses. If you or your hands are reluctant to learn new commands and key assignments, you can make Word imitate the word processor you know. You won't get a complete match, but you can simulate the most frequently used commands.

For example, if you're accustomed to reaching for the F10 key to save a document with the WordPerfect program, record:

as a macro and assign the F10 key as the control code. (Notice that Word uses Ctrl-F10 to choose and carry out the Transfer Save command, saving the file under its previous name.)

If you want Word to activate the new key assignments each time you start Word, save the macros that change key assignments in NORMAL.GLY. If, instead, you want to choose when to activate them, save the macros in a separate glossary named, for example, KEY-MAP.GLY. Then, when you want to activate the new key assignments, load or merge KEY-MAP.GLY. Either way you can change your mind about key assignments by deleting the macros. Deleting macros and loading, merging, and saving glossaries are done with the Transfer Glossary commands described in detail in Chapter 8.

WORKING WITH MACROS

Whether you use macros that you create or macros that Word supplies, the techniques for working with them are the same. The following sections summarize what you learned about running macros and deleting macros. In addition, you'll learn how to repeat, cancel, and print macros.

Running Macros

You have three ways to run a macro that's in glossary memory. Whichever way you choose, first move the cursor to where you want to start running the macro, unless you're sure the macro does that for you. Then:

- If the macro has been assigned a control code, such as Ctrl-C, simply type the control code. The commands and keystrokes contained in the macro are carried out—starting at the cursor position.

- If you know the name of the macro, you can type the name and press the F3 key. The macro name disappears, and the macro starts running from the cursor's location.

■ To see a list of macros and glossary entries, choose the Insert command and press the F1 key or, with the mouse, point to the *from* field and Click-R. (Macro names are usually given the extension *.mac* to distinguish them from glossary entries.) To choose a macro from the list, move the highlight to the macro name you want and press the Enter key to run the macro. If you're using a mouse, point to your choice and Click-R.

When using a macro for the first time, it's wise to protect your work by saving any unsaved changes before you run the macro. The Undo command can undo the last command or action taken by the macro—but not the entire macro. If the macro does something dreadful, you can use the Transfer Clear command to clear the document without saving the damage, and then you can reload the previously saved copy of the document.

Repeating and Canceling Macros

You can repeat macros the same way that you repeat single commands— by pressing the F4 key. (In versions of Word prior to version 5.0, you must run the macro again to repeat it.)

You can interrupt a macro by pressing the Escape key. Word stops and displays the message:

```
Enter Y to resume macro or Esc to cancel ▮
```

You can press Y to restart the macro where you left off or press the Esc key again to stop it altogether. If you stop the macro, only the commands and keystrokes that are not yet carried out are canceled. Those that were carried out are unchanged.

Deleting and Printing Macros

Macros are deleted and printed in the same way that other glossary entries are. Use the Transfer Glossary Clear command to delete macros. This command prompts you to enter the name(s) of the macros you want to delete. You can type them, separating multiple names with commas, or select them from a list of glossary entries.

You can use the Print Glossary command to print an entire glossary, including macros as well as other entries. Once you choose the command, Word prints the contents of the glossary currently in memory. More details about both of these commands are given in Chapter 8.

THERE'S MORE

In this chapter you became acquainted with macros, started using them, learned how to run the macros that Word supplies, and created a macro by recording keystrokes.

Word offers another way to create macros—to write them. When you write macros, you can include special instructions (like the Pause instruction) that can't be recorded in macros. These special instructions let you program macros to calculate, to repeat themselves conditionally, to ask you for information, and to perform tasks only if specified conditions are met or perform alternative tasks if the conditions are not met. Once you're at ease with the notion of macros and with the techniques for recording and running them, explore the more advanced macro options described in the *Using Microsoft Word* manual.

Chapter 17

Style Sheets

In the book-publishing field, book designers draw up "spec sheets" to outline the formatting specifications for published works. Typesetters, proofreaders, editors, and artists use spec sheets to guide them as they transform an author's raw text and sketches into an attractive and marketable book. Adherence to the spec sheet ensures consistency from one page to the next. In the business world, companies often have style manuals to guide people as they prepare memos, letters, and reports.

With the introduction of built-in *style sheets,* Microsoft took a giant step toward accommodating the need for formatting standards. Word lets you create style sheets that contain formatting specifications that Word can interpret and apply to text. Instead of looking up the format specifications for a block of text on a spec sheet or in a style manual, you tell Word what kind of text it is. Then Word looks up the formatting instructions for you. Instead of your issuing all the commands necessary to produce that format, Word issues them for you.

Equally important, style sheets can save you time—whether you're trying to conform to a house style or not. The styles contained in style sheets are really formatting macros: Each style can replace several formatting commands with a single command. One significant difference between macros and styles is that once you apply a style to some text, it becomes linked to that text. If you change the formatting instructions of the style, any text that has been linked to it is also changed. A macro that is changed has no effect on text to which it was previously applied.

Creating and using styles for frequently repeated formatting instructions and for seldom-used but complex formats can save you much time and trouble.

USING A STYLE SHEET

Without knowing much about the content or makeup of style sheets, you can begin using them to format documents. Word provides a few ready-made style sheets that you can try. Before you can use a style sheet to format a document, however, you must first attach it to the document.

Attaching a Style Sheet

You can attach a style sheet to a document before you begin typing the document or after you type it. To attach a style sheet to a document:

1. Choose the Format Stylesheet Attach command:

   | Esc | F | S | A | *or* | Format Click-L | Stylesheet Click-R |

2. When you see:

   `FORMAT STYLESHEET ATTACH:` █

   type the name and, if necessary, the path of the style sheet you want to attach. As usual, you can request and choose from a list of style sheets instead of typing in a response. In the list, Word includes files in the current document drive and directory that end with the filename extension *.STY*. (You can specify another drive and directory before you request the list.)

3. Carry out the command.

Let's create a letter and format it as we type it using the style sheet called SEMI.STY that Word provides. SEMI.STY is designed to format letters in a standard semiblock style. You can find it and a style sheet called FULL.STY (for full-block letters) on the Utilities Disk. Use the DOS COPY command to copy SEMI.STY and FULL.STY from the Utilities Disk to your current document disk or directory. Start Word or use the Transfer Clear Window command so that you have a blank window in which to start typing a new document. Choose the Format Stylesheet Attach command. When prompted for a style sheet name, type:

SEMI

and press the Enter key.

SEMI.STY is now available for use. Because it is attached to the document you're about to create, it will be loaded each time you load the document. The next step is to find out what styles are contained in the style sheet.

Short View of Available Styles

Three kinds of styles can be in a style sheet: character styles, paragraph styles, and division styles. *Character styles* specify character formats only, such as boldface italics, underlined uppercase letters, and superscripts in a smaller font. *Paragraph styles* control formatting options available through the Format Paragraph command, such as alignment, indents, and line spacing. As a bonus, paragraph styles can also incorporate character formats and tab formats so that you can, for example, center a heading and make it boldface with one command, or indent a table and set tabs for it with one command. *Division styles* determine the general layout, such as the margins, page size, page numbering, and all the other options offered by the Format Division commands.

An individual style in a style sheet usually governs the formatting of a distinct part of a document. For example, one style might control the placement and format of the date in a letter, another style might control the format of the complimentary closing, and another might determine the treatment of a numbered list within the document.

*If you have the
Special Edition
with disk
included, consult
the Introduction*

Each style in a style sheet is assigned a key code that can be used to apply the style. Much like the control codes used to play back macros, key codes combine the Alternate key with one or two other keys. For example, in SEMI.STY, Alt-DA is the key code for the style that formats the date in a letter.

When you're not familiar with the styles and key codes in a style sheet, you can use the Format Stylesheet command to list and select available styles. You will need to specify whether you want to see Character, Paragraph, or Division Styles. Let's first take a look at the character styles available in SEMI.STY. If you haven't already done so, follow the instructions in the previous section to clear the screen and attach SEMI.STY.

To see a list of available character styles, choose the Format Stylesheet Character command and then press the F1 key. For SEMI.STY, you see the following list:

```
Character Standard                          UC Character 1 (UNDERLINED)
Character Summary Info ((C) 1984-6)
```

The first style listed, *Character Standard,* is Word's default character style without any special formatting. Word adds this style to style sheets although you don't see it in the style sheets themselves. Applying this style is equivalent to pressing Alternate-Spacebar to restore characters to normal format. The second listing, *Character Summary Info,* is not really a style. It's a copyright message embedded in the style sheet. The third listing, *UC Character,* is more typical of listings you see for styles:

```
UC Character 1 (UNDERLINED)
 /      /       /       /
Key code  Usage  Variant  Remark
```

Four pieces of information are given about the style: the key code, the usage, the variant, and a remark. The *key code* tells you what keys you can press in combination with the Alternate key to apply the style to selected text. The *usage* tells you whether the style formats characters, paragraphs, or divisions. The *variant* is an identifier used to distinguish between different styles having the same usage. A set of special variant names (such as *Standard, Page number,* and *Footnote ref*) is used for styles that are applied automatically. Usually, a variant name is a number that has no significance by itself. For most purposes, you can ignore the variant. The *remark* tells you the purpose of the style. In this case, the remark tells you that this style underlines selected characters. In a well-written style sheet, the remarks and the key codes provide good clues to what a style does and what it's used for.

Now let's take a look at the paragraph styles available with SEMI.STY. Choose the Format Stylesheet Paragraph command and then press the F1 key. You see this list of paragraph styles:

```
SP Paragraph Standard (STANDARD PARAGR) LH Paragraph 10 (ADJUSTABLE LETTERHEAD)
RA Paragraph 14 (shift-◄─┘ RETURN NAME) DA Paragraph 7 (DATE)
IA Paragraph 11 (INSIDE ADDRESS/Mr. Ji) SA Paragraph 13 (SALUTATION / Dear...)
CL Paragraph 21 (COMPLMNTRY CLOSING/Si) NA Paragraph 8 (AUTHOR'S NAME (BELOW S)
TI Paragraph 9 (AUTHOR'S TITLE (AFTER) RI Paragraph 17 (REF INITIALS, ENCLOSU)
```

There is a paragraph style for each distinct part of a letter:

	Corresponding Style	
Parts of a Letter	*Key Code*	*Remark*
Return address	RA	(shift-◄─┘ RETURN NAME)
Date	DA	(DATE)
Recipient's address	IA	(INSIDE ADDRESS/Mr. Ji)
Salutation	SA	(SALUTATION / Dear...)
Body of letter	SP	(STANDARD PARAGR)
Complimentary closing	CL	(COMPLMNTRY CLOSING/Si)
Author's name (below signature)	NA	(AUTHOR'S NAME (BELOW S)
Author's title (after name)	TI	(AUTHOR'S TITLE (AFTER)
Reference information: Initials (author/ preparer), enclosures, CC (copies to)	RI	(REF INITIALS, ENCLOSU)

Some of the remarks seem to be incomplete because they are truncated in the display to include only some of a possible 28 characters. In the remark for the return-address style, the author reminds you to press Shift-Enter at the end of each line of the address rather than the Enter key alone. (The way that the return address is formatted requires that the entire address be treated as one paragraph.)

In addition to the styles corresponding to the parts of a letter, you see a style having the key code *LH* and labeled with the remark, *ADJUSTABLE LETTERHEAD*. This style was added to the style sheet to accommodate letter-head stationery. If you're preparing a letter that will be printed on letterhead stationery, you don't need to type a return address. Instead, you need to allow extra space for the preprinted letterhead, and that's what the LH style does for you.

When you format a letter, most of the formatting is done with paragraph formats. But margins and page size are determined by division formats. Let's see what the options are for division styles in this style sheet. Choose the For-mat Stylesheet Division command and then press the F1 key to see a list of division styles. Most letters, as well as other kinds of documents, have only one division, so you see only one division style:

```
S/ Division Standard (SEMI-BLOCK LETTE)
```

Because this style has been assigned an automatic variant name, *Standard,* it is automatically applied to the document. Now let's start typing a letter and apply styles from SEMI.STY to see what SEMI.STY can do for us.

Applying Styles from a Style Sheet

You can apply styles to a document in two ways. The quickest is to press the key code. For example, press Alt-DA to format the date in a letter. If you don't know the key code, you can choose the appropriate Format Stylesheet command to view a list of character, paragraph, or division styles (as you did in the previous section) and then choose the style you want from the list.

Style-sheet formatting works like direct formatting using the Format command: You can format text as you're typing by applying styles before you type the text, or you can go back to previously typed text and apply styles. If you format as you're typing, the style you choose affects everything you type until you choose another style or change the format with formatting commands. If you apply a style to previously typed text, the style you choose affects highlighted text only.

When using SEMI.STY, it might be best to format as you're typing so that you can see the letter take shape as you type it. The style sheet inserts all the extra tabs and line spacing necessary. You don't need to press the Tab key or the Enter key to add the indents and blank lines you normally want in a letter.

When using a style sheet, turn on the *style bar* so that you can see the codes for the styles appear as you apply them. To turn on the style bar, change the response to the *show style bar* command field of the Options command to *Yes.*

Let's suppose you'll be printing on letterhead stationery: You need extra space at the top to allow room for the preprinted name, logo, address, and so on. Press Alt-LH. *LH* appears in the style bar to the left of the cursor to indicate that the first paragraph has the letterhead style. This first paragraph won't have any text in it. It's only a space maker that adds two blank lines. In combination with the top margin, it allows two inches at the top of the page for the letterhead. Now press the Enter key to move to the next paragraph. Again, *LH* appears next to the second paragraph. All paragraphs will have the letterhead format until you choose a new format.

The first item you usually want to type in a letter is the date, so press Alt-DA. The style code for the second paragraph changes to *DA*, and the cursor jumps over to the middle of the screen, where the date normally appears in a semiblock style letter. Now type the date. For example, type:

April 25, 1990

and press Enter.

To type the address, press Alt-IA (for Inside Address). The cursor jumps back to the left margin where you want the address positioned. Type the name and address of the person the letter is going to, pressing the Enter key at the end of each line. In this case, type:

Johnny Appleseed
25 Apple Blossom Road
Springfield, IL 60432

Press Alt-SA to prepare for the salutation. The cursor skips down a line to leave blank space between the address and the salutation. Type:

Dear Johnny,

and press Enter.

Now you're ready to type the body of the letter, so press Alt-SP to indicate that you want standard paragraph formatting. For semiblock letter style, this means the first line of each paragraph is indented. After applying the standard paragraph format, the cursor moves five spaces to the right for the first-line indent. Type the body of the letter, pressing the Enter key once at the end of each paragraph:

I am pleased to offer you a position with our firm as Horticultural Consultant for the Midwest region. What impressed us most about your background are the volunteer activities you have engaged in throughout the prairie states.

As you know, PlantRight is sprouting several new branches and can offer an industrious young twig like yourself ample growth opportunity. Please call me at your earliest convenience so that we can discuss salary, benefits, and starting date.

Notice how the standard paragraph style not only indents each paragraph for you but also adds a blank line between paragraphs.

To close the letter, press Alt-CL and type the closing:

Sincerely,

and press Enter. Now press Alt-NA to position the author's name under the closing and type the name:

Pete Moss

and press Enter. The style adds enough space to insert a signature above the name.

Press Alt-TI to type the author's title under the name. You might want to break long titles by pressing Shift-Enter where you want to start a new line. Shift-Enter starts a new line without starting a new paragraph, and the title style indents the second line three spaces. Type:

Vice President,

and press Shift-Enter. Then type:

Trees and Shrubs

and press Enter.

At the end of a letter, it's customary to put the author's and the typist's initials. Notes about enclosures and who receives copies are also appended. Suppose you forget the key code for formatting this reference information. Choose the Format Stylesheet Paragraph command and press the F1 key to see a list of available paragraph styles. Use the direction keys to move the highlight to the style labeled with the remark *REF INITIALS, ENCLOSU* and press Enter. The command applies the selected style to the currently highlighted paragraph. Now type the initials:

PM:vn

and you're done.

Figure 17-1 shows you what the letter formatted with the semiblock style sheet looks like when it's printed.

You can easily reformat a document by attaching a new style sheet if the style sheet uses the same key codes and different, but corresponding, style definitions. For example, Word provides another style sheet for letters called FULL.STY. It includes the formatting instructions needed to produce a letter in full-block style. With full-block style, none of the main parts of the letter are indented. By attaching FULL.STY to the letter you've recently prepared, you'll see an immediate transformation. Choose the Format Stylesheet Attach command, type *FULL* in the command field, and press Enter. The results of attaching FULL.STY to your letter are shown in Figure 17-2 on page 324.

Now switch back to SEMI.STY so that you can learn how to alter it in the next sections. Choose the Format Stylesheet Attach command again, type *SEMI* in the command field, and carry out the command.

Alt-LH

Alt-DA

Alt-IA

Alt-SA

Alt-SP

Alt-CL

Alt-NA
Alt-TI
Alt-RI

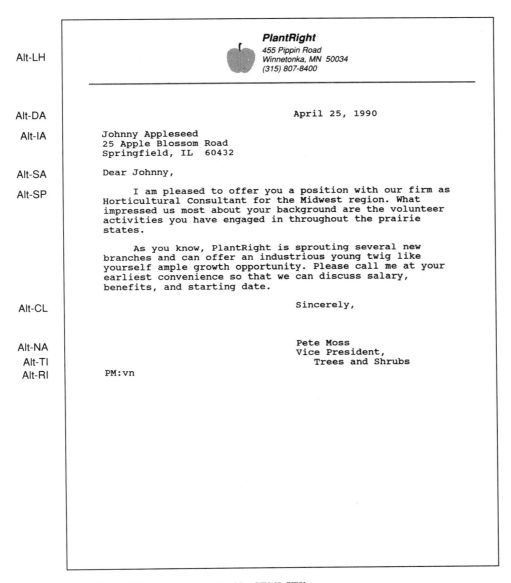

Figure 17-1. *Letter formatted by SEMI.STY.*

Alt-LH

PlantRight
455 Pippin Road
Winnetonka, MN 50034
(315) 807-8400

Alt-DA

April 25, 1990

Alt-IA

Johnny Appleseed
25 Apple Blossom Road
Springfield, IL 60432

Alt-SA

Dear Johnny,

Alt-SP

I am pleased to offer you a position with our firm as
Horticultural Consultant for the Midwest region. What
impressed us most about your background are the volunteer
activities you have engaged in throughout the prairie
states.

As you know, PlantRight is sprouting several new branches
and can offer an industrious young twig like yourself ample
growth opportunity. Please call me at your earliest
convenience so that we can discuss salary, benefits, and
starting date.

Alt-CL

Sincerely,

Alt-NA

Pete Moss

Alt-TI
Alt-RI

Vice President,
    Trees and Shrubs
PM:vn

Figure 17-2. *Letter formatted by FULL.STY.*

Recording a Style

The easiest way to create new styles and to add them to a style sheet is to type and format text, and then to record the format in the style sheet. Frequently, letters and other documents include numbered or unnumbered lists. In this section, you'll create a style that you can use to format lists in any type of document.

Hanging indents provide an attractive format for lists. With hanging indents, the item numbers or markers (sometimes called bullets) stick out from the rest of the text. Each item in the list is treated as a separate paragraph, and the first line of each paragraph is outdented (given a negative left indent).

Let's add a section that includes a list to the Johnny Appleseed letter. Move the cursor to the end of the first paragraph and press the Enter key. Start typing the new section:

Your duties will include:

and press the Enter key again. Now comes the list. The list will be indented from the rest of the letter, and each item in the list will be marked by a hyphen. You'll type the first item in the list and format it with the Format Paragraph command. Press the Tab key before and after you type the hyphen. Type:

- *Preparation of budgets, forecasts, and quarterly reports for submission to the Head Office.*

To create the hanging indent:

1. With the cursor still in the first item of the list, choose the Format Paragraph command.

2. Type *1* in the *left indent* field.

3. Type *-.5* in the *first line* field.

4. Type *.5* in the *space before* field to allow one-half line of extra space between items in the list.

5. Press the Enter key.

6. Choose the Format Tabs Set command.

7. Type *.8* in the *position* field, choose *Right* in the *alignment* field, and press the Ins key.

8. Type *1* in the *position* field, choose *Left* in the *alignment* field, and press the Enter key.

The right-aligned tab is for positioning the markers or numbers for entries in a list. Right-alignment ensures that the numbers marking a numbered list line up like this:

    8.
    9.
    10.
    11.

and not like this:

    8.
    9.
    10.
    11.

The second tab, which is left-aligned, ensures that the first character following the number or marker is aligned with the rest of the paragraph. Your first item in the list should now look like this:

```
-  Preparation of budgets, forecasts, and quarterly
   reports for submission to the Head Office.
```

Now let's record this format in a style sheet. To record a style:

1. Move the cursor to the text formatted in the style you want to record. In this case, move the cursor to the list item you formatted.

2. Choose the Format Stylesheet Record command. You see these command fields:

```
FORMAT STYLESHEET RECORD key code: █        usage: Character(Paragraph)Division
                       variant: 1           remark:
```

3. Type an easy-to-remember 1-letter or 2-letter code for the style in the *key code* field. For example, type *IL* in the *key code* field for the indented list format that you're recording now.

4. In the *usage* field, highlight the kind of style you're recording: Character, Paragraph, or Division. In this case, choose *Paragraph*.

5. You can usually accept the proposed response that appears when you move the cursor to the *variant* field. Most styles are assigned a number as a variant. When you format a standard character, paragraph, division, page number, footnote, running head, heading, outline, or index, you need to assign a special variant name so that the style is automatically applied. To see a list of options for variant labels, press the F1 key when the highlight is in the *variant* field. If a variant name is already assigned to a style, the key code for the style is shown next to the variant. In this example, choose *1*, as proposed.

6. Type a note in the *remark* field that tells you what the style does or what kind of text it is used for. For example, type *INDENTED LIST* to identify the format you're recording now. Use uppercase letters to make the remark easy to spot in a style sheet.

7. Press the Enter key to carry out the command.

You've just added a new style to the style sheet attached to the current document. If you did the previous exercises in this chapter, you inserted the style in SEMI.STY that is attached to the Johnny Appleseed letter. In addition to creating a new style, you assigned the style to the first item in the list. You should see the key code *IL* to the left of that paragraph.

Continue typing the rest of the list and watch the newly recorded style do the formatting for you. Remember to press the Tab key before and after each hyphen marking an entry in the list and to press the Enter key after each entry. Type:

- *Hiring and firing.*
- *Establishment of local nurseries and seed beds.*
- *Field management of planting crews.*

So far, you've learned to attach, use, and alter a style sheet by recording a new style. You can easily do these tasks without leaving the main menu that you're familiar with and without learning the details of how style sheets are composed. When you're ready to venture away from the main menu and examine style sheets more closely, move on to the next sections.

WORKING IN THE GALLERY

You can use the Gallery command to view or print an entire style sheet. You can also use it to directly edit individual styles or to create new styles from scratch. After you choose the Gallery command, the style sheet that is attached to the document appears in the window. Below the style sheet display is the Gallery menu, with commands similar to the commands that are on the main menu:

```
GALLERY: Copy Delete Exit Format Help
         Insert Name Print Transfer Undo
```

Commands on the Gallery menu affect style sheets only. The Exit command takes you back to the main menu where you view and work on documents.

Viewing and Printing Style Sheets

As soon as you choose the Gallery command, you see the style sheet that is attached to the active document. The name of the style sheet is shown in the lower right corner of the gallery window. Figure 17-3 shows what you see when you view SEMI.STY.

```
1   S/ Division Standard                      SEMI-BLOCK LETTER, 6" WIDTH
        Page break. Page length 11"; width 8.5". Page # format Arabic. Top
        margin 1.67"; bottom 1"; left 1.25"; right 1.25". Top running head
        at 1". Bottom running head at 0.83". Footnotes on same page.
2   LH Paragraph 10                          ADJUSTABLE LETTERHEAD SPACE
        modern b 12. Flush left, space after 2 li.
3   RA Paragraph 14                          shift-◄─┘ RETURN NAME, ADDR
        modern b 12. Flush left, Left indent 3.2", space before 1 li (keep
        in one column, keep with following paragraph).
4   DA Paragraph 7                                              DATE
        modern b 12. Flush left, Left indent 3.2", space after 1 li (keep
        in one column, keep with following paragraph).
5   IA Paragraph 11                          INSIDE ADDRESS/Mr. Jim Smith
        modern b 12. Flush left, Left indent 0.5" (first line indent -
        0.5"), right indent 2.8" (keep in one column, keep with following
        paragraph).
6   SA Paragraph 13                              SALUTATION / Dear...
        modern b 12. Flush left, space before 1 li (keep in one column,
        keep with following paragraph).
7   SP Paragraph Standard                        STANDARD PARAGRAPH
        modern b 12. Flush left (first line indent 0.5"), space before 1
        li.
8   CL Paragraph 21                          COMPLMNTRY CLOSING/Sincerely
        modern b 12. Flush left, Left indent 3.2", space before 1 li (keep
                                                               ─SEMI.STY─
```

Figure 17-3. *Display of style sheet called SEMI.STY.*

Each paragraph in the style sheet represents one style, or set of formatting instructions. For example, the style that formats standard divisions (the default division style) looks like this:

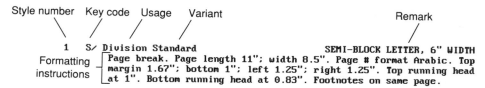

The first line of the style contains the same information you see when you use the Format Stylesheet command to view a list of styles. It tells you the key code, usage, variant, and remark. (Word numbers the styles starting with 1 and displays the numbers to the left of each style.) The remaining lines detail the formatting instructions for the style.

You can scroll up and down to see more of the style sheet, as you do with a document. Press Ctrl-PgDn now to see the end of the style sheet, where the style that you recorded for indenting lists is stored.

You can print a copy of the style sheet that's in view by choosing the Print command. To view or print a style sheet that isn't attached to the current document, you need to load it into memory with the Transfer Load command described in the next section.

The Transfer Commands

The Transfer commands on the Gallery menu are almost identical to those on the main menu. You can load style sheets from disk into memory with the Transfer Load command, save them on disk with the Transfer Save command, clear them from memory with the Transfer Clear command, delete them with the Transfer Delete command, merge two or more style sheets with Transfer Merge, rename them with Transfer Rename, and set a default directory for finding and saving style sheets with Transfer Options.

Using the Transfer Load command to load a style sheet into memory does not attach the style sheet to any document. That can only be done with the Format Stylesheet Attach command from the main menu or by pressing Y in response to the message *Enter Y to attach new style sheet...* when you leave the Gallery menu. Using the Transfer Clear command does not detach a style sheet from any document. You can detach a style sheet from a document by choosing the Format Stylesheet Attach command, pressing the Delete key, and carrying out the command.

Editing Style Sheets

All changes that you make to a style sheet while in the gallery are made with commands from the Gallery menu and with the Insert or Delete keys. You cannot type directly in the style sheet window.

You use the direction keys to move the highlight in the window up and down from one style to another. The highlight always highlights at least one entire style at a time. It is used to mark the style that you want to edit or the place where you want to insert a new style. You can extend the highlight to select more than one style at a time. You would do this, for example, when you want to delete two or more adjacent styles.

The commands used to edit style sheets are:

Copy	Insert
Delete	Name
Format	Undo

The Copy command copies the highlighted style(s) to the scrap, and the Delete command (or the Delete key) deletes the highlighted style(s) to the scrap. From the scrap you can, if desired, reinsert the style(s) with the Insert command (or the Insert key). You can insert the style(s) back in the same style sheet or in another style sheet after it has been loaded with the Transfer Load command. You would, for example, want to reinsert a style in the same style sheet when you want to create a new style by copying an existing one and making minor changes to it. You can move a style from one location in a style sheet to another by first deleting it and then inserting it. You might want to move styles around within a style sheet so that related styles are grouped together.

You can also use the Insert command to create new styles from scratch. It enables you to assign the new style a key code, define the usage and variant, and write a remark. You then use the Format command to define the formatting specifics for the style. The Format command also lets you change the formatting specifics for existing styles, and the Name command allows you to change the key codes, variants, or remarks for styles.

After making changes to a style sheet file, you must save the file to preserve the changes. As with document files, Word checks for unsaved changes to a style sheet file before it allows you to quit, clear memory, or load another style sheet.

Let's try some of the commands in the Gallery menu. In the next sections, we'll use the Copy and Insert commands to copy styles from one style sheet to another, the Insert and Format commands to create a new style, and the Format command to change an existing style.

Copying styles from one style sheet to another

Some standard elements of a document rarely vary from one document to another. For example, lists can be found in almost every kind of document: letters, reports, resumes, and articles. Although you might want to have different style sheets for different kinds of documents, you'll probably find that some styles, such as the style you create to format lists, are suitable for more than one style sheet. Rather than re-create those styles in each style sheet, you can copy them from one style sheet to another.

To see how it's done, we'll copy the indented list style that you created in a previous section from the style sheet named SEMI.STY to the one named FULL.STY. To copy a style from one style sheet to another:

1. Highlight the style you want to copy. In this case, highlight the style labeled with the remark *INDENTED LIST*.

2. Choose the Copy command. The style appears in the scrap without being removed from the style sheet.

3. Use the Transfer Load command to load the style sheet in which you want to insert the copy. After choosing Transfer Load, type *FULL* in the *style sheet name* field and press the Enter key to load *FULL.STY*. If there are any unsaved changes to the current style sheet, SEMI.STY in this case, Word gives you the opportunity to save them before loading another style sheet.

4. Move the highlight to the place where you want to insert the copy, and press the Insert key or choose and carry out the Insert command.

Now that you have FULL.STY in view, let's add another style to it. This time, you'll use the Gallery commands to create the style instead of creating the style by recording a format as you did before.

Creating styles from scratch

Two commands come into play when you create a style using the Gallery menu: the Insert command and the Format command. First you need to use the Insert command to assign a key code and to identify it with a usage, variant, and remark. Then you need to use the Format command to specify the formatting instructions for the style.

Let's create a style that formats characters in boldface italics. Move the highlight to where you want to insert the style. Because you're creating a character style, move the highlight to the other character style in the style sheet. (It has the key code *UC* and the remark *UNDERLINED*.) You can insert styles anywhere, but grouping similar styles together makes it easier to read style sheets and find styles. After the highlight is in position:

1. Choose the Insert command. You see:

```
INSERT key code: []         usage:(Character)Paragraph Division
         variant: 2         remark:
```

2. Type *BI* for the key code and choose *Character* for the usage.

3. Skip the variant field, letting Word assign a variant number, and type:

   BOLDFACE-ITALICS

   in the *remarks* field.

4. Press Enter to carry out the command.

The boldface-italics style is inserted and highlighted, but it does not yet include the formatting instructions that make characters bold and italic.

To define the formatting instructions for the new style:

1. Choose the Format command while the highlight is on the style.

2. Because you assigned the style a character usage, Word chooses the Character subcommand for you and displays the Format Character command fields:

```
FORMAT CHARACTER bold: Yes No      italic: Yes(No)        underline: Yes(No)
          strikethrough: Yes(No)   uppercase: Yes(No)     small caps: Yes(No)
          double underline: Yes(No) position:(Normal)Superscript Subscript
          font name: PicaD         font size: 12          font color: Black
          hidden: Yes(No)
```

3. Choose *Yes* in the *bold* and *italic* fields.

4. Carry out the command.

The style now includes instructions to format characters in boldface and italics. By creating this style, you can give one command (Alt-BI) to apply more than one character format (boldface *and* italics). One of the benefits of adding frequently used character formats to style sheets (even single formats like boldface or underlining) is that you then have an alternative to using the speed-formatting keys, which have to be combined with Alt-X when you have a style sheet attached to a document. Without a style for designating bold-faced characters, for example, you would have to type Alt-XB to use the speed-formatting keys Alt-B.

You can create paragraph and division styles in the same way that you create character styles. First use the Insert command to identify the style, and then use the Format command to specify the formatting instructions for the style. What you see after you choose the Format command depends on the usage you choose with the Insert command. If you choose a paragraph usage, Word presents this menu of subcommands:

```
FORMAT: Character Paragraph Tab Border pOsition
```

As mentioned before, a paragraph style can include character and tab format-ting. (It can also include border formatting—a feature that allows you to draw lines around a paragraph—and absolute positioning of a paragraph.) You can, in turn, choose each of these subcommands to assign formats to the paragraph style. The command fields you see when you choose these com-mands are identical to those you see when you choose the equivalent commands from the main menu.

If you're formatting a division style, Word displays these subcommands when you choose the Format command:

```
FORMAT DIVISION: Margins Page-numbers Layout line-Numbers
```

which are identical to the Format Division subcommands found on the main menu.

Changing a style

You can use the Format command on the Gallery menu to check and change the formatting instructions in an existing style. With the style sheet in view in the gallery, simply highlight the style you want to change and choose the Format command. To see how it's done, let's change the margins in the division style of FULL.STY. Check the name of the style sheet in the gallery window. If it is not FULL.STY, use the Transfer Load command to load FULL.STY. Then:

1. Highlight the style having the key code *S/* and labeled with the *Division Standard* usage and variant.

2. Choose the Format command and then the Margins subcommand. Type *1* in the *left* and *right* margin command fields to reduce the margins from 1.25" to 1".

3. Carry out the command.

The instructions in the style are immediately changed. If you exit to a document to which FULL.STY is attached, you see that the document has also changed to fit into the new margins.

THE DEFAULT STYLE SHEET: NORMAL.STY

When you create a new document, Word looks for and attaches a style sheet called NORMAL.STY. NORMAL.STY does not contain style definitions until you insert them, so it does not, initially, have any effect on the documents you create.

You can change the default formats that Word usually applies to documents by adding standard character, paragraph, and division styles to NORMAL.STY. You might, for example, want page numbers printed for most documents and the first lines of paragraphs automatically indented. You can add a division style to NORMAL.STY that includes instructions to print page numbers and a paragraph style that indents the first lines of paragraphs. By assigning either of these styles the *Standard* variant, the formatting instructions in that style are automatically applied to your text. They become the new default formats. You can override these formatting instructions by attaching a different style sheet to the document, by applying different styles to the text, or by formatting the document with the Format commands found on the main menu.

In addition to using NORMAL.STY to change default formats for most (or standard) text, use it to store your most commonly used formats for special text. Examples of special text are lists, titles, headings, and tables. What you put in NORMAL.STY depends on the kind of documents you most often prepare. For example, if you usually prepare letters, you might use NORMAL.STY to store formats for the parts of a letter. You are not confined to using the formats you define in NORMAL.STY. When styles are assigned a variant that is not automatic (any numbered variant), they are not applied to text unless you apply them with the key code or the Format Stylesheet command. By putting commonly used formats in a style sheet called NORMAL.STY, you simply make them readily available. You can have more than one style sheet called NORMAL.STY, but they must be on separate disks or in separate directories.

PART IV

APPENDIXES

Appendix A
Getting Acquainted with DOS

Before you can start Word, you must first start DOS, the Disk Operating System. By familiarizing yourself with the most useful DOS commands, you'll feel comfortable working in the DOS environment and be ready to use some very handy tools that DOS provides.

STARTING THE DISK OPERATING SYSTEM

Whenever you start your computer, it looks for DOS on the floppy disk in drive A and loads it into memory. If there is no disk in drive A, it checks to see if DOS is on a fixed disk in the C drive. This book assumes that DOS is already on your fixed disk.

After DOS is loaded into memory, it normally asks you to enter the date and the time or, if you have a built-in, battery-operated calendar/clock, to confirm the current date and time. DOS uses this information to record the date and time that each document is created or changed.

When you answer the date and time questions or give commands to DOS, always complete your answer or command by pressing the Enter key, which is labeled with a bent arrow. If you make a mistake while typing, you can back up and erase it with the Backspace key, which is above the Enter key and is labeled with a left arrow. Whenever you type numbers on a computer keyboard, be sure to use the number keys and not, for example, the letter *l* (for one) or the letter *O* (for zero).

To start DOS:

1. If you have a floppy-disk system, put your DOS disk in drive A. Drive A is the left or the top drive in a two-drive system. If you have a fixed disk (drive C), DOS is already on it, so leave drive A empty with the door open.

2. If your computer is off, turn it on. If the components of your system must be turned on individually, turn on your printer, your monitor, your disk drive(s), and then your computer. If your computer is already

on, restart it by holding down the Control (Ctrl) and the Alternate (Alt) keys as you press the Delete (Del) key:

3. If the current date displayed by DOS is correct, press the Enter key to confirm it. If it needs to be changed, type in the correct date and then press the Enter key. Use hyphens or slashes to separate parts of the date. For example, type:

    1/2/90

    if today's date is January 2, 1990.

4. If the current time displayed is correct, press the Enter key to confirm it. If it needs to be changed, type in the correct time and then press the Enter key. Use colons to separate units of time. For example, type:

    8:00

    if the correct time is 8 o'clock in the morning. DOS uses a 24-hour clock, so add 12 hours to afternoon or evening times. For example, type *14:00* for 2 o'clock in the afternoon. (Although it's rarely necessary to be so precise, seconds and hundredths of seconds can be appended to the time using colons, as before, to separate units of time.)

When you see the *A>* prompt (on a floppy-disk system) or the *C>* prompt (on a fixed-disk system), you know that DOS is running and ready for you to give the command to start Word.

UNDERSTANDING DOS FILENAMES

Programs and documents are stored on a disk as *files,* each with a unique name. When you create a new document, you give it a *filename*. A filename can be from one through eight characters long and can include letters, numbers, and many symbols found on your keyboard, but no spaces. Acceptable symbols are:

! @ # $ % & ( ) - _ { } ' ~

The following symbols cannot be used as part of a filename:

¦ < > / \

A filename can be followed by an *extension,* which can be up to three characters long. You can use any of the characters allowed in a filename. A period separates the filename from the extension. (Often, programs reserve certain extensions for their own use.)

Here are a few sample document filenames with extensions:

CHAPTER1.DOC	README.DOC
PICKLES.DOC	RESUME.DOC
8-15MEMO.DOC	JAN_SALE.RPT

Notice how symbols are used instead of spaces to separate words or numbers in a filename. Filename extensions are usually used to indicate, in a general way, what is in a file. For example, the extension .DOC tells you (and Word) that there is a document stored in a file.

THE DOS PROMPT AND THE CURRENT DRIVE

The *DOS prompt* A> (or C> for a fixed disk) tells you that DOS is started and is waiting for you to tell it what to do next by typing a *command.* The DOS prompt also tells you which drive is the *current drive.* That's where DOS looks for any files that it needs to carry out your commands.

Initially, the current drive is the drive where DOS resides. You can change the current drive so that DOS will automatically look in another drive for files. To make another drive the current drive, type the letter of the drive followed by a colon at the DOS prompt. For example, at the *A>*, type:

B:

and press the Enter key to change the current drive from A to B.

In most cases, instead of *changing* the current drive, you tell DOS where to look for individual files that aren't in the current drive. You do this by including the name of the disk drive with the filename. For example, typing:

B:CHAPTER1.DOC

tells DOS that it can find the file CHAPTER1.DOC on the floppy disk in drive B. When specifying a file, always put a colon after the drive name and don't put any spaces between the drive name and the filename, or between the filename and the extension.

LOOKING AT A DISK'S DIRECTORY

A *directory* is a list of all files on a disk. It displays the name of each file, the date and time each file was created or last changed, the size of each file (measured in bytes), the total number of files, and the amount of free space (in bytes) remaining on the disk. Recall that a byte is the amount of space needed to store one character. It takes about 3000 bytes (3 KB) to store one single-spaced document page.

When checking a directory to see if you have enough room for more documents, allow twice the space you think you'll need for additional documents because Word always keeps the previous copy of a revised document (and assigns the previous copy the same filename as the new document with an extension of .BAK, which stands for backup). In addition, Word needs some of your disk space to jot down notes to itself in temporary files. So allow some extra space (from 20 to 40 KB) for Word. Don't be too concerned with exact amounts of disk space: Word lets you know when you're running out. If you don't have enough room left on a disk to store a file, Word lets you put it on another disk.

To view the directory of a disk in the current drive, type:

DIR

at the DOS prompt (*A>* or *C>*) and press the Enter key. To view the directory of a disk that is not in the current drive, type the drive name and a colon after the DIR command. Let's try it now. Insert one of the Word disks in drive B. (If you have a fixed disk and one floppy-disk drive, the floppy-disk drive is referred to as both A and B.) Now type:

DIR B:

and press the Enter key.

You should now see a list of files similar to the one shown in Figure A-1. (For now, don't try to figure out what's inside each file you see listed. Simply try to get a general idea of what kind of information you see in a directory.)

```
Volume in drive B is WORD PROGRM
Directory of  B:\

WORD     EXE    235649   12-04-88    5:18p
MW       HLP    107779   11-27-88    5:50p
        2 File(s)       17408 bytes free
```

Figure A-1. *The directory display of a Word disk (a single-level directory).*

Figure A-2 focuses on a single entry from the directory and identifies each column of information.

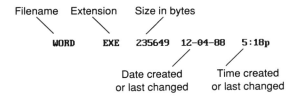

Figure A-2. *A directory entry.*

For a long directory, type:

DIR/P

to make the computer pause after showing the first screenful of filenames. Then press any key to see the next screenful or the rest of the directory.

❑ NOTE: *You can type uppercase or lowercase letters when you type commands or information for DOS.*

HIGHER-CAPACITY FLOPPY-DISK AND FIXED-DISK DIRECTORIES

Higher-capacity floppy disks and fixed disks can contain hundreds of files. It would be very time-consuming if you had to view all of them in the same directory, or if DOS had to search through hundreds of files to find the one you want. DOS provides a way to organize files into subdirectories so that you can view a subdirectory that lists a smaller group of related files rather than viewing a list of all files on a disk.

Setting up subdirectories is similar to setting up a filing system for paper files. If you have a filing cabinet full of file folders, you wouldn't want to search through the entire cabinet to find one file. You might assign a different category of files to each drawer. Then, within each drawer, you might further subdivide your files by grouping related files together and inserting labeled partitions that identify the subdivisions. To find a particular file, you would have to first go to the right drawer and then find the right subdivision in that drawer. Hopefully, the organization is logical and the labels on the drawer and on the subdivisions guide you to the place where your file is stored.

Making a Subdirectory

To create a subdirectory, use the MD (Make Directory) command. You create and name the subdirectory at the same time. For example, type:

MD \SALES

at the DOS prompt, and then press the Enter key to create a subdirectory called Sales. Follow the same rules for naming subdirectories that you use for naming files. As with filenames, each subdirectory must have a unique name. If you try to create a subdirectory using a name that is already in use, DOS tells you it is unable to create the directory.

The Root Directory and the Current Directory

Like the current drive, the *current directory* is the place where DOS expects to find any programs or files that you refer to in DOS commands. When you start DOS, the current directory is the *root directory* and is represented by a single backslash (\).

The root directory is created by DOS when you format a disk. If no subdirectories exist, the root directory is the only directory. If you create subdirectories, the root directory is the top-level directory and usually contains only a few DOS files that must be in the root directory, such as AUTOEXEC.BAT and CONFIG.SYS, which you will learn about later.

You can change the current directory before you give a command or you can include a subdirectory's name in a command so that DOS can find what it needs to carry out the command.

To change the current directory, use the CD (Change Directory) command. For example, to change the current directory to the Sales subdirectory, type:

CD \SALES

at the DOS prompt and press the Enter key.

Now that the Sales directory is the current directory, you can subdivide it by creating new subdirectories with the MD (Make Directory) command. For example, type:

MD SOFTWARE

and press the Enter key; then type:

MD HARDWARE

and press the Enter key again. Because these commands are given while Sales is the current directory, they create two subdirectories—Software and Hardware—that are on a level below the Sales directory.

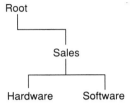

A directory on any level can be made the current directory. In the above example, you could change the current directory to Hardware, but first let's take a look at paths and pathnames.

Paths and Pathnames

A *path,* or *pathname,* spells out the route that DOS has to travel to get to a file. DOS first wants to see the drive, then the root directory, the subdirectory, the sub-subdirectory, and lastly the filename with parts of the path separated by *backslashes* (\). For example, the complete path to a file called HAMMER.RPT in the Hardware subdirectory would look like this:

If C is the current drive and the Sales directory is the current directory, you could drop *C:\SALES* from the path because DOS would assume that's where you want to start looking. The path now looks like this:

HARDWARE\HAMMER.RPT

A subdirectory is actually a special kind of file. When you refer to it, DOS expects you to give its address or path. For example, if you wanted to see a list of all files in the Hardware subdirectory, you would type:

DIR C:\SALES\HARDWARE

and press the Enter key. Or, if you wanted to make Hardware the current directory, you would type:

CD C:\SALES\HARDWARE

As usual, if C is the current drive, you don't have to include *C:* in the path.

343

Subdirectories, like other kinds of files, are listed in the directory they reside in. For example, if you asked to see the Sales directory, you might see a directory listing similar to the one shown in Figure A-3.

```
Volume in drive C has no label
Directory of  C:\SALES

.              <DIR>      11-18-90   12:04p
..             <DIR>      11-18-90   12:04p
HARDWARE       <DIR>      11-18-90   12:08p
SOFTWARE       <DIR>      11-18-90   12:09p
ANNUAL    RPT    30888    11-22-90   11:35a
HOTLIST   DOC     1098    11-29-90    2:45p
EMPLOYEE  DOC     3780    12-01-90    8:53a
         7 File(s)   1196032 bytes free
```

Figure A-3. *The directory display of the Sales subdirectory (a multilevel directory).*

Notice in Figure A-3 that both the names of files and the names of subdirectories (labeled with <DIR>) are in the directory for Sales. (The first two subdirectories displayed are special names DOS gives the *current directory* [.] and the *parent directory* [..] immediately above it.) Just as you might store miscellaneous or broad category files at the beginning of a file drawer labeled Sales, you can put files directly under the directory called Sales, rather than in the Hardware or Software subdirectory.

Changing the DOS Prompt

When you have multiple directories, it's easy to lose track of which directory you're in. With the PROMPT command, you can change the DOS prompt so that it displays the current directory along with the current drive. (You can also customize the prompt so that DOS will greet you with any message you like.)

You might want to create a prompt that tells you the current drive and current directory with a minimum number of characters, such as:

C:\SALES\HARDWARE>

This prompt tells you that *C* is the current drive and that the current directory is *HARDWARE*, which is a subdirectory of *SALES*. To create this kind of prompt, type:

PROMPT pg

at the *A>* or *C>* prompt, and press the Enter key. The *$p* tells DOS to display the current drive and directory. The *$g* tells DOS to append an angle bracket (>) at the end of the prompt. Once you give this PROMPT command, DOS displays the customized prompt throughout your work session. Each time you start DOS, you must give the PROMPT command again—unless you put it in an AUTOEXEC.BAT file so that the command is automatically executed each time you start DOS. (See the end of this appendix for more information about AUTOEXEC.BAT files.)

To restore a prompt to a simple current drive indicator like A> or C>, type:

PROMPT

and press the Enter key.

Removing a Subdirectory

After making a subdirectory, you might decide that you don't really have use for it. The RD (Remove Directory) command erases empty directories. For example, to remove the subdirectory called Software, you would type:

RD C:\SALES\SOFTWARE

If the directory that you want to remove is the current directory, you must first change to a different directory (with the CD command) because DOS won't remove the current directory. DOS won't remove a directory that has files or other subdirectories in it either: You first have to copy the files you want to save to another directory and then delete all files and remove any subdirectories.

The PATH Command

Application programs such as Word are started by typing a command. DOS finds the instructions for carrying out the command in a file with a .COM or .EXE filename extension. When you type the command *WORD* to start the Word program, DOS looks for the executable file WORD.EXE.

If you use multiple directories, you have to type the full path to the WORD.EXE file if it is not in the current directory. To enable you to start Word from any directory without having to specify the path, you can give a PATH command to DOS that tells it where to search for the WORD.EXE file.

For example, if you store the Word program in a directory called WORDIR in the C drive, the following PATH command tells DOS where to look for WORD.EXE:

PATH C:\WORDIR

Whenever you give the command to start Word, DOS will look for WORD.EXE in WORDIR if it can't find it in the current directory. You can list more than one path in a PATH command by separating the paths with semicolons. If, for example, you have a program that starts with the command DRAW, and the DRAW.EXE file resides in a directory called Artwork, you might type your PATH command like this:

PATH C:\WORDIR;C:\ARTWORK

This PATH command would enable you to simply type *WORD* or *DRAW* to start the Word or Draw program, regardless of which directory is currently active.

DOS remembers a PATH command throughout a work session. Each time you start DOS, you must give the PATH command again unless you put it in an AUTOEXEC.BAT file so that the command is automatically executed each time you start DOS. The Setup program described in Appendix B creates or alters an AUTOEXEC.BAT file to include a PATH command that tells DOS where to find Word.

FORMATTING A DISK

Before the computer can store files on a document disk, the disk has to be formatted. *Formatting a disk* is similar to drawing lines on the unlined pages of a notebook and numbering the pages before you start writing. You only have to format a disk once—the first time you use it.

Fixed disks are formatted when they are installed. The intricacies of formatting a fixed disk are beyond the scope of this book. If your fixed disk has never been formatted, see your DOS manual or, better yet, get some expert help. If you have a fixed disk, you still need to know how to format floppy disks because you will use them to make backup copies of files on your fixed disk. Should the fixed disk ever fail or become damaged, all is not lost if you have backup copies on floppy disks.

Formatting a floppy disk erases everything that's on the disk. Although you don't have to format a used disk that you want to recycle, formatting is a fast way to erase everything so that all the storage space is free for new files. Always check a disk's directory before formatting it, though, to be sure no files are on it that you want to keep.

The program that you use to format floppy disks is part of DOS, but it's in a separate file, called FORMAT.COM, on the DOS disk. FORMAT.COM is usually stored in the DOS directory of a fixed disk. (As explained in Appendix B, you can also format floppy disks with the Setup program that comes with Word. However, this is a roundabout method that requires more disk handling.)

❑ CAUTION: *Use extreme care not to format a fixed disk by mistake. Always include the floppy-disk drive name (*A: *or* B:*) when you type the FORMAT command.*

Let's format a floppy disk now so that it'll be ready to use. To start, insert the disk you want to format in drive B and close the drive door. (If you have a fixed disk and only one floppy-disk drive, the floppy-disk drive is referred to as both A and B.) If you have a dual-drive floppy-disk system, insert your DOS disk in drive A. When you see the *A>* or *C>* prompt, type:

DIR B:

to see if there is anything on the floppy disk that you intend to format. If there are files on the disk in drive B, replace it with another disk, unless you're sure you want to erase the files. If you see the message:

```
General Failure error reading drive B
Abort, Retry, Fail? _
```

DOS is telling you it can't use the disk yet because it has never been formatted. Press A (for Abort) to cancel the DIR command and return to the *A>* or *C>* prompt.

When you're sure you want to format the disk in drive B, type:

FORMAT B:

and press the Enter key. You see the message:

```
Insert new diskette for drive B:
and strike ENTER when ready_
```

The term *new diskette* refers to the floppy disk you want to format. If you're not sure you put the correct disk in drive B, now is your last chance to check. If you are sure, press the Enter key.

When DOS is done formatting the floppy disk, you see the message:

```
Format complete

    362496 bytes total disk space
    362496 bytes available on disk

Format another (Y/N)?_
```

This time, press N for No, followed by the Enter key, to leave the FORMAT program. Notice that DOS tells you how much storage space is available on your blank disk. When DOS displays the system prompt, remove the formatted disk from drive B and label it to indicate that it has been formatted and is ready to use.

DELETING AND RENAMING FILES

Word provides you with commands for deleting files or changing filenames, so you might never have to use the DEL (Delete file) or REN (Rename file) commands that DOS provides. However, it's often more convenient to delete or rename files using the DOS commands.

To delete a file called OUTADATE.DOC, you would type:

DEL OUTADATE.DOC

and press the Enter key. As with all DOS commands, you need to tell DOS the complete path to a file you want to delete, unless the file is in the current drive and current directory. For example, if the current drive is A and you want to delete OUTADATE.DOC from the disk in drive B, you would type:

DEL B:OUTADATE.DOC

In the same example, if the file is in a subdirectory called Sales, you would type:

DEL B:\SALES\OUTADATE.DOC

To change the name of a file called OLDNAME.DOC to NEWNAME.DOC, you would type:

REN OLDNAME.DOC NEWNAME.DOC

and press the Enter key. As with other file-related DOS commands, you must specify the drive and directory where OLDNAME.DOC can be found if it is not in the current drive and directory.

MAKING BACKUP COPIES

To protect your work, develop a habit of making backup copies at least once a day of any word-processing work you do. When you receive new software packages, such as Word, it's wise to make a backup copy of each disk in the package before you do anything else with it.

If you have two floppy-disk drives, you can easily copy files from one floppy disk to another. Many computer systems have a fixed disk and only one floppy-disk drive. With one floppy-disk drive, you copy an entire floppy disk or single files from one floppy disk to another by exchanging disks during the copying process. DOS calls the disk you copy *from* the *source disk* and the disk you copy *to* the *target disk*.

The commands DISKCOPY and COPY are handy tools for copying entire floppy disks or individual files.

The DISKCOPY Command

The DISKCOPY command makes an exact duplicate of an entire disk. Unlike the COPY command, DISKCOPY works only with floppy disks (not fixed disks), and it formats the target disk before it begins copying if the disk has not been formatted before. If the floppy disk you're copying is a DOS disk, DISKCOPY will copy the entire disk, including any parts of the operating system stored in hidden files.

If you have no backup copies of your Word disks, make them now with the DISKCOPY command. DISKCOPY resides in a file called DISKCOPY.COM on the DOS disk or in the DOS directory or the root directory of a fixed disk.

First write-protect your Word disks by placing a write-protect tab over the notch on the side of each 5¼-inch disk or by opening the write-product window of each 3½-inch disk. (See illustrations in Chapter 1.) This will prevent you from accidentally altering or erasing your original disks.

Now check to see that the *A>* or *C>* prompt is on the screen. If you have two floppy-disk drives, put the DOS disk in drive A. Then type:

DISKCOPY A: B:

and press the Enter key. When DOS prompts you to insert the source disk in drive A, put one of your Word disks in drive A and press any key to confirm that the disk is in place and the drive door is closed. When DOS prompts you to insert the target disk in drive B, put a blank disk (or one that does not have any files on it that you want to keep) in drive B and press any key.

If you have only one floppy-disk drive, type:

DISKCOPY

and press the Enter key. DOS will prompt you to insert the source disk (in this case, the Word disk you want to copy) and exchange it with the target disk (a blank disk) when necessary. Depending on the amount of memory in your computer, you might be prompted to switch disks repeatedly.

You know that the copy is complete when DOS asks you if you want another copy. You can remove both disks, label the copy, and store the original away in a safe place. Use the copy when you set up and work with Word.

Now press Y for Yes to copy another Word disk. As before, Word prompts you to insert the source and target disks. You can repeat this process until all of your original Word disks have been copied. After all disks are copied, press N for No when asked if you want to make another copy.

Using the COPY Command

You can back up individual files or an entire directory with the COPY command that comes with (and is an intrinsic part of) DOS. When you use the COPY command, the target disk must be a previously formatted disk. If the target disk already has files on it, the newly copied files will be added without affecting the existing files unless you try to add a file with the same name as an existing file. In that case, the newly copied file will replace the existing file.

If you have the Special Edition with disk included, consult the Introduction

To see how to copy a single file, let's copy the README.DOC file from the Utilities 1 disk (or the Utilities disk if you have 3½-inch disks) to another formatted disk. README.DOC contains last-minute information on the Word program that didn't make it into the user manuals. When you run the Setup program, take a look at this file to see if it has any information that is useful to you.

First look for the *A>* or *C>* prompt. If you have two floppy-disk drives, insert the Utilities 1 disk (or the Utilities disk) in drive A and a formatted disk in drive B. Now type:

COPY A:README.DOC B:

and press the Enter key.

If you have only one floppy-disk drive, insert the source disk (in this case, the Utilities 1 or Utilities disk) in the drive. Now type:

COPY A:README.DOC B:

and press the Enter key.

When DOS prompts you to insert the disk for drive B, remove the Utilities 1 or Utilities disk and put in a formatted disk. When you're ready to proceed, press any key. DOS continues to ask you to exchange disks until it is done copying.

When the copy operation is complete, you see a message telling you that one file was copied. The copy of the file will also have the name README.DOC.

Wild Cards

You can use what DOS calls *wildcards* when specifying files that you want to copy with the COPY command. An asterisk (*) stands for any number of unspecified characters. A question mark (?) stands for any single unspecified character. For example, you can type:

*.DOC

to represent all document files. It stands for any filename with the extension .DOC. If you want to copy all files in a directory, you can use:

.

to represent all filenames and filename extensions.

If only one directory—the root directory—is on a disk, *.* represents all files on the disk. For example, if you do not have multiple directories, the command:

COPY A:*.* B:

tells DOS to copy all the files on the disk in drive A to the disk in drive B. (When no directory is specified, DOS assumes you mean the current directory.) The copied files will have the same names as the original files, and DOS displays the name of each file on the screen as it's being copied. After all the files have been copied, you see a message telling you how many files were copied.

Copying to and from a Fixed Disk

Files on a fixed disk should be copied onto floppy disks in case the fixed disk becomes damaged. You can use the COPY command to copy files to and from the fixed disk. Follow the instructions given in the preceding section, substituting *C:* for *A:* or *B:*, when appropriate. Because your fixed disk probably has multiple directories, be sure to specify the directory path for a file being copied to or from the fixed disk whenever the file's directory is not the current directory. COPY can also be used to copy files from one directory to another on the same disk.

The COPY command is easy to use and initially will serve all of your backup needs. When you're willing to invest more time in learning what DOS has to offer, investigate a pair of commands called BACKUP and RESTORE. These are powerful tools that can save you time and floppy-disk space when backing up a fixed disk. With BACKUP, you can select individual files or groups of files based on their filenames, the directory they reside in, the date they were last changed, and whether or not they were changed since they were last backed up. Files copied with BACKUP can only be used after they have been recopied to a fixed disk with the RESTORE command. For more information on BACKUP and RESTORE, see your DOS manual or *Running MS-DOS* by Van Wolverton (Microsoft Press).

ABOUT CONFIG.SYS AND AUTOEXEC.BAT FILES

Each time you start the operating system, DOS looks for two special files named CONFIG.SYS and AUTOEXEC.BAT. Both files can contain lists of special setup commands that you want DOS to automatically execute.

You can create and edit these files as you would create and edit text files, but they must be saved without Word's usual formatting. (They must be saved with a *text only* format.) Each line of text in a CONFIG.SYS or AUTOEXEC.BAT file is a separate DOS command. DOS looks for CONFIG.SYS and AUTOEXEC.BAT files on the DOS disk or in the root directory of the disk used to start DOS. The Setup program (described in Appendix B) helps you create or alter CONFIG.SYS and AUTOEXEC.BAT files.

A CONFIG.SYS file contains commands that can't be given by typing them at the keyboard like other DOS commands. These commands tell DOS the special configuration requirements for your particular hardware and software system. For example, if you use a mouse, the command DEVICE=MOUSE.SYS tells DOS to look for and read a file called MOUSE.SYS, which tells DOS how to use the mouse.

An AUTOEXEC.BAT file contains commands that can be typed at the keyboard but are put in an AUTOEXEC.BAT file so that you don't have to type them each time you start DOS. Examples of commands found in an AUTOEXEC.BAT file are the PROMPT and PATH commands that you met in previous sections.

Appendix B
Setting Up and Starting Word

*If you have the
Special Edition
with disk
included, consult
the Introduction*

The Setup program that comes with Word leads you through the steps of copying the Word program and accessory files that you will need or find helpful when using Word. In most cases, you only have to use the Setup program once—before you use Word for the first time. Depending on the type of system you have, there might be a few other things you will want to do in preparation for using Word. I'll explain those additional setup tasks that are either necessary or recommended for your system.

WHAT'S ON THE DISKS YOU RECEIVE?

The table in Figure B-1 lists the disks that your Word package contains.

5¼-inch Floppy Disks	3½-inch Floppy Disks
Program 1	Program
Program 2	
Spell	Spell/Thesaurus
Thesaurus	
Utilities 1	Utilities
Utilities 2	
Utilities 3	
Printer 1	Printers
Printer 2	
Utilities/Printers	Utilities/Printers
Learning Word Essentials—Keyboard	Learning Word—Keyboard
Learning Word Essentials—Mouse	Learning Word—Mouse
Learning Word Advanced Lessons	

Figure B-1. *The disks you receive with Microsoft Word version 5.0.*

The *Program 1* and *Program 2* disks contain the Microsoft Word word-processing program. If you are using 3½-inch disks, you have one disk named *Program*.

If you have the Special Edition with disk included, consult the Introduction

The *Spell* disk contains a spelling checker that you can use to check for spelling errors in Word documents. The *Thesaurus* disk puts an electronic thesaurus at your fingertips. With it, you can look up words to find their synonyms. On the 3½-inch disks, the spelling checker and thesaurus are combined on the *Spell/Thesaurus* disk.

The *Utilities* disks (three disks if you have 5¼-inch disks; one disk if you have 3½-inch disks) store the Setup program and several other programs and files that are useful accessories. Here you'll find the Help and Hyphenation files, some ready-made style sheets and glossaries, as well as a file called README.DOC. README.DOC contains corrections to the Word manuals and notes about changes made to Word after the manuals were printed. The Setup program offers you the opportunity to look at the README.DOC file to see if it contains anything relevant to your specific system or application.

The *Printer 1* and *Printer 2* disks (the *Printers* disk if you are using 3½-inch disks) store files containing information that Word needs to work with specific printers. Most of these files have the filename extension .PRD, which stands for printer description.

The *Utilities/Printers* disk contains files that wouldn't fit on the other disks, including one called MOUSE.SYS that enables your computer to work with a mouse. (If you have 3½-inch disks, MOUSE.SYS resides on the *Utilities* disk.)

The *Learning Word* disks contain tutorials that help you get a hands-on feel for how Word works. You can use the Learning Word program by itself, or you can access lessons while you're working with the Word program.

WHAT DOES THE SETUP PROGRAM DO?

For both fixed-disk systems and floppy-disk systems, the Setup program:

- Creates a *working copy* of the Word Program disk on another floppy disk or in the directory you specify on a fixed disk.

- Copies printer information file(s) to your working copy of the Word Program disk or to the Word program directory of the fixed disk.

- Creates or alters the AUTOEXEC.BAT file to help Word run effectively.

- Copies the mouse information file (MOUSE.SYS) to your DOS disk or into the Word program directory of a fixed disk. Setup also creates or alters the CONFIG.SYS file to include a DEVICE command that tells DOS where to find the mouse-information file.

Word needs to know what kind of printer(s) you'll be using. After you choose the option to copy printer information, you select a printer from the list that Setup provides. If you will be using more than one printer, you'll want Setup to copy a printer description file for each printer that you'll be using. You can select only one printer at a time, but you can choose the printer-setup option again to select an additional printer. If you can't find your printer on the list displayed by Setup, see the section called ''Additional Setup Tasks'' in this chapter.

If you have the Special Edition with disk included, consult the Introduction

Choose the mouse option only if you have a mouse. If you're setting up a floppy-disk system, Setup alters your *working copy* of the DOS disk. You must use this altered DOS disk to start the operating system when you want to use the mouse with Word.

Setup Tasks for Floppy Disks

If you are setting up a floppy-disk system, the Setup program offers you the options to:

- Format blank floppy disks for storing documents.

- Copy Help and Hyphenation files to a document disk if they will not fit onto your Program disk.

Because new disks need to be formatted before you can store documents on them, the Setup program offers to format disks for you. (Setup simply runs the DOS FORMAT program described in Appendix A.)

Because the Help and Hyphenation files won't fit on a 360 KB Word Program disk, the Setup program offers to copy them onto the *formatted,* blank disks that you will use to store documents. The Help and Hyphenation files take up about 132 KB of space on each disk, but having these files on your document disks might be more convenient than switching to a Utilities disk each time you ask for help or automatic hyphenation.

Setup Tasks for Fixed Disks

If you're setting up a fixed disk, the Setup program can:

- Copy the Learning Word program and the Help and Hyphenation files to the fixed disk.

- Copy the Spell program to the fixed disk.

- Copy the Thesaurus program to the fixed disk.

*If you have the
Special Edition
with disk
included, consult
the Introduction*

Because of the greater storage capacity of fixed disks, the Setup program offers you the options to copy the major accessory programs to the Word program directory of your fixed disk. Copy as many of the accessories as you have room for because having them on the fixed disk will make them easier to access and faster to use.

HOW TO USE THE SETUP PROGRAM

How you use the Setup program depends on whether you are setting up a floppy-disk system or a fixed-disk system.

Setting Up a Floppy-Disk System

To set up Word on a floppy-disk system, you'll need:

- The Word Program disks, the Utilities disks, and the Printer disks.

- A DOS disk (version 2.0 or later). The DOS disk you use should be a copy, not the original, and it should have the FORMAT.COM file on it. Check its directory with the DIR/P command to see if FORMAT.COM is there.

- One blank, unformatted floppy disk for creating a working copy of Word. Optionally, additional unformatted disks to format for storing documents.

- The brand name and model of your printer(s).

To run the Setup program, you first need to start DOS (as explained in Appendix A). When you see the *A>* prompt, replace the DOS disk in drive A with the Utilities 1 disk (or the Utilities disk if you have 3½-inch disks). Then type:

SETUP

and press the Enter key to start the Setup program.

The Setup program will lead you through the setup procedure by telling you what to do next, asking you questions, giving you lists of options to choose from, and telling you when to remove or insert disks.

Setting Up a Fixed-Disk System

To set up Word on a fixed disk, you'll need:

- The Word Program disk, the Spell and Thesaurus disks, the Utilities disks, and the Printer disks.

- The Learning Word disks if you want to run the Learning Word program from your fixed disk.

- The name of the directory you want to copy the Word program to. If the directory doesn't exist yet, Setup will create it for you and assign the name you want. Whatever name you give it, this directory is referred to as the *Word program directory.*

- The brand name and model of your printer(s).

If you have the Special Edition with disk included, consult the Introduction

To run the Setup program, you first need to start DOS (as explained in Appendix A). When you see the *C>* prompt, insert the Utilities 1 disk (or the Utilities disk if you have 3½-inch disks) in drive A. Then type:

A:SETUP

and press the Enter key to start the Setup program.

The Setup program tells you what to do next, asks you questions, gives you lists of possible answers to choose from, and tells you when to remove or insert disks.

ADDITIONAL SETUP TASKS

In some situations you either need to or might want to perform additional setup tasks. Most of these situations depend on what kind of equipment you have. Glance through the sections that follow to see if any of them apply to you.

If You Can't Find Your Printer on the List

If you can't find your printer on the list that the Setup program displays, you can select one of Word's generic printers. These are listed at the very end of the printer list. *Standard printer* is for dot-matrix printers that don't have backspace capability. *Standard printer with support for backspace* is for dot-matrix printers with backspace capability. *Standard printer with support for form feeds* is for dot-matrix printers that recognize a form-feed character at the end of a page. And *Standard daisywheel printer* is for daisy-wheel and thimble printers.

The printer description file for dot-matrix printers without backspace capability (called TTY.PRD) is already on your Word Program disk. The generic printer description files enable almost any printer to work, but they do not support advanced features such as proportional spacing, microspacing, italics, boldface, or other special printing effects.

If you have the Special Edition with disk included, consult the Introduction

In addition to providing ready-made files that enable you to use the most widely used printers, Word provides programs (in files called MAKEPRD.EXE and MERGEPRD.EXE) that let you tailor-make your own printer description files for less widely used printers or printer-font combinations. See the booklet *Printer Information for Microsoft Word* for instructions on using these programs.

If You Have a Serial Printer

If you have a serial printer, you must regulate how the computer sends characters to the printer. You do this through the MODE command that comes with DOS. If, after consulting your DOS manual and printer manual, you're not sure how to use the MODE command or what parameters to include in it, ask your dealer for help. Once you know how to use MODE, it's a good idea to put the MODE command into your AUTOEXEC.BAT file so that the computer is prepared to talk to your printer each time you start DOS.

If You Have Higher-Capacity Disks

If you don't have a fixed disk but have 5¼-inch disks that hold 1.2 MB or 3½-inch disks, you can take advantage of their higher storage capacity by combining Word and part of DOS on one disk. This way, you will need only one disk to start both DOS and Word. (You cannot use this procedure with 5¼-inch disks that hold only 360 KB.)

To combine Word and DOS on one disk:

1. Format a blank disk as a *system start* disk. To do this, insert your DOS disk in drive A. Then, type:

   FORMAT B: /S

   at the *A>* prompt and press the Enter key. (Typing */S* after the *B:* tells DOS to create a system start disk. DOS will copy to the disk the files that are necessary for starting DOS.)

2. When the Format program asks for a new disk, insert a blank, unformatted disk in drive B. (If you have only one floppy-disk drive, remove your DOS disk from drive A and insert the blank, unformatted disk; DOS will treat the drive as both drive A and drive B.)

3. Press the Enter key to format the disk and copy DOS to it.

4. When the Format program is finished, it will ask if you want to format another disk. Press N for No, and then press the Enter key.

5. Run the Setup program as described earlier, using the new system start disk when Setup asks for a blank disk or your DOS disk.

You can now use the disk to start DOS and then, without having to change disks, to start Word.

If You Add Equipment Later

You might purchase a mouse or a printer after you've set up your working copy of Word. In that case, run the Setup program again, choosing only those options that apply to the new equipment. If you have a floppy-disk system, insert your *working copy* of the Word Program disk when the Setup program asks you to insert the Word Program disk.

Appendix C
Summary of Commands

STARTING AND STOPPING WORD

Starting Word

	Type:
Start Word without loading a document	word
Start Word and load specified document	word *filename*
Start Word and load document last worked with in window #1	word/1

Stopping Word

	Command
Stop the Word program and return to DOS	Quit

ENTERING TEXT

	Keys
Start new paragraph	Enter
Start new line (within same paragraph)	Shift-Enter
Start new division	Ctrl-Enter
Start new column	Ctrl-Enter
Start new page	Ctrl-Shift-Enter
Enter nonrequired hyphen	Ctrl- – (hyphen)
Enter nonbreaking hyphen	Ctrl-Shift- – (hyphen)
Enter nonbreaking space	Ctrl-Spacebar
Enter character not found on key top	Alt-(ASCII code for character); works with numeric keypad only

CHOOSING COMMANDS WITH THE KEYBOARD

	Keys/Command
Move to and from menu	Esc
Choose a command, subcommand, or option in a command field	Press key corresponding to uppercase letter
Move to next menu item or option in a command field	Spacebar
Move to previous menu item or option in a command field	Backspace
Move to next command field	→ or Tab
Move to previous field	← or Shift-Tab
Request a list of possible responses	F1 key
Move to response on list	Direction keys
Carry out command	Enter
Cancel command and return to text	Esc
Cancel command and return to menu	Ctrl-Esc
Get help with specific command	Alt-H
Get tutorial help with specific command	Alt-H, T, L

SCROLLING

	Keys
Up	
Up one line	Scroll Lock ON, ↑
Up one windowful	PgUp
Up to beginning of document	Ctrl-PgUp
Down	
Down one line	Scroll Lock ON, ↓
Down one windowful	PgDn
Down to end of document	Ctrl-PgDn
Left	
Left ⅓ windowful	Scroll Lock ON, ←
Left to beginning of line	Home
Right	
Right ⅓ windowful	Scroll Lock ON, →
Right to end of line	End

MOVING THE CURSOR

	Keys/Command
Up	
Up one line	↑
Up one paragraph	Ctrl-↑ *or* F9
Up to top of window	Ctrl-Home
Up to beginning of document	Ctrl-PgUp
Down	
Down one line	↓
Down one paragraph	Ctrl-↓ *or* F10
Down to bottom of window	Ctrl-End
Down to end of document	Ctrl-PgDn
Left	
Left one character	←
Left one word	Ctrl-← *or* F7
Left one sentence	Shift-F7
Left to beginning of line	Home
Right	
Right one character	→
Right one word	Ctrl-→ *or* F8
Right one sentence	Shift-F8
Right to end of line	End
To a Specific Place	
To next window	F1
To previous window	Shift-F1
To specified page number	Esc, J, P (Jump Page)
To next footnote, or from footnote reference mark to related footnote text and back	Esc, J, F (Jump Footnote)
To specified text	Esc, S (Search)
To specified format	Esc, F, E (Format sEarch)

HIGHLIGHTING TEXT

	Keys
Word left	F7
Word right	F8
Current line	Shift-F9
Sentence left	Shift-F7
Sentence right	Shift-F8
Previous paragraph	F9
Next paragraph	F10
Entire document	Shift-F10
Block:	
1. Move cursor to beginning of block	Direction keys
2. Extend cursor	F6
3. Move cursor to end of block	Direction keys

EDITING TEXT

	Keys	*Command*	*Command Field*
Deleting			
Delete character left	Backspace		
Delete highlighted text to scrap	Del *or*	Delete	to: {}
Delete highlighted text (no scrap)	Shift-Del		
Delete highlighted text to glossary		Delete	to: *glossary name*
Inserting			
Insert contents of scrap	Ins *or*	Insert	from: {}
Insert scrap after deleting highlighted text	Shift-Ins		
Insert glossary entry: choose glossary name from list		Insert	from: F1
Replace glossary name in document with glossary entry	F3		

(continued)

EDITING TEXT. *continued*

	Keys		*Command*	*Command Field*
Copying				
Copy highlighted text to new location:				
1. Copy to scrap			Copy	to: {}
2. Move cursor to new location	Direction keys			
3. Insert from scrap	Ins	*or*	Insert	from: {}
Copy highlighted text to glossary			Copy	to: *glossary name*
Moving				
Move highlighted text to new location:				
1. Delete to scrap	Del	*or*	Delete	to: {}
2. Move cursor to new location	Direction keys			
3. Insert from scrap	Ins	*or*	Insert	from: {}
Searching and Replacing				
Find text			Search	
Find and replace text			Replace	
Replace selected text with scrap	Shift-Del			
Find format			Format sEarch	
Replace format			Format repLace	
Miscellaneous				
Overtype (on/off)	F5			
Repeat last command	F4			
Repeat last search command	Shift-F4			
Reverse last edit or format change	Shift-F1	*or*	Undo	
Help:				
General			Help Index	
Tutorial			Help Tutorial	
Help specific to highlighted command	Alt-H			
Tutorial help specific to highlighted command	Alt-H, T, L			
Run other programs			Library Run	

WORKING WITH WINDOWS

	Keys	*Command*
Split an existing window horizontally		Window Split Horizontal
Split an existing window vertically		Window Split Vertical
Open a footnote window		Window Split Footnote
Close a window		Window Close
Move to the next window	F1	
Zoom a window	Ctrl-F1	

FORMATTING CHARACTERS

You can assign most character formats by using either Alt-key combinations or the Format Character command. You can also use the Format Character command to view character formats that have already been assigned. If a style sheet is attached to a document, you must first type Alt-X to use the pre-defined Alt-key assignments listed here. For example, type Alt-XB for Alt-B.

	Alt-Key	*Command*	*Command Field*
Change font	---	Format Character	font name:
Change font size	---	Format Character	font size:
Bold	Alt-B	Format Character	bold: Yes
Double underline	Alt-D	Format Character	double underline: Yes
Italic	Alt-I	Format Character	italic: Yes
Normal character	Alt-Spacebar	Format Character	*all fields*
Small capitals	Alt-K	Format Character	small caps: Yes
Strikethrough	Alt-S	Format Character	strikethrough: Yes
Superscript	Alt-+	Format Character	position: Superscript

(continued)

FORMATTING CHARACTERS. *continued*

	Alt-Key	*Command*	*Command Field*
Subscript	Alt-−	Format Character	position: Subscript
Underline	Alt-U	Format Character	underline: Yes
Uppercase	---	Format Character	uppercase: Yes
Hidden text	Alt-E	Format Character	hidden: Yes

FORMATTING PARAGRAPHS

You can assign most paragraph formats by using either Alt-key combinations or by using the Format Paragraph command. When the paragraph format requires a measurement, the Alt-key combination assigns a fixed measurement, as shown in parentheses under the column heading Alt-Key (Fixed Measure). In these cases, the Format Paragraph command is more flexible because you can type any measurement in the appropriate command field.

	Alt-Key (Fixed Measure)	*Command*	*Command Field*
Paragraph Alignment			
Align paragraph flush left	Alt-L	Format Paragraph	alignment: Left
Align paragraph flush right	Alt-R	Format Paragraph	alignment: Right
Center paragraph	Alt-C	Format Paragraph	alignment: Centered
Justify paragraph	Alt-J	Format Paragraph	alignment: Justified
Indenting Paragraphs			
Indent first line	Alt-F (to next tab)	Format Paragraph	first line: *positive measure greater than left indent*

(continued)

FORMATTING PARAGRAPHS. *continued*

	Alt-Key (Fixed Measure)	*Command*	*Command Field*
Outdent first line (hanging indent)	Alt-T (1/2 inch)	Format Paragraph	first line: *negative measure equal to or less than left indent*
Indent left side	Alt-N (to next tab)	Format Paragraph	left indent:
Increase (nest)	Alt-N (to next tab)		
Decrease	Alt-M (to previous tab)		
Indent right side	---	Format Paragraph	right indent:
Line Spacing			
Set spacing between lines in paragraph	Alt-1 (Single) Alt-2 (Double)	Format Paragraph	line spacing:
Add extra space before paragraph	Alt-0 (1 line)	Format Paragraph	space before:
Add extra space after paragraph	---	Format Paragraph	space after:
Miscellaneous			
Normal paragraph	Alt-P	Format Paragraph	*all fields*
Prevent page break in paragraph	---	Format Paragraph	keep together: Yes
Prevent page break between paragraphs	---	Format Paragraph	keep follow: Yes
Avoid widows and orphans when printing		Print Options	widow/orphan control: Yes
Tabs			
Set, view, move, or clear tabs		Format Tab Set	
Clear tabs		Format Tab Clear	
Clear all tabs and reset tabs at every 1/2 inch		Format Tab Reset-all	

FORMATTING DIVISIONS

	Command	Command Field
Division Boundaries		
Start division on same page and column	Format Division Layout	division break: Continuous
Start division in new column	Format Division Layout	division break: Column
Start division on new page	Format Division Layout	division break: Page
Start division on next odd-numbered page	Format Division Layout	division break: Odd
Start division on next even-numbered page	Format Division Layout	division break: Even
Page Numbering		
Print page numbers	Format Division Page-numbers	PAGE-NUMBERS: Yes
Position page numbers	Format Division Page-numbers	from top: from left:
Continue page numbering from previous division	Format Division Page-numbers	numbering: Continuous
Start new page numbering for division at page number	Format Division Page-numbers	numbering: Start at:
Change format for page numbers	Format Division Page-numbers	number format:
Margins and Page Size		
Set page size	Format Division Margins	page length: width:
Set top margin	Format Division Margins	top:
Set bottom margin	Format Division Margins	bottom:
Set left margin	Format Division Margins	left:
Set right margin	Format Division Margins	right:
Set gutter margin	Format Division Margins	gutter margin:
Multiple Columns		
Print in multiple columns	Format Division Layout	number of columns:
Assign space between multiple columns	Format Division Layout	space between columns:

(continued)

FORMATTING DIVISIONS. *continued*

	Command	Command Field
Footnotes		
Create footnote	Format Footnote	
Change footnote reference mark	Format Footnote	reference mark: (leave blank for auto-numbering)
Position footnotes on same page as reference marks	Format Division Layout	footnotes: Samepage
Position footnotes at end of division/document	Format Division Layout	footnotes: End
Move between footnote and reference mark	Jump Footnote	
Open footnote window	Window Split Footnote	
Running Heads		
Create running head and assign general position	Format Running-head	*all fields*
Assign exact position for running heads at top of page	Format Division Margins	running-head position from top:
Assign exact position for running heads at bottom of page	Format Division Margins	from bottom:
Format text of running head	Format Paragraph	*all fields*

If you have the Special Edition with disk included, consult the Introduction

STYLE SHEETS

	Command
General	
Attach style sheet	Format Stylesheet Attach
Apply character style	Format Stylesheet Character
Apply paragraph style	Format Stylesheet Paragraph
Apply division style	Format Stylesheet Division
Record style	Format Stylesheet Record

(continued)

STYLE SHEETS. *continued*

	Command
Gallery Menu	
Go to Gallery menu	Gallery
Exit Gallery menu	Exit
Create new style	Insert
Format new style	Format
Change format of highlighted style	Format
Change name of highlighted style	Name
Copy style	Copy, Insert
Delete style	Delete
Move style	Delete, Insert
Undo last change to style sheet	Undo
Print style sheet	Print
Style sheet file handling	Transfer

FILE HANDLING

	Command	Command Field
Document Files		
Load document file	Transfer Load	
Save document file	Transfer Save	
Save all open files	Transfer Allsave	
Delete any file	Transfer Delete	
Merge document files	Transfer Merge	
Rename document files	Transfer Rename	
Change current document drive/directory	Transfer Options	
Clear window	Transfer Clear Window	
Clear entire workspace	Transfer Clear All	
Display summary sheet when saving file first time	Options	summary sheet: Yes

(continued)

371

FILE HANDLING. *continued*

	Command	Command Field
Glossary Files		
Load glossary file	Transfer Glossary Load	
Merge glossary files	Transfer Glossary Merge	
Save glossary file	Transfer Glossary Save	
Clear glossary memory	Transfer Glossary Clear	
Delete glossary file	Transfer Delete	
Style Sheet Files		
Load style sheet	Gallery Transfer Load	
Merge style sheet	Gallery Transfer Merge	
Delete style sheet	Gallery Transfer Delete	
Save style sheet	Gallery Transfer Save	
Clear style sheet from window	Gallery Transfer Clear	
Rename style sheet	Gallery Transfer Rename	
Change default style sheet drive/directory	Gallery Transfer Options	

PRINTING

If you have the Special Edition with disk included, consult the Introduction

	Command	Command Field
Print document (after loading it)	Print Printer	
Print glossary	Print Glossary	
Print style sheet	Gallery Print	
Print summary sheet with document	1. Print Options 2. Print Printer	summary sheet: Yes
Print summary sheet without document	Library Document-retrieval Print:	marked files: Summary
Use computer as typewriter	Print Direct	
Send printer output to file instead of to printer	Print File	
Merge documents while printing	Print Merge	
Repaginate without printing	Print Repaginate	

(continued)

PRINTING. *continued*

	Command	*Command Field*
Temporarily stop queued printing	Print Queue Pause	
Restart queued printing, continuing from where you left off	Print Queue Continue	
Restart queued printing, starting from the beginning	Print Queue Restart	
Cancel queued printing	Print Queue Stop	

Printing Options

	Command	*Command Field*
Print draft	Print Options	draft: Yes
Print more than one copy	Print Options	copies:
Print highlighted section of document	Print Options	range: Selection
Print specified pages	Print Options	range: Pages page numbers:
Print hidden text	Print Options	hidden text: Yes
Print summary sheet with document	Print Options	summary sheet: Yes
Avoid widows and orphans	Print Options	widow/orphan control: Yes
Print while editing (queued printing)	Print Options	queued: Yes

If you have the Special Edition with disk included, consult the Introduction

OPERATING OPTIONS

	Command	*Command Field*
Set current document drive/directory	Transfer Options	setup:
Display summary sheet when saving file first time	Options	summary sheet: Yes
Change display mode	Options	display mode: (press F1 and select)
Change colors	Options	colors: (press F1 and select)
Turn off audible alarm	Options	mute: Yes
Hide menu	Options	show menu: No

(continued)

OPERATING OPTIONS. *continued*

	Command	*Command Field*
Hide screen borders	Options	show screen borders: No
Display line numbers in status line	Options	line numbers: Yes
View document with actual line breaks	Options	show line breaks: Yes
View hidden text	Options	show hidden text: Yes
View some normally invisible characters (paragraph mark, new line mark, and optional hyphen)	Options	show non-printing symbols: Partial
View all normally invisible characters	Options	show non-printing symbols: All
View style bar	Options	show style bar: Yes
View ruler line	Options	show ruler: Yes
Change cursor speed (0–9)	Options	cursor speed:
Change default unit of measure (in, cm, p10, p12, pt)	Options	measure:
Change default tab width	Options	default tab width:
Change automatic date or time formats	Options	date format: time format:
Change decimal character	Options	decimal character:

DOCUMENT-RETRIEVAL MENU

	Command	*Command Field*
Access Document-retrieval menu	Library Document-retrieval	
Return to main menu	Exit	
Load file	Load	
Copy marked files	Copy	delete files after copy: No
Move marked files	Copy	delete files after copy: Yes
Delete marked files	Delete	

(continued)

DOCUMENT-RETRIEVAL MENU. *continued*

	Command	*Command Field*
Print summary sheets and/or documents for files marked in document-retrieval window	Print	range: All
Search for files	Query	
Determine which files are listed in document-retrieval window	Query	
Control amount of information shown for listed documents	View	
Sort listed documents	View	sort by:
Make changes to summary sheet	Update	

HYPHENATION, THESAURUS, AND SPELLING

	Command	*Command Field*
Automatically hyphenate words	Library Hyphenate	
Find synonyms for highlighted word	Library thEsaurus	
Check document for spelling errors	Library Spell	
Spell Menu		
Return to main menu	Exit	
Correct word	Correct	
Leave word as is	Ignore	
Reverse last correction	Undo	
Spelling Options		
Check all letters in words	Library Spell Options	lookup: Complete
Assume first two letters of words are correct	Library Spell Options	lookup: Quick
Ignore words in all caps	Library Spell Options	ignore all caps: Yes
Automatically view alternative spellings	Library Spell Options	alternatives: Auto

If you have the Special Edition with disk included, consult the Introduction

Appendix D
Shortcut Keys and Toggle Keys

SHORTCUT KEYS

Shortcut keys are fast alternatives to using menu commands. They are usually function keys or function-key combinations. If you assign a shortcut key to a macro, you must press Ctrl-X and then the shortcut key(s) to access the original key assignments listed here.

	Shortcut Keys	*Equivalent Menu Command*
Insert from scrap	Ins	Insert from: {}
Insert from glossary	F3	Insert from: *glossary name*
Copy to scrap	Alt-F3	Copy to: {}
Delete to scrap	Del	Delete to: {}
Undo last action	Shift-F1	Undo
Set tab	Alt-F1	Format Tab Set
Format running head (Top—All pages)	Ctrl-F2	Format Running-head
Format running head (Bottom—All pages)	Alt-F2	Format Running-head
Change font	Alt-F8	Format Character
Repeat last edit command	F4	
Repeat last search command	Shift-F4	Search
Jump to page	Alt-F5	Jump Page
Look up synonyms	Ctrl-F6	Library thEsaurus
Check spelling	Alt-F6	Library Spell
Turn printer display on and off. (When this option is on, line breaks appear on screen as they will when printed.)	Alt-F7	Options show line breaks:
Switch between last two display modes used	Alt-F9	Options display mode:
Load document	Ctrl-F7	Transfer Load

(continued)

SHORTCUT KEYS. *continued*

	Shortcut Keys	*Equivalent Menu Command*
Print document	Ctrl-F8	Print Printer
Preview document	Ctrl-F9	Print preView
Save document (and formatting)	Ctrl-F10	Transfer Save
Record style	Alt-F10	Format Stylesheet Record
Get help	Alt-H	Help

TOGGLE KEYS

Toggle keys alternate between turning something on and turning it off. For most toggle keys, Word displays a two-letter code in the status line to let you know when a toggle key is turned on. A few toggle keys listed here are not covered in this book. They are included so that you will know which keys to press to turn them off if you accidentally turn them on.

	Keys	*Code Displayed When On*
Type uppercase letters	Caps Lock	CL
Column selection	Shift-F6	CS
Extend highlight	F6	EX
Use direction keys to draw lines	Ctrl-F5	LD
Show layout	Alt-F4	LY
Mark revisions	Esc, F, M, O, Y, ↵ (to turn on)	MR
	Esc, F, M, O, N, ↵ (to turn off)	
Use direction keys to type numbers	Num Lock	NL
Overtype	F5	OT
Record macro	Shift-F3	RM
Use direction keys to scroll	Scroll Lock	SL
Run macros step-by-step	Ctrl-F3	ST
Zoom window	Ctrl-F1	ZM
Choose display mode	Alt-F9	no code
Printer display	Alt-F7	no code

Appendix E
Summary of Mouse Activities

CHOOSING COMMANDS

	Location of Pointer	Point To:	Mouse Button
Choose command, subcommand, or option in command field	Command area	Command, subcommand, or option	Click-L
Choose option in command field and carry out command	Command area	Option	Click-R
Move to command field	Command area	Command field	Click-L
Request list of possible responses	Command area	Command field	Click-R
Carry out command	Command area	Capitalized command word	Click-L
Cancel command	Command area	Anything	Click-LR
Get help with specific command	Status line	?	Click-L

SCROLLING

	Location of Pointer	Point To:	Mouse Button
Up	Left window border	Position from top of scroll bar that matches distance you want to scroll	Click-L
Down	Left window border	Position from top of scroll bar that matches distance you want to scroll	Click-R

(continued)

SCROLLING. *continued*

	Location of Pointer	Point To:	Mouse Button
Left	Bottom window border	Position from left end of scroll bar that matches distance you want to scroll	Click-L
Right	Bottom window border	Position from left end of scroll bar that matches distance you want to scroll	Click-R
Thumbing:			
Up/down	Left window border	Position on scroll bar relative to position you want to be in document	Click-LR
Left/right	Bottom window border	Position on scroll bar relative to position you want to be in document	Click-LR

MOVING THE CURSOR AND HIGHLIGHTING TEXT

	Location of Pointer	Point To:	Mouse Button
Character	Text area	Character	Click-L
Word	Text area	Any character in word	Click-R
Sentence	Text area	Any character in sentence	Click-LR
Line	Selection bar	Line	Click-L
Paragraph	Selection bar	Any line in paragraph	Click-R
Whole document	Selection bar	Any line in document	Click-LR
Block	Text area	1. Beginning of block 2. End of block	Hold-L Rel-L

EDITING TEXT

	Location of Pointer	Point To:	Mouse Button
Copy highlighted text	Text area	New location for highlighted text	Shift+Click-L
Move highlighted text	Text area	New location for highlighted text	Ctrl+Click-L

WORKING WITH WINDOWS

	Location of Pointer	Point To:	Mouse Button
Split existing window horizontally	Right window border	Line where you want new window to start	Click-L
Split existing window vertically	Top window border	Column where you want new window to start	Click-L
Open footnote window	Right window border	Line where you want footnote window to start	Shift+Click-R
Close window	Window you want to close	Top or right window border	Click-LR
Move window border	Window you want to move	1. Lower right corner 2. New position for lower right corner	Hold-L Rel-L
Zoom a window	Window you want to zoom	Window number (upper left corner)	Click-R

FORMATTING

	Location of Pointer	Point To:	Mouse Button
Copy character formatting to highlighted text	Text area	Character whose format you want to copy	Alt+Click-L
Copy paragraph formatting to highlighted text	Selection bar	Paragraph whose format you want to copy	Alt+Click-R
Turn on ruler	Window where you want to turn on ruler	Upper right corner of window	Click-L
Turn off ruler	Window where you want to turn off ruler	Upper right corner of window	Click-LR
Set tab stop	On ruler	Position where you want to set tab	Click-L
Move tab stop	On ruler	1. Tab stop you want to move	Hold-R
		2. New location	Rel-R
Clear tab stop	On ruler	Tab stop you want to clear	Click-LR

Appendix F
Symbols in the Scrap

Word uses the following graphic symbols to represent special characters that have been copied or deleted to the scrap.

Symbol	Represents
·	Space
→	Tab character
↓	Newline character
¶	Paragraph mark
§	Division mark
—	Optional hyphen
⊟	Automatic page numbers
♣	Automatic footnote numbers
♥	Timeprint
⬛	Dateprint
■	End of row in column selection

INDEX

Italicized page numbers indicate graphics.

Special Characters and Numbers

Janet Rampa

Born and raised in Wilmington, Illinois, Janet Rampa studied philosophy and literature at the University of Illinois. An early enthusiast of word processing with microcomputers, she set up and managed the word-processing department at Sybex Computer Books and edited two bestselling word-processing books, *Introduction to WordStar* by Arthur Naiman and *Introduction to Word Processing* by Hal Glatzer. She was a cofounder of TechArt Associates, a microcomputer software development and training group in Berkeley, California. She now resides in Los Altos, California.

The manuscript for this book was prepared and submitted to Microsoft Press in electronic form. Text files were processed and formatted using Microsoft Word.

Cover design by Greg Hickman
Interior text design by Darcie S. Furlan
Illustrations by Becky Geisler-Johnson
Principal typography by Carol Luke

Text and display composition by Microsoft Press in Times Roman, using the Magna composition system and the Linotronic 300 laser imagesetter.